ALIEN STRONGHOLDS ON EARTH

SECRET UFO BASES EXIST ALL AROUND US

By Timothy Green Beckley and Sean Casteel

With Diane Tessman, Tim R. Swartz, Nigel Watson, Scott Corrales, Regan Lee, Hercules Invictus, Joshua Shapiro, Donald Worley, Carol Ann Rodriguez

INNER LIGHT/GLOBAL COMMUNICATIONS

P.O. Box 753
New Brunswick, NJ 08903

mrufo8@hotmail.com

ALIEN STRONGHOLDS ON EARTH
Secret UFO Bases Exist All Around Us
By Timothy Green Beckley and Sean Casteel

Copyright © 2019 by Timothy Green Beckley
dba Inner Light/Global Communications

All rights reserved. No part of these manuscripts may be copied or reproduced by any mechanical or digital methods and no excerpts or quotes may be used in any other book or manuscript without permission in writing by the Publisher, Inner Light/Global Communications except by a reviewer who may quote brief passages in a review.

Published in the United States of America

Inner Light/Global Communications
PO Box 753
New Brunswick, NJ 08903

Staff Members:
Timothy G. Beckley: Publisher
Carol Ann Rodriguez: Assistant to the Publisher
Sean Casteel: General Associate Editor
Tim R. Swartz: Formatting, Graphics and Editorial Consultant
William Kern: Editorial and Art Consultant

www.ConspiracyJournal.com

Order Hot Line: 1-732-602-3407

PayPal: MrUFO8@hotmail.com

CONTENTS

ALIEN BASES EXIST ALL AROUND US! By Tim Beckley – 1

SECTION ONE – In Your Own Backyard! – 2

CHAPTER ONE – WE FOUND A BASE IN THE CALIF. FOOTHILLS AT NIGHT! – 4

CHAPTER TWO – JUST OUTSIDE THE CITY OF ANGELS – THE TUJUNGA CANYON CONTACTS – 8

CHAPTER THREE – MYSTERY OF ALIEN INFESTATIONS by Don Worley – 12

SECTION TWO - Hidden in Plain Sight – 19

CHAPTER FOUR – THE UFO BASE 40 MILES FROM THE WHITE HOUSE – 20

CHAPTER FIVE – CONTACT IN CALVERT – 27

CHAPTER SIX – UMMO ON EARTH – 32

CHAPTER SEVEN – WE ARE AMONGST TRUE COSMIC FRIENDS (THE FRIENDSHIP CASE) – 37

SECTION THREE - The Desert - Alien Hotspots – 47

CHAPTER EIGHT – FROM THE DESERT SANDS CAULDRONS OF MAGIC WILL FLOW – 48

CHAPTER NINE – MOJAVE BY STARLIGHT – 54

CHAPTER TEN – MIDNIGHT MADNESS IN THE DESERT – 60

CHAPTER ELEVEN - HAUNTED DESERTS: UFOS IN THE EMPTINESS By Scott Corrales – 64

SECTION FOUR - Go Tell It On The Mountains – 81

CHAPTER TWELVE – HIGH IN THE ANDES – 82

CHAPTER THIRTEEN – THE MAGIC OF SEDONA'S RED ROCKS – 98

CHAPTER FOURTEEN – AIN'T NO MOUNTAIN HIGH ENOUGH - MOUNT SHASTA – 114

CHAPTER FIFTEEN – MIND CONTROL, REPTILIANS AND THE SUPERSTITION MOUNTAINS – 120

CHAPTER SIXTEEN – STAR CENTER OLYMPUS By Hercules Invictus – 130

SECTION FIVE - Pyramids As Alien Bases – **141**

CHAPTER SEVENTEEN – SEARCHING FOR FLYING TORTILLA BASES IN MEXICO – **144**

CHAPTER EIGHTEEN – THE MEXICAN ADVENTURE CONTINUES – **155**

SECTION SIX - Hidden Hangars Beneath The Sea – **164**

CHAPTER NINETEEN – BY THE SEA, BY THE BEAUTIFUL SEA By Tim Beckley – **166**

CHAPTER TWENTY – OCEANIC CELESTIAL EVENTS – **172**

CHAPTER TWENTY ONE – CANADA'S UNDERWATER WONDERS – **178**

CHAPTER TWENTY TWO – DEEP SEA ALIEN DIVING
– Interview with Preston Dennet – **182**

CHAPTER TWENTY THREE – ARE UNDERSEA BASES USED FOR
ALIEN ABDUCTIONS? By Sean Casteel – **192**

SECTION SEVEN - Underground Alien Bases – **200**

CHAPTER TWENTY FOUR – ALIENS GO UNDERGROUND by Nigel Watson – **202**

CHAPTER TWENTY FIVE – THE DULCE BASE – **208**

CHAPTER TWENTY SIX – MILITARY MIND CONTROL AND UFO
EXPERIENCE By Tim R. Swartz – **214**

Timothy Green Beckley

ALIEN STRONGHOLDS ON EARTH!

Introduction
ALIEN BASES EXIST ALL AROUND US!
By Timothy Green Beckley

They are said to walk amongst us. And, if this is true, surely they have to be living nearby, even if in seclusion.

Some UFO bases are believed to be located high in the mountains – such as Mount Shasta, Mount Olympus, and at the tiptop of the Andes.

Some are located way back in the jungles of Mexico and along the Amazon.

Still others require diving and sonar equipment to pinpoint the aliens' water world.

Others are "hidden" in plain sight. They could be in what seem to be abandoned buildings. Or out-of-the-way castles or mansions that can house a sizable encampment of Ultra-terrestrials. They might be along darkened trails that lead to the swamplands of America, or in the unpopulated areas of Australia's Outback.

For decades we have collected the many reports that have come our way, relegating some to the waste basket because they lack credibility. Others remain in our "grey basket," because they have yet to be proven or disproven, while the remainder might lead us to some well-deserved discoveries if we manage to enter the star gate on the end of sundown.

It's believed – and we are seeking concrete proof – that at least some of those researchers who have gone in search of alien "hangouts" have never returned with accounts of what they came across. Raymond Bernard comes to mind. He entered the jungles of Brazil in search of a cavern base and might have gotten snatched by the reptilians or Richard Shaver's "Dero," who want to remain well secluded from the prying eyes of the human race.

We welcome you to join us in our quest to seek out the truth about such engaging cosmic matters. Who knows? Maybe one of us might make an important discovery that will further our research into the bizarre planet we live on.

mrufo8@hotmail.com

Mr. UFO's Secret Files – YouTube channel

ALIEN STRONGHOLDS ON EARTH!

SECTION ONE

IN YOUR OWN BACK YARD

One thing I discovered - an alien base or stronghold doesn't necessarily have to be tucked way out of the way. They are frequently located in places that are easily approachable. You might have to sneak up to them in the dead of night (like if you were hanging out around Area 51 waiting for one of those Bob Lazar craft to come over at 10 PM on Wednesday), but if you keep a cool head about you and tell your companion to "keep it down," this may be a golden opportunity to come across something very strange and unusual.

Our first few cases are comprised of episodes where the witnesses to something truly strange and unusual happen to come across an encampment of Ultra-terrestrials by accident. It wasn't planned. They didn't go out in anticipation of meeting up with someone piloting a craft that was manufactured "off world." It was a fluke. A blunder. A coincidence that sent them out into the night. Maybe they were on their way to a convenience store, or out to get a breath of fresh air. It doesn't really matter, for they encroached upon forbidden terrain. If they are among the lucky ones, they returned to their daily lives with perhaps shaken limbs. Maybe some never came back. We will never know for sure.

ALIEN STRONGHOLDS ON EARTH!

Wherever they come from they are all around us in every neighborhood.

ALIEN STRONGHOLDS ON EARTH!

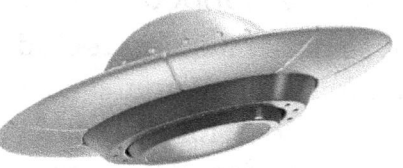

Chapter One
WE FOUND A BASE IN THE CALIFORNIA FOOTHILLS AT NIGHT!

Editor's Note: This rather sensational report came to us via Sandra L. Edison, publisher of "The Network Newsletter," a New Age publication that is actually a mail forwarding service for those interested in UFOs and other "offbeat" subjects who wish to correspond with each other. Though the author of this bizarre story does not want her name used "because she is busy in the motion picture business," Sandra Edison says the witness seems very reliable and trustworthy.

* * * * * * * * * *

This report was sent to us by one of our members, Alex R. of California. In it, she tells of an interesting and sometimes frightening "adventure" she shared with her friend Annemarie.

Alex's narrative begins: "I have been reading recently about all the alleged underground alien labs and facilities and took particular interest in a rumor purporting an underground base of this kind to be located in the Lancaster/Palmdale area near the Tehachapi Mountains. There may be some truth to this, as my friend Annemarie and I had something very weird happen to us there.

"Annemarie had, some years ago, purchased some undeveloped land in that area and had not done anything with it nor had she been to see it. In the early 1980s, she took an interest in the property as the Lancaster/Palmdale area was 'coming into its own.' Homes were being built, and businesses were moving there. Since this was the case, she felt sure that the value of the property would increase, and she was thinking of selling it. However, she had not seen it. Her ex-husband had bought it and declared it was in a 'great' location. He deeded it over to her after the divorce. He had given her a rather crude map with some landmarks by which we would be able to identify the property.

"We drove the nearly two hours to Lancaster/Palmdale and began our search.

ALIEN STRONGHOLDS ON EARTH!

The map was not much help, however, because it had been made when the area was still undeveloped and most of the natural landmarks were gone – removed to make room for houses. Every time we found what looked like a road which would take us somewhere, it turned into a dead-end. The area we were in was now full of cul-de-sacs for the housing development that would soon be built on it. After about two and a half hours of driving, we stopped for a cool drink.

"By now, neither of us was really that interested in finding Annemarie's property, but we figured that the day was still young so we'd press on. We got back on the main highway and decided to look for dirt roads in the hopes that the land was still undeveloped and that we had missed it in looking in the developed areas. At last, a broad, well-kept dirt road appeared. At first we thought it might be the entrance to someone's farm or ranch, but, since there wasn't a mailbox, we decided to proceed.

"After about half a mile, something odd happened. The dirt road became a wide, beautifully paved asphalt road, with a single white dividing line. We were astounded at this but were glad as the dirt road was taking its toll on Annemarie's car. We had driven about two miles when, up ahead, we saw what looked like a dust storm coming out of the mountains. Annemarie slowed down and we watched. It was not a storm but a vehicle, a car, coming towards us at full speed. 'Let's get out of here,' I said. 'I don't think that would be a good idea,' said Annemarie.

"She came to a complete stop, right in the middle of the road. 'Are you crazy?' I said. 'Stay calm and let me do the talking,' she said.

The car, a drab olive green, late model sedan, was, by now, up on the road, still driving full speed. They were heading directly for us. I was afraid that they would not stop in time and they would hit us.

The car stopped, brakes screeching, within inches of us, and two men got out. A third man remained in the car. They were young men, in their mid-thirties, dressed in pale blue coveralls (no name plates or insignias) and 'baseball' caps. One had sandy-colored hair, the other was white-blonde. The third man was in the front of the car, talking on a radio microphone. All wore wraparound sunglasses. Somehow, I knew that we might be in terrible trouble and that we were somewhere we didn't belong!

"The sandy-haired man came up to the driver's side of the car; the blonde was on my side, the passenger side. He kept his right hand in his pocket at all times. I wondered if he was carrying a gun. 'Good morning, ladies!' said sandyhair. 'Where are you going?' Annemarie showed him the map. 'We're trying to find my property,' she said. 'Can you help us?' He studied the map.

"'You haven't been here for a while, have you?' he said. 'All of these places on the map have been removed or destroyed.' He looked at the map again. 'This place looks like it might be on the other side of town. Why don't you look there?'

ALIEN STRONGHOLDS ON EARTH!

He was extremely polite, smiling all the while he spoke, yet he terrified me and Annemarie. The blonde man never spoke, nor did he smile or look at me. The third man remained on the radio. (Running the "make" on Annemarie's car?)

"'We'll be happy to escort you ladies back to the main road.' Though it sounded like a polite suggestion, it was actually an ORDER to LEAVE NOW! Annemarie said nothing, merely backed up slowly and drove back, still slowly, to our place of entrance into this 'forbidden' area. The men and their car stayed close behind us and followed us for several miles.

Could there be an underground UFO base in the Lancaster/Palmdale area near the Tehachapi Mountains?

"Annemarie and I did not speak during this time. I think we were too scared. Then, instead of going back to the main part of the city, she took the freeway onramp and headed back home. I noticed that she kept looking in her rearview mirror. 'What's wrong?' I asked. 'Someone is following us,' she said. I was too frightened to turn around so I lowered my sun visor and looked in the vanity mirror. There, a few car lengths behind us, was another late model sedan, medium blue in color, being driven by a man in a green coverall, wearing a cap and wraparound sunglasses. His two companions were dressed the same way.

"'What do they want from us?' I asked. 'They probably want to make sure that we go back home and don't try to come back,' said Annemarie. 'Ken (her ex-

ALIEN STRONGHOLDS ON EARTH!

husband) told me that he heard about the government using parts of that area for secret experiments,' she said. 'Maybe we were about to break in on one of them.' Then she laughed and I joined her. It broke the tension. They stayed with us until we were about halfway home. Then they began to back off, getting further and further away. After a while, we didn't see them anymore. When we arrived home, Annemarie dropped me off and we agreed to meet later (after we had showered and freshened up) for dinner.

"At about 7:30 P.M., she and I met at a local restaurant and we talked about our adventure. We were now curious about what had happened and wondered if we should go back or if we would be able to find the road again. (We lived in the San Fernando Valley and were not at all familiar with the Antelope Valley area.) We then got further into our mutual interest in UFOs. We jokingly considered the possibility that the 'men' we had seen were really aliens.

"We left the restaurant at about 10:30. The restaurant is situated in a very busy traffic area and is also near a freeway and a very busy motor hotel. There is constant noise and traffic at all hours. It is never quiet there.

"However, this night, things were to be different! When we came out of the restaurant, the street was DESERTED! This was on a Saturday night, one of the busiest nights of the week for this restaurant! There were no cars going by, no people, no sounds of traffic. In fact, there was no sound of any kind! When Annemarie and I spoke to each other, our voices sounded hollow, far away.

"'I've never seen it so quiet,' I said. 'Neither have I,' Annemarie said. Then, as if on command, we both looked up. There, at a level just over our heads, was a SPACECRAFT! We could not see the craft itself very clearly, but it was outlined by white lights which ran all around it. It was the shape of an elongated triangle. It remained in its position for what seemed a few minutes. Then it moved away. Suddenly, as if someone had turned up the volume on a TV set, all the normal sounds returned.

"We walked to our cars and Annemarie checked her watch. 'Oh, my God,' she said. 'What's the matter?' I asked. 'What time do you have?' she asked. I looked at my watch and was stunned to see it was 12:35 A.M. We had been looking at the spacecraft for two hours and five minutes?!

"That was the final straw and all the fright we wanted to have for one day. We agreed never to go out to look for that 'forbidden' area and Annemarie sold her property soon after this incident. There may be more than just rumors about what is going on in the Tehachapi Mountains! We were chased away and given a good scare! Keep looking for the truth, but use caution!"

ALIEN STRONGHOLDS ON EARTH!

Chapter Two
JUST OUTSIDE THE CITY OF ANGELS
THE TUJUNGA CANYON CONTACTS

Says researcher Ann Druffel: As far as I can tell, the witness involved in this case had no early childhood experiences of UFO encounters or abductions by aliens. So why they singled her out is hard to say.

According to her own thinking, Mrs. De Long feels she may have stumbled upon a secret alien base and somehow the UFOnauts were alerted to her presence and selected her as an unofficial spokesperson for their cause. Their reason for such an open contact is a frequently delivered message – that humankind should learn to live in peace.

Mrs. De Long's cosmic adventures took place in Tujunga Canyon on the outskirts of Los Angeles. According to UFOInsight.com, the sightings go back as early as 1953.

"The first case on record occurred on the evening of 22nd March 1953. Sara Shaw and Jan Whitley, who at the time lived in an isolated cabin in the Tujunga Canyon, were awoken by a bright light outside their home. The pair went to investigate and the next thing they realized they were outside their cabin, running, scared and confused, and with no memory of how they had ended up outside. Furthermore, according to their watches, two hours had passed in what seemed to them to be only seconds.

It was only when they made their report to NICAP years later, and following hypnotic regression, that the missing time was revealed.

"According to Sara, while under regression, several 'thin humanoids dressed in black' somehow entered their cabin through the closed window. They were taken to a 'Saturn-shaped UFO' which hovered nearby over a stream. Sara cooperated with her unwelcome hosts. Jan, on the other hand, would put up substantial

ALIEN STRONGHOLDS ON EARTH!

resistance, becoming quite hysterical, and was ultimately 'taken away, protesting violently'

"Sara would describe stepping into a 'solid beam of light' that would lift her 'about the same angle as an escalator' but with no steps. The humanoids would examine Sara, using what she believed to be an 'X-ray-type device.' She wasn't sure how long the procedure took to complete, but the next thing she realized, the humanoids were 'informing' her telepathically of cures for cancer. She failed to remember the details, feeling beyond overwhelmed with the situation. The humanoids themselves appeared to have white skin and elongated heads that were neither 'wider at the top or the bottom!' Following this, she and Jan found themselves back in the 'beam of light' which returned them to their cabin."

Mrs. De Long claims that there is a a flying saucer base - complete with at least three spaceships and two interplanetary pilots - tucked away in the mountains above Sunland and Tujunga, California.

Much has been written on the subject of the Tujunga Canyon sightings. Preston Dennett has been on top of the situation, as has ace veteran UFOlogist Ann Druffel, who has published an entire book on the matter.

But no matter. I spent several hours chatting with Mrs. De Long on the telephone back when her epic encounter first got a bit of press coverage (it certainly was not headline copy).

She said she had discovered a flying saucer base – complete with at least three

ALIEN STRONGHOLDS ON EARTH!

spaceships and two interplanetary pilots — allegedly tucked away in the mountains above Sunland and Tujunga, California.

And, from their Big Tujunga Canon base station, the two spacemen have been calling quite regularly on several Foothill residents, bringing messages from outer space. Mrs. De Long said she had repeated contacts with two space people.

Her 12-year-old son, Charles, and a man, Charles Kisner of Montrose, have also seen, listened to and talked with the visitors from outer space.

Mrs. De Long said several of the contacts have occurred in the Big Tujunga Canyon area, near a reservoir.

Because of the repeated contacts in the same area, Mrs. De Long maintains that spacemen are using the area around the dam as their Earth base of operation.

To fortify her claim, Mrs. De Long cites the experiences of a Los Angeles couple who followed a flying saucer across the foothills and into the canyon area.

The pair were found by sheriff's deputies, lost near the Big Tujunga Canyon Road.

They told officials they had followed the large saucer-shaped object into the area and became lost when it disappeared with the approaching dawn.

Mrs. De Long, supported by her son, said the spaceship was probably the one she and four other witnesses had seen. According to Mrs. De Long, she, her husband, Kisner and Charles, were first contacted in July while traveling through the isolated canyon at night. She said a bright light appeared to be following the car, and that the four occupants "began to feel uneasy."

The spaceship then appeared behind the car, traveling along close to the ground with three multi-colored rays extending from the rounded contours of the UFO. Sure that something big was coming their way, the group returned the next night to the same general Foothill area.

Again the saucer-shaped object appeared. This time, however, the frightened occupants of the Rambler were introduced to "Kronin." Introducing himself in a blaze of bright light, the spaceman told them not to be afraid, that he meant no harm. Mrs. De Long said that in spite of the spaceman's easy manner, she was "very frightened."

After reassuring the car's occupants again, "Kronin" chatted briefly about atmospheric conditions and the food he ate on "Clarion," his home planet.

"Kronin" then disappeared, promising to keep in touch, Mrs. De Long recalled.

The next night, Mrs. De Long, Charles, and Kisner traveled again to Big Tujunga Canyon, hoping to catch a glimpse of the space travelers. Their hopes were not for nothing. Mrs. De Long said "Kronin" appeared outside the car, materializing in a cloud of vapor. As the car moved along the highway, "Kronin" kept pace, chatting in a low-pitched voice with the three Foothills residents.

ALIEN STRONGHOLDS ON EARTH!

Mrs. De Long had brought her tape recorder along, and was able to record the spaceman's conversation. In a gravelly low voice that would be expected of a spaceman "Kronin" spoke about his visit to Earth.

Mrs. De Long said he called her an Earth Angel and said he was contacting people on Earth to try to forestall a possible world war. He reported that people on other planets were concerned with the war-like activities on Earth.

Before disappearing, the spaceman asked the car's occupants to face to their left and see the beautiful beam from his spaceship. "It was absolutely fantastic," Mrs. De Long said. "This multi-colored ray stretched from his mother ship and right through a large mountain in the canyon."

She said "Kronin" was a large man, over six feet tall, and that he had no eyes. "He told us he saw through thought control," Mrs. De Long said. After disappearing, "Kronin" said he would contact them again when atmospheric conditions were just right.

UFO researcher Ann Druffel

ALIEN STRONGHOLDS ON EARTH!

Chapter Three
MYSTERY OF ALIEN INFESTATIONS
By Don Worley

Don Worley investigated, by his own estimation, over 300 UFO cases. Not so much sightings of unexplained objects in the sky, but more about what happens at ground level to those observers who have been selected for close-level, often repeated encounters. He was an active representative of both the Tucson-based Aerial Phenomena Research Organization (APRO) and Dr. J. Allen Hynek's Center for UFO Studies (CUFOS), as well as a frequent contributor to Tim Beckley's "UFO Universe" and "UFO Review" publications." Don passed away in January 2018. The following has been extracted and updated from an issue of "UFO Review."

* * * * * * * * * *

When Coral and Jim Lorenzen of the Tucson-based UFO group APRO sent me into the isolated strip mines area of south central Indiana, I was little prepared for what I was to uncover. The intensity and boldness of the aliens during the 1966-67 sighting wave was unbelievable. Domed discs and oval-shaped craft were being seen by many witnesses and at close range.

For example, on the Curry and Smith farms, burnt circles 20 feet in diameter were found. So much was going on that there was really no way to keep up with it all in the limited time I could spend on the scene. As a result of all the activity, many people thought that the UFOs must be hiding in the bottom of the strip mine lakes, though no "hard" evidence to prove this theory was ever forthcoming.

One amazed farmer, George Pratt, said he often watched UFOs playing around over his farm. The round, yellow, bright light came so often from the strip mines nearby that he used the expression "It came up," like he was talking about the moon or sun.

"This thing came all summer long in the evening," Pratt said. "It didn't make

ALIEN STRONGHOLDS ON EARTH!

any sound, but it sure tore up my radio. It would set up there for about 15 minutes then usually move off to the south. As the days grew longer in the summer, it was a round sliver thing in the daylight. People laughed at me in town, but when they came out here on the road they would spot it on the way. About 14 others have seen it. One night three of them jets came in from Terre Haute and chased the light. I could see their wing lights and hear their motors. That thing flitted about the sky like a firefly and played a game with the jets. They never could get near it. I don't know. I still don't believe they come from space."

In those young wild days, I was startled at the scope of the infestation in the strip mines area, but now we know that it was really nothing new and probably not even comparable to events elsewhere.

Alien abduction researcher Don Worley investigated, by his own estimation, over 300 UFO cases.

There are Instances where the concentration seems to be in just a small locality affecting few persons. When Bernice Neblett moved to her small island home near Vancouver, British Columbia, she discovered that she was in the midst of a teeming UFO swarm. For weeks she watched all kinds of strange flying objects around her lonely island. She learned that they were not going to hurt her. She even named one "the red flasher," and one night actually heard laughter issue from the small barrel-shaped craft.

A somewhat wider radius was involved during the latter part of 1976 and early 1977 in Michigan's Upper Peninsula. Briar Mountain (near the town of Norway) was the focal point of a 20 miles-in-diameter area that has seen intense UFO activity over a period of three decades. Most of the 50 employees of the ski lodge on Briar Mountain have seen as many as 20 or more UFOs. To them, it was a disconcerting sight to see glowing craft zipping down the slopes much like skiers would. One observer, a shocked publishing magnate, returned home with his friends

ALIEN STRONGHOLDS ON EARTH!

and remained silent about what they had seen at the lodge.

Infestations also occur over bodies of water. Many Canadians living on the shores of Lake Ontario, between Oakville and Toronto, are convinced that a base for UFOs exists under the restless water of the lake. For years many witnesses have seen lights shooting in and out of the lake, and a number of photos have been taken. Harry Picket, an aeronautical engineer, pilot, and owner of an aircraft research firm, has watched the lights for years from his Niagara-on-the-Lake home. The orange lights are seen to hover, fly in erratic patterns, and sometimes zip straight up in the air and out of sight. What are all these lights and why are they being seen in these locations?

South America has been an incredible hotbed of UFO activity for ages. Near the little town of Demerval Lobo, in northeastern Brazil, in the spring of 1984, the antics of egg-shaped craft were so prevalent that laborers working in the fields abandoned their jobs and fled.

Everyone was certain there was a UFO base nearby. In an area formed by the Brazilian town of Odios, Mente Alogre, and Santarem, in the Amazon River basin, it was believed a base existed under the water. Fishermen pulled up their lines because of the boldness of the objects. Charles Tucker and an investigator from the USA as well as a Brazilian Air Force investigator, went into the region in the summer of 1981. I never found out what happened to them, but I'm sure they came up empty-handed on the hidden base theory.

At another South American locations, so many UFOs were seen shooting out of or entering the gulfs of San Maties and San Jorge that they became commonplace and receive little attention. Several Argentine UFO groups, after accumulating years of data, became convinced that submerged alien bases surely exist in the sea off the southern coast of Patagonia.

Another phenomenon in other areas has been the perplexing underground motor sounds. The sound of underground motors can often affect many witnesses, but the case that occurred at Michael Richardson's hillside tin mine (located 61 miles south of Marble Bar in Australia), was by its isolated nature heard by few. Three Aborigines stopped by "Max's" camp and called his attention to the motor sounds he had already begun to hear emanating from the hills above his camp. A search was made of the rugged area where no vehicle could travel, but no cause for the sound was apparent and it continued even as they searched for its origin.

But it is the "other" events that took place during the motor sounds period that are really quite interesting.

On May 19, 1978, Max was visited by a tall, "normal-looking" male wearing overalls. We cannot say exactly normal, since the visitor's left hand looked transparent, "as though it had been burned and it was new skin." This person, whose speech as normal, arrived in a Land Rover with unusually small wheels bearing a

ALIEN STRONGHOLDS ON EARTH!

plate number that Max later checked and found to be registered to someone else. The name and place of residence the man gave also proved to be false. The man seemed obsessed with beryllium and kept questioning Max on it. This is an interesting sideline of the case, because I recall that in one high intensity cow mutilation area of Colorado, the sweet smell of beryllium often filled the air and even the wind didn't disperse the odor.

It was a hot day, but the stranger refused any liquid refreshment during the two hours he was there. Max asked him to aid in lifting some iron sheets and Max discovered the man had no strength at all. He began to tremble, then toppled over. Max had to help him up.

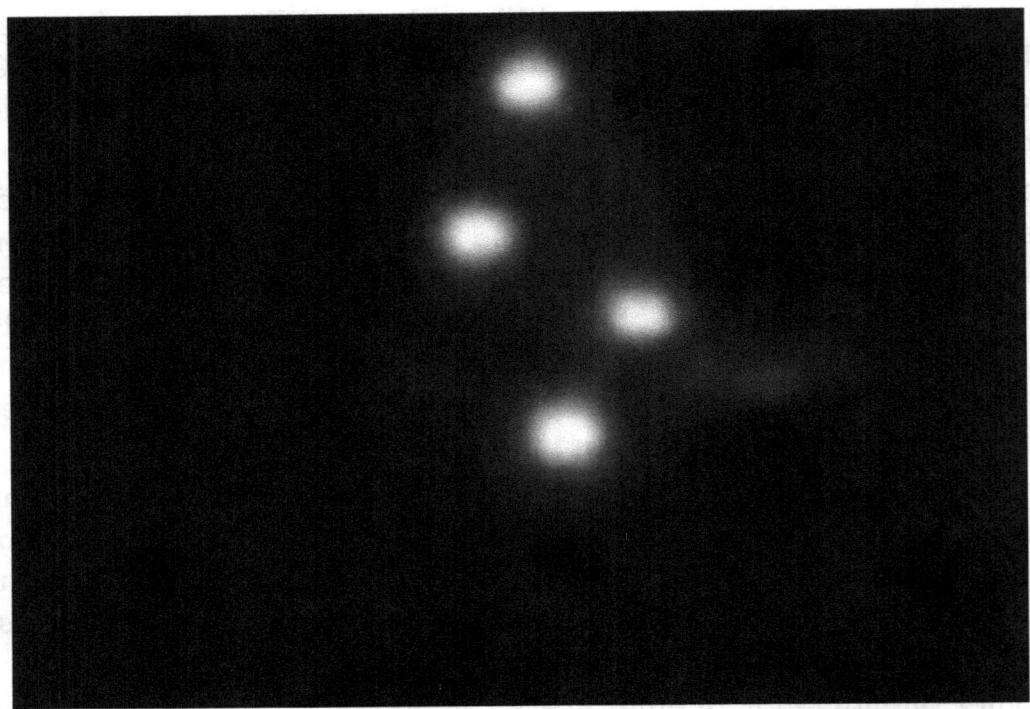

The Yakima Indian Reservation, located in south central Washington State has seen UFO activity for some ten years.

About a week later, Max had retired to his bed under the stars. Suddenly, the night sky brightened as a glowing object came at him from two kilometers away. As it sped low overhead it became an enormous zeppelin-sized orange glowing craft with a revolving white light. The following morning, Max found that his compass heading had been altered, his dog now possessed boundless energy, and he also had surprising energy. He could now lift 180 pound pipes with no effort at all.

About one week later, something in the sky projected a brilliant beam which bathed Max's entire camp in bright light for about three minutes. The period of "charged power" and "super-energy" at Hillside Mine lasted over two weeks. It would be foolish not to suspect that whatever was making the motor sounds in the hills above the camp also was capable of the other strange things that occurred.

ALIEN STRONGHOLDS ON EARTH!

We are offered additional clues about concentrations when we note other broader scale infestations and the mind staggering phenomena that can become associated with them. Landings, contact with UFO occupants, surgical cow mutilation, and encounters with ape-like entitles often begin to occur. Campers around Big Bear Lake on the eastern edge of the San Gabriel Mountains in California had seen some 30 UFOs over the course of three weeks.

They also encountered great ape-like figures. It was also discovered that you could pick up strange mechanical sounds upon planting a microphone on the forest floor. Within one hundred miles of Calvert, Texas, there were missile silos, radar units, as well as Air Force and Army bases. However, all the multiple phenomena that engulfed this region in 1973 did not seem to have anything to do with these establishments, since alien concentrations also occur in areas not having defense establishments. There were many UFO reports, plus landings, alien contact, mutilations, and, again, strange underground sounds.

The Yakima Indian Reservation, located in south central Washington State, is a region of hundreds of square miles of rugged forest land. During periods of high UFO activity, forest lookouts In fire control towers watched glowing objects maneuvering over distant ridges and moving about down into the canyons. Most of the other usual phenomena we have come to expect was present. When aerial activity was the heaviest, Chief Fire Control Officer, Bill Vogel, reported a sound similar to turbines or large truck motors which could be heard running underground. It sounded like a truck laboring to get up a hill and never getting there, it was reported.

Meanwhile, just south of the reservation and north of the Columbia River, another investigator (who formerly worked twenty years as a Los Angeles law enforcement official) reported yet another unbelievable situation. The area had been the scene of much UFO activity for some ten years. One ranch family believed the UFOs must be engaged in some kind of mining operation. The source of the machinery sound seemed deep underground. Ape-like entities (Big Foot critters) had shown up so much that the ranch horses and dogs no longer went into a panic when they appeared.

This family also claimed they had seen weird animals, such as pure white and black cougar-like cats with long front legs, short back legs, and a ringed tall. They also reported a pink flamingo-like bird, huge beaver-tailed porcupines, strange insects (such as pure white "black widow" spiders), and enormous moths. The family thought some of the creatures they had seen could be tropical in nature. I came away convinced of the reality of their claims.

The great profusion of assorted UFOs and other eerie happenings in the forested northwestern region of New Jersey in the 1975-76 time period was also most amazing. This sparsely settled region of hills, lakes, swamps, and forests in the

ALIEN STRONGHOLDS ON EARTH!

counties of Morris, Warren, Hunterdon, and Sussex was the site of another one of those macabre infestation scenes. Great sky flashes, brilliant ruby-red UFOs, and an estimate that there could have been as many as 600 sightings of ape-entities gives you some Idea of the "problem" that afflicted the inhabitants.

The hairy ones seemed to do a lot of howling and crying all over the place and left many tracks. We are primarily concerned here with the truck sounds reported by so many citizens for several years. Near White Meadow Lake, N.J., witnesses reported sounds resembling underground construction work or subterranean machinery. The sound of a truck climbing a hill was frequently described. The sounds would often last much of the night. One housewife thought they came from the direction of high voltage lines in a distant woods. Another witness, who had heard the sounds off and on for several years, pinpointed their location as that of a water storage tank behind his home. He also heard the sound of a baby crying, which came from the same direction.

This identical baby crying sound has been known to come from the throat of the ape entitles. Another couple in the same area discovered a row of tiny unusual footprints in their yard. Dr. Harley Rutledge, a respected physicist, conducted a valuable five-year study of an intense area in southeastern Missouri. He did not solve the burning mystery of an alien presence in such abundance. A number of investigators have espoused the "magnetic fault line" theory. Like many theories, I'm afraid it has too few facts to support it and would still leave much unexplained.

What are we to think about these disturbing underground sounds? Due to descriptions that often tally, I do assume that the witnesses are accurate and the sounds are coming from beneath the ground. I believe they are not being fooled by a massive stereophonic sound penetrating everywhere and only appearing to come from the Earth. Don't think for a moment that I am in any fashion being swayed toward a foolish "they-originate-from-under-the-Earth theory." One fact is proven beyond all doubt by the alien infestation modus operandi. That fact is, there must exist a space-time dimensional entrance (and exit) from our plane to some other realm. The "nuts-and-bolts boys" will have to bow out on this one. No explanation they could ever give would ever provide them with a leg to stand on.

In any event, it's pretty certain that the government will never reveal the truth about these awesome matters. They know that on the day that Earth's masses awaken to the realization of the fanatic stellar ultra-technology we called UFOs, social disintegration could become a very real possibility.

What are the aliens doing in these infested areas? Make no mistake, the UFO Intelligence Is up to something. At present, its motives and ultimate purpose lie beyond our limited awareness and comprehension. Comparatively, we are like blind slugs. The aliens' covert Influence upon all things human may be much more than we suspect.

ALIEN STRONGHOLDS ON EARTH!

Eyewitness reports from all over the world indicate the possibility of an alien presence in secret underground bases.

ALIEN STRONGHOLDS ON EARTH!

SECTION TWO

HIDDEN IN PLAIN SIGHT

Most people don't realize it, but you might not have to go far out of your way to come across an alien base. They are, as this title suggests, hidden in plain sight. It's easy for some ultra-terrestrials to get lost in a crowd because it's said they look so human that they could be walking the street easily "camouflaged" as an earthling.

There is one case I remember where a woman saw a UFO land on the outskirts of town. She got a pretty good look at the craft's occupants from her hiding place. A day or two later she was in the supermarket checkout line and, with two or three customers in front of her, she recognized a man whom she had seen disembarking from the spaceship just outside of the city. She tried to keep up with him as he proceeded outside the door, eventually following him right out into the parking lot where he seemingly vanished. This despite the fact that he was only a few feet ahead of her as he exited the store.

So keep your eyes open and be alert – but for safety's sake we don't want you being part of the "411" movement! – do keep at an adequate distance at least until you figure out what the aliens modus operande might be.

ALIEN STRONGHOLDS ON EARTH!

Chapter Four
THE UFO BASE 40 MILES FROM THE WHITE HOUSE
By Sean Casteel

In the course of his decades of research, publisher, editor and writer Timothy Green Beckley has run across evidence that the Ultra-terrestrials, as he prefers to name the occupants of UFOs – not being able to pin point their actual source or path of origin – have established strongholds or bases right under our very noses. Some of these bases or "hot spots" appear to be occupied by "friendlies" and others by those who are here with very negative vibes on sinister missions.

In "Alien Blood Lust" Beckley tells the horrific story of a Long Island, New York talk show host who was taken to a large "meeting hall" which fronted for the secret world headquarters of a strange group of alien "androids" who called themselves "The Council of Ten Men."

The talk show host, identified as J. P. Paro, was a friend of John Keel's and describes the incident thus:

"In the recesses of the building was a hidden laboratory in which what appeared to be several corpses were laid out on examination tables. Next to the 'corpses' were rows of test tubes and bottles filled with blood," Ms Paro recounted. "Each bottle was labeled with names, such as 'CHARLES' and 'SUSAN.' The Ten handled some of the bottles and sampled their contents orally and without facial expressions." The whole scene sickened the witness, and she was greatly disturbed by the experience. Hopefully your initial search for an Alien Base will not lead you in such a morbid direction.

Beckley reveals that way back in the mid 1970's he stumbled upon a UFO base located a scant 40 miles from the White House. At the time he filed a full report from which we extract some fascinating details.

"The setting sun loomed like a gigantic fireball on the horizon," Beckley writes,

ALIEN STRONGHOLDS ON EARTH!

"as Captain C.S. Wilson prepared to land his Eastern Airlines jumbo jet at Washington's National Airport during the early evening hours of November 19, 1975. The veteran pilot, with more than 10,000 flight hours to his credit, had descended from 24,000 to 15,000 feet when he caught sight of several cylindrical-shaped objects crossing from east to west in front of his plane at a distance of five miles."

Wilson at first thought it was a formation of three to four conventional aircraft, and the idea that the objects were a kind of missile that could change direction and target his plane also crossed his mind. The commercial airliner, carrying 85 passengers, was en route to Washington, D.C., from West Palm Beach, Florida, when the incident occurred. The weather was perfectly clear and visibility unlimited.

"Attempts to identify the aerial denizens were futile," Beckley writes. "NASA, which maintains a base near Richmond, Virginia, from which rockets are launched for atmospheric research, denied that any missiles had been fired at the time of the sighting. Due to the serious nature of Captain Wilson's report – and the fact that it took place inside highly-restricted military airspace – a Defense Department spokesman admitted that his agency was anxious to investigate the matter further."

The following night, Beckley continues, a multitude of highly luminous "fireballs" were spotted up and down the East Coast. Sightings were particularly heavy in the Washington, D.C., area.

Robert Hitt, the director of the Chesapeake Virginia Planetarium, had just delivered a lecture that night and was in the process of setting up a telescope on the roof when a UFO streaked by overhead. The object was a brilliant green and was falling straight down. It turned deep orange and finally bright red before it dropped below the horizon. The director said he expected to hear the rumbling sound of the object landing or the noise of a crash but was surprised by its silence instead.

"If someone painted a picture of it," Hitt said, "as it changed from bright green to red, you wouldn't believe it. It was the most incredible night of my life!"

Beckley acknowledges that many of his readers are probably aware that during the summer of 1952 UFOs buzzed the nation's capital on several occasions, causing near panic in military circles. The UFOs were tracked as blips on radar, seen simultaneously from both the ground and the air, and chased by our fastest military planes. But what is not as generally well-known is that sightings of UFOs over the D.C. area are not rare at all. In fact, they are quite common.

"Since the late 1940s," Beckley writes, "government employees, high-ranking military personnel and police officers, as well as a host of other responsible individuals, have spotted strange, pulsating craft soaring above such landmarks as the Pentagon, the Washington Monument and the White House. Al-

ALIEN STRONGHOLDS ON EARTH!

Frame from an 8mm film taken by George Adamski near Washington DC

though to the public, the military brass has repeatedly tried to dismiss these sightings as nothing more esoteric than 'meteorite showers' or 'temperature inversions,' officially a large percentage of the cases remain on the books as UNSOLVED.

"My own files contain adequate testimony," he continues, "which suggests that UFO witnesses have been threatened with instant dismissal from their government jobs if they dare to break the cloud of secrecy that hangs ominously over the Capitol Hill cover-up. Apparently it has become routine procedure to go so far as to transfer those in the Armed Forces who have been among the observers of UFOs over D.C. 'The powers that be' will go to great lengths to prevent what they consider to be 'essential' information leaking out."

To bolster his case for a secret UFO base hidden somewhere in Virginia, Beckley tells the story of Martha Long, a longtime resident of Warrenton, Virginia. Martha, beginning in 1953, when she was ten years old, underwent several UFO sightings, encounters with the UFO occupants and "missing time" episodes, which today are understood to be an indicator that an alien abduction experience has taken place.

At the age of fourteen, while with her brother, Roger, Martha was out in the early morning hours delivering newspapers on their rural route when they sighted a luminous figure standing in the road.

ALIEN STRONGHOLDS ON EARTH!

"It was on my brother's side of the road," Martha recalls, "so he saw it first and started yelling 'What's that?' Roger slowed the car and stopped. All I can definitely remember is coming face-to-face with this 'man' – if you could call him that – standing there on the road, our headlights reflecting off his silvery suit."

Martha told Beckley that the being was taller than average height, nearly seven feet tall, and was heavy-set in a muscular way. She thinks that the humanoid's head was covered with a helmet or hood. She definitely saw his face, but something prevents her from recalling the details of what it looked like. When asked if the being disappeared or just walked away, Martha said, "My memory eludes me. The last thing I can clearly recollect is that he seemed about to step into the path of our car. He walked onto the road and then paused in front of our car, as my brother started to hit the brakes."

Beckley says that Martha is convinced that the UFO occupants have been keeping tabs on her over the years and that at times they may even be reading her mind. After she got married and had children of her own, Martha claims that UFOs would often pace her automobile in the late afternoon and evening hours as she returned home from routine errands at the grocery store or the post office.

Several of Martha's sightings have been of a routine nature – lights in the sky – while others have been quite spectacular. On numerous occasions, she's seen them hovering just above the ground.

Meanwhile, other residents of Warrenton, Virginia, and the surrounding communities have come to take these metallic, sometimes glowing, ships for granted. "They come in and out of here so often," she told Beckley, "that nobody bothers to get excited any longer. I've personally seen these UFOs hover within a few feet off the ground so often that I've long since lost count."

Martha talked about just how rural her hometown is.

"Back when I was growing up," she said, "around the time of my initial sighting, our telephone directory consisted of a page and a half. And we didn't even have yellow pages. People in the city might think we're a little backward, but in reality we're just as aware as anyone living in New York, Boston or Washington. After all, we have TV down here too!"

Another sighting in the Warrenton area involved Sheriff's Deputy John Payne. While on routine patrol in December 1973, he noticed a bright object blinking on and off in the sky to the north. Stepping on the gas pedal, Payne began to pursue the craft. He followed it until he had climbed a hill off Route 55, where he was able to get a clear look at it.

The deputy took a pair of binoculars and peered through them. He was able to see that the object had red, blue and green lights streaming from top to bottom. In a subsequent report in an area newspaper, several residents listening to the police

ALIEN STRONGHOLDS ON EARTH!

Flying Objects Near Washington Spotted by Both Pilots and Radar

Air Force Reveals Reports of Something, Perhaps 'Saucers,' Traveling Slowly But Jumping Up and Down

band radio channel heard several officers excitedly commenting that "all hell is breaking loose" and that UFOs were all over the county. At that same time, in nearby Prince William, Virginia, two more UFOs were seen hovering over the southwestern portion of the tiny town.

"None of the sightings made on that day have ever been explained," Beckley writes, "and it doesn't seem likely that they ever will be."

"I'm not afraid to admit I've seen UFOs around here," Linda Bernhardt of Remington, Virginia told Beckley, "and so have others. Over the years I've seen all kinds of odd shapes in the sky, so you could never convince me that they were anything but spaceships. Of course they're from other planets. Where else could they possibly be from? I mean, they travel so gracefully, yet upon occasion can reach supersonic speeds without creating a ripple in the air. None of our own aircraft can do that."

ALIEN STRONGHOLDS ON EARTH!

Beckley moves on to talk about Bull Run Mountain, which an investigative columnist named Drew Pearson claimed was the location of a secret military installation that was created by tunneling into the mountain's base. The installation was intended to shelter important military and political officials in case of a nuclear attack while the rest of the country fended for itself. Further controversy ensued when it was learned that those to be admitted there were mostly personal friends of the president.

"And while the underground facilities at Bull Run Mountain were designed to be top secret," Beckley writes, "and its very existence denied, everyone in Washington seemed to know about it. Pearson even appeared on the Johnny Carson Show, where he and Carson joked about not being on the list of the 'special' few who would be permitted to go underground in the event of a holocaust. Needless to say, once the cat was out of the bag, the base was shut tight, though rumor has it that the underground caverns still contain enough food and supplies to comfortably take care of several hundred key individuals should the occasion arise."

One of the reasons Bull Run Mountain was selected for such an "honor" is because its natural caverns are said to be among the largest in the United States. Huge "rooms" carved out by nature's own hand millions of years ago are nearly perfect for the intended purpose. High ceilings and a wide expanse would make it almost unnecessary to do any "retouching." Millions of dollars could be saved by not having to dig or tunnel with heavy machinery.

"Needless to say, if Uncle Sam and the Pentagon brass knew of Bull Run Mountain's natural cavern formations in the 1950s," Beckley writes, "no doubt the occupants of UFOs could have discovered them eons ago and used them to their own advantage. If flying saucers are coming here from other worlds, the most practical thing for any alien race to do would be to construct bases right here on our planet so that they wouldn't have to travel senselessly back and forth the vast distance to their home planet. Time and energy could be saved and a lot more accomplished."

Beckley further reasons that, given that the U.S. is among the most powerful nations on Earth, the UFOs would want to be as close as possible to our seat of government. Also, the fact that most UFO sightings in the D.C. area take place at low altitudes leads one to suspect that the UFOs are flying "under the radar" there in one of the most closely guarded airspaces in the world.

In any case, the way sightings tend to cluster around the rural parts of Virginia outside of Washington – so frequently that the locals barely take notice of them anymore – combined with the "open secret" of the alleged military base at Bull Run Mountain, it is reasonable to assume that some kind of human and/or alien base exists there. Whether our scientists and military are working side-by-

ALIEN STRONGHOLDS ON EARTH!

side with the UFO occupants in rural Virginia remains to be seen, but the undeniable presence of SOMETHING in the area demands further study and analysis.

For those seeking further confirmation of this alien base we suggest a search of our YouTube channel. Under "Mr UFOs Secret Files" search for "Startling UFO Sightings of a Washington Whistle Blower," which is a video interview we did with the late security officer Paul Dickey.

Is there a secret base located under Bull Run Mountain, Virginia?

ALIEN STRONGHOLDS ON EARTH!

Chapter Five
CONTACT IN CALVERT

If you want to choose a state at random to seek out alien bases it might be a toss-up between California, New Mexico and the commonwealth of Texas, where the eyes are upon you for sure – but they are likely alien eyes, notes Tim Beckley, who reported on some very strange incidents over the town of Calvert.

In a 1975 article he wrote for the now defunct "UFO Report," entitled "Calvert, Texas: Flying Saucer Way Station," Timothy Green Beckley scribes: "Evidence continues to mount that alien beings have established bases in selective regions around the globe. Data now being meticulously sifted through and evaluated by researchers strongly suggests that the crews of these so-called flying saucers are currently in the process of carrying out a program that will ultimately affect all mankind – a program that may prove to be of monumental proportions."

Since the early 1950s, according to Beckley, the United States Southwest has been the focal point for repeated UFO activity. Sometime in the mid-1960s, the Air Force reported in a highly classified document that Texas ranked third in continual visits by UFOs. Beckley then tightens his focus to the tiny Texas town of Calvert.

"With a population slightly more than 2000," he writes, "Calvert is essentially like many other peaceful ranching communities nestled deep in this country's cattle raising belt. What makes Calvert so unique is that in this area – divided by the Brazos River and hidden away in Texas's Robertson County – UFOs have virtually become nightly callers. Witnesses have included a bank president and a retired Navy officer, as well as law enforcement officials. In addition to the many multiple-witness sightings constantly being reported around Calvert, there has also been a parallel flurry of related ground level phenomena."

Those other elements include interference with normal radio reception; unexplained tracks on the ground; mysterious deaths and disappearances of livestock; credible reports of landings and contacts with UFO occupants; and pecu-

ALIEN STRONGHOLDS ON EARTH!

liar noises coming from unknown sources deep underground.

Beckley says it is no surprise that this area of Texas is also heavily dotted with military security systems designed to defend this country in case of enemy attack. Within a radius of 100 miles of Calvert are numerous underground missile silos, mobile radar units, Air Force and Army bases, as well as many top-secret installations that require special clearance from the Pentagon in order to know their purpose. That purpose, one assumes, is something vital to the protection of our nation.

The editor-in-chief of the town's only newspaper, a woman named Gracia Unger, told Beckley that there have probably been more sightings of unexplained phenomena above this tiny town than anywhere else in North America. Unger

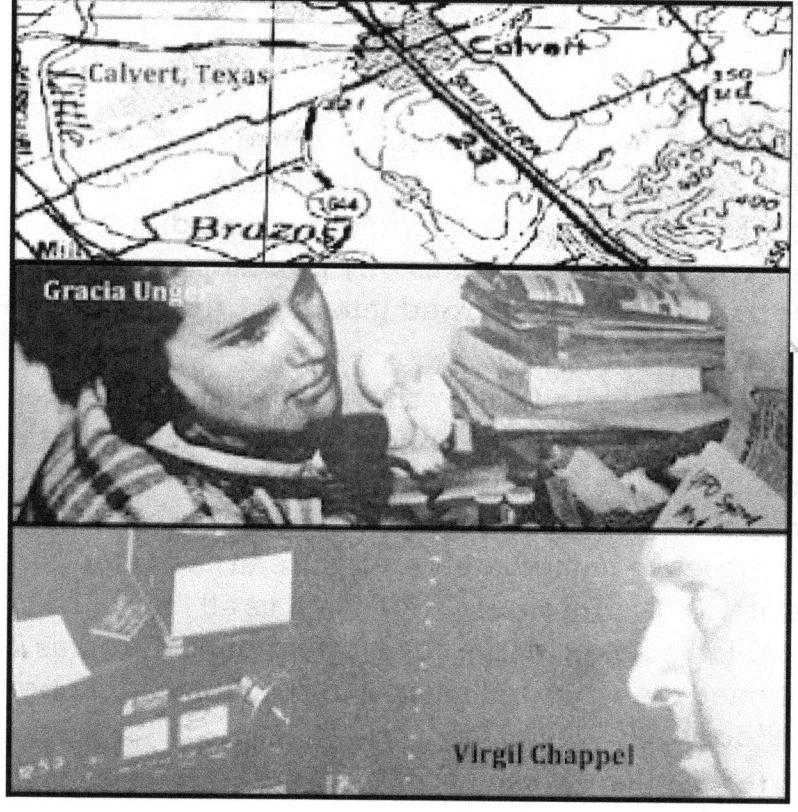

said that reports of UFOs in the area date back many years, but reached near-epidemic proportions during November and December 1973.

"I know something weird is going on around these parts!" Unger said. "Unfortunately, I have found it exceedingly difficult to get any substantial cooperation on this UFO problem from some eyewitnesses and the government. Though I've personally investigated more than 200 valid sightings – and had a good number of my own – there is a lot more happening which folks aren't willing to talk about with anyone! Those who have encountered these things are thought of as being crazy. It more or less comes down to this: people who have seen UFOs believe in them, and people who have not been exposed to the phenomenon directly laugh at those who have."

Unger said that the discs are nothing new, neither to the town nor to her. Local sightings date back to the late 1890s.

ALIEN STRONGHOLDS ON EARTH!

"Many of the events that have transpired over the ensuing years," she continued, "have gone far beyond mere aerial appearances. From time to time, some remarkable – no, incredible – ground level mysteries have occurred which tie in directly with UFOs, and have convinced me that Calvert is being used as a waystation by these beings."

At the time of Beckley's interview, Unger said that she had seen a variety of strange craft, "at least 50 of them." Her first sighting took place in 1956, when she was twelve years old.

"I often think about what happened," she said, "and can vividly recall the details of my experience because it shook me so."

Unger was with her father, an executive for Southern Pacific Railroad, and they were in the family car returning home after a visit with friends of the family. The time was around 3 A.M., and they were driving along Highway 6, a few miles east of Calvert.

"With absolutely no advance warning," she recounted, "from out of the blackness of space, came these two glowing objects, which proceeded to follow us down a rather deserted stretch of road. We were really frightened and didn't know what to expect. Finally, curiosity getting the best of us, my Dad stopped the car and we got out and watched as the two objects merged into one, growing larger by degrees, like a balloon being blown up.

"Eventually it moved off," Unger continued, "hovering about 30 feet in the air over a nearby pasture. Without making a sound, this object began shining a large and extremely powerful searchlight on a herd of resting cattle. Next it moved in our direction, coming to within 25 feet of us, throwing its eerie spotlight upon us in the process. Our instincts told us to leave immediately and we returned to the car. The UFO – we didn't know what it was then, of course – followed us all the way into Calvert and then zipped off to a high position in the sky, turning pinkish-red as it soared upward. My father cautioned me not to tell anyone about the incident because he said no one would believe us."

Beckley's article also offers the testimony of many other credible witnesses to UFO activity in high concentrations there in Calvert. Just as Gracia Unger can be assumed, with her journalistic training, to be able to sort and present the facts of what's happened to her and the Calvert area, so are many others equally trustworthy observers, including a bank manager and several local business owners, people unlikely to fabricate such a story, even for laughs.

The list of witnesses also includes local law enforcement officials. One sheriff's deputy spoke to Beckley but asked not to be named since it might endanger his job.

"We get sightings almost every night," the deputy said, "but what can we do? Our hands are literally tied. After all, the government keeps saying that flying

ALIEN STRONGHOLDS ON EARTH!

saucers don't even exist. We're not in the business of chasing ghosts. What would we do if we caught an alien being anyway?"

Beckley writes: "That reputable individuals have seen strange objects above Calvert cannot be denied. The existing evidence is now overwhelming. But why have the ufonauts chosen this sector of the Southwest as a base?"

For an answer, Beckley quotes a longtime independent researcher and local witness named Tommy Blann.

"Calvert lies right in the middle of one of the greatest concentrations of military installations," Blann declared, "to be found anywhere in this country. To give you an idea of what I mean, there's Gray Air Force Base in Killeen, about 60 miles northwest of Calvert. Around the perimeter of this base, the government has set up mobile radar units, positioned on the back of flatbed trucks. These units can be moved about the badlands from one spot to another at a moment's notice, supposedly for the express purpose of tracking enemy missiles coming in from the Gulf of Mexico.

"Nicknamed the 'Red Eye Radar Units,'" Blann went on, "I have been told by a reliable source that they have picked up speeding unidentified objects on a number of occasions. A UFO was supposedly monitored on these radar screens for more than ten minutes. Apparently it reached the point where jet interceptors almost had to be scrambled to check out and identify the 'bogie.' From what I'm led to believe, the object shot off into space moments before a red alert was to be sounded."

Blann said that the now-defunct Project Blue Book, a program conducted by the Air Force to investigate UFO reports, published graphs that showed that Central Texas has always been among the hottest of UFO hotspots. This area is also known for its tight security, which cloaks in a veil of extreme secrecy the various scientific and military research projects being developed there.

There are also at least three strategically-placed underground missiles silos in this area of Texas, Blann told Beckley.

"No one really seems to have any idea of what goes on in these particular silos," Blann said, "but we have been told these installations are extremely important to the well-being of our country. Other than that, we are kept in the dark."

Meanwhile, the Army base Fort Hood is located within 15 miles of Calvert. Many UFO witnesses have claimed that they either originated at – or headed in the direction of – Fort Hood. On several occasions, base officials have debunked the UFOs seen there as misinterpretations of conventional objects such as flares and balloons sent aloft as part of some routine nighttime test. Near-paralyzed witnesses have, in most instances, refused to accept these explanations.

Moreover, the world's largest airport, Dallas-Fort Worth, is located just 80 miles due north of Calvert. As many as a dozen UFO sightings on any given night alleg-

ALIEN STRONGHOLDS ON EARTH!

edly take place there. Airport regulations require, as a matter of air safety, that operation crews and public safety officers immediately report anything they can't identify.

The mere thought that so much UFO activity takes place less than 100 miles from Calvert is unsettling enough. Yet the facts cannot be denied, Beckley writes.

"We have come to learn that UFOs are frequently seen around or near key space and military installations," he says. "No doubt they are keeping a close surveillance on the development of our technology, just as we maintain a watchful eye on any important advancement made by foreign adversaries."

But if the UFOs really are maintaining a base in the area, where are they hiding?

Tommy Blann offers this possibility, saying he personally knows of caverns which exist beneath farmland on the outskirts of town.

"There is a complex network of caves and tunnels," he says, "which connect somewhere underground. A check of geological survey maps will show that Calvert is built directly on top of a fault line which zigzags for miles in all directions."

Ranchers and farmers in the area have reported hearing peculiar noises coming from deep beneath their feet. It appears to them as if a steady droning noise is originating from all directions but is loudest when ears are placed to the ground. This has led Blann to conclude that "UFOs operating around here have established bases for themselves far beneath the Earth's crust."

Blann also theorized that the aliens may be using the silent underground hot mineral streams that crisscross that part of the state as a large hydrodynamic generator, thus supplying the space visitors with all the energy they need without having to construct anything aboveground which would give their presence away.

"Many UFO investigators are watching the heavens above this area in Texas," Beckley writes. "The general consensus is that an event of tremendous universal importance will occur here in the not-too-distant future. On this point, almost all eyewitnesses to Calvert's UFO mystery agree."

To Beckley's way of thinking such a prediction held true as UFOs went so far as to fly over the Bush family compound on their roundabout over the nearby town of Stephenville. Readers can research this case further on their own if they are not aware of it already. Some startling photos were taken and at one point the string-like UFO with its multitude of colored lights appeared over the county court house.

ALIEN STRONGHOLDS ON EARTH!

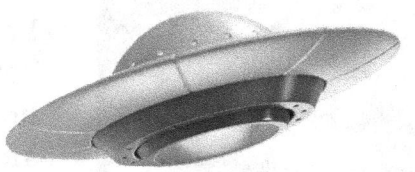

Chapter Six
UMMO ON EARTH

Perhaps at first we should simplify matters involving this most intriguing series of events which indicates aliens are underfoot and all around us. Tim Beckley provides us with this intriguing summation on what has become known widely as the UMMO case, going so far as to set it up in caps at the beginning for emphasis.

THE ALIENS ARE AMONG US! THEY WISH TO COMMUNICATE! AND HAVE EVEN CONSTRUCTED CITIES IN REMOTE PLACES WHILE THEY ARE HERE!

The story of UMMO starts with a series of letters and phone calls to various Spanish UFO researchers in 1965 that purportedly came from an extraterrestrial race. While the most commonly reported method of ET contact is clearly by telepathy, the aliens in this case tried a more direct, decidedly earthly method of communication. The letters contained highly detailed discourses on such weighty topics as physics and medicine that could only have been written by experts on the cutting edge in those rarified fields that are light years beyond what a lay hoaxer could have come up with. One of the letters also predicted that a UFO sighting would occur on a certain day at a certain location in Spain, and the ship did indeed appear on schedule and at the appointed place. It was a rare event in the annals of Ufology, a supposed alien prediction that actually came true. The race behind the letters and activity claimed to have come from a planet named UMMO, saying that they had arrived on Earth in 1950 and had been biding their time before contacting trustworthy Earthlings. They had come in response to a weak signal inadvertently sent out into space by a Norwegian ship conducting ionospheric research in 1934. It was later verified that both the ship and its experiments were indeed real-world events.

The case even involves photographic evidence!

ALIEN STRONGHOLDS ON EARTH!

UMMO and the Extraterrestrial Papers (2012), edited by Timothy Green Beckley

The first landing took place near the Basses-Alps in France. The aliens from UMMO also claimed to have built an underground base in France as well, and later to have established other strongholds, including in isolated, small cities, much like the aliens in the science fiction hit "District Nine." The story kicks into higher gear when two additional sightings occurred near Madrid in 1966 and 1967. In both instances, the bottom side of the ship displayed the letters UMMO as well as a distinctive pictorial mark seen throughout the book that resembles our own notation for Uranus.

The UMMO phenomenon is an anomaly unto itself in the world of UFOlogy. It is as yet a still unsolved mystery and cannot be easily dismissed in spite of how unlikely it would appear to be on the surface. Is this a genuine case of extraterrestrials reaching out to make contact with mankind in terms humans can understand? Something more direct and open than New Age channeling or the searching through by regressive hypnosis of people claiming to be abductees?

According to veteran UFO researcher and author Antonio Huneeus, "A vast number of technical and sometimes philosophical communications have been mailed in manila envelopes to no less than 20 and probably many more Spanish and French UFOlogists. There are allegedly also networks of correspondents in Canada, Australia, Yugoslavia, and other countries, although there is no concrete proof of this."

ALIEN ENTITIES AND THE COMMON MAILMAN

In other words, established UFOlogists in various parts of the world have been receiving what are essentially letters in the mail from extraterrestrials. How is that for direct and open communication? There has never been any proof that the letters were fabricated by some "earthly" intelligence agency or by a persistent

ALIEN STRONGHOLDS ON EARTH!

and well-informed hoaxer. It has also never been proven that the letters were what they purported to be: communiques from intelligent beings from the planet UMMO, who, by their own admission, have been visiting Earth secretly since 1950.

The aliens in question claim that their planet orbits a star which we catalog as Wolf 424, located 14.6 light years away from our sun. Wolf 424 is named after one of its discoverers, a French astronomer named Etienne Wolf, who worked in conjunction with fellow Frenchman Pons Rayet.

UFOlogist Antonio Ribera wrote the book, *Perfect Case*, which dealt with two UFO landings in the mid-1960s near Madrid.

THE UMMO SHIPS LAND IN PLAIN SIGHT

The late Spanish writer and UFOlogist Antonio Ribera is among the main sources for the continued credibility of the UMMO phenomenon. Ribera wrote a classic book, "A Perfect Case," which chronicled two UFO landings in the mid-1960s near Madrid.

The first landing took place on February 6, 1966, at about 6 P.M. Half a dozen witnesses observed the flight path and landing of a perfectly round saucer with three legs and a diameter of approximately 33 feet. One of the closer witnesses clearly saw an emblem on the ship similar to our astronomical symbol for Uranus. The symbol was visible in a series of controversial photos taken of the alleged UMMO ships as well as being seen by eyewitnesses at the scene.

It was around this same time that a Spanish UFO buff named Fernando Sesma began to receive by mail a number of technical papers relating to and supposedly written by the OEMMI, the inhabitants of UMMO. The second landing incident, which took in June 1967, was actually predicted several days before it happened in a written message mailed to Sesma and two other correspondents. Even the precise geographical coordinates of the landing were provided. All of the details of the 1966 sighting were repeated, to include the size, shape and symbol on the object.

Seven clear photos of a classic flying saucer with a large UMMO symbol were

ALIEN STRONGHOLDS ON EARTH!

taken that day but were later labeled as a hoax by Dr. J. Allen Hynek's Center for UFO Studies (CUFOS) and Ground Saucer Watch in Phoenix, Arizona. Nevertheless, Spanish UFOlogist Ribera continued to stand by the photos as genuine.

TECHNICAL PAPERS TOO COMPLEX TO SIMPLY DISMISS

In the wake of the two sightings, the list of correspondents quickly grew to the aforementioned 20 people mostly residing in several Spanish cities. The envelopes contained no return address, which meant the correspondence was only one-way. But a steady stream of highly technical papers, some dealing with the nature of the universe and the basis for intelligent life in the cosmos, continued for some time.

Photo of a UFO with UMMO markings on its underside. Taken on the outskirts of Madrid in 1967.

Huneeus is careful to point out that the content of UMMO material is different from that of most contactee cases because the letters don't contain messianic messages of doom and salvation. The method used is always by mail and not direct or telepathic contact. Unlike George Adamski and countless other "cosmic souls" trying to convert our confused human species, the authors of the UMMO papers write things like, "In no way do we wish – and we sternly warn you about this – to see you fall into the temptation of switching your religious, scientific and politico-economic ideas for ours. It would be a mistake for you to adopt our ideas, concepts and statements at face value."

Meanwhile, there is little reason to call the affair a simple hoax, Huneeus says,

ALIEN STRONGHOLDS ON EARTH!

because we must consider the duration and complexity of the material involved.

"One must remember," he says, "that some of the papers on advanced physics, cosmology, biology and space propulsion actually astounded a number of respected Spanish and French scientists and engineers."

Or, as Dr. Jacques Vallee, the venerated computer expert and UFO researcher, theorizes, "If these concepts were not of extraterrestrial origin, then they must have originated with people who knew perfectly the ultimate advances of modern physics and had extrapolated beyond them."

THE HIDDEN BASES OF THE "PEOPLE" FROM UMMO

The extraterrestrials, if one accepts that explanation, could possibly look human enough to pass among us unnoticed. These same human-looking aliens most likely congregate in groups together, perhaps even building cities of their own and establishing small colonies throughout the Earth.

"At the beginning of their history," Ribera writes, "they would have to live in burrows, like rabbits. Later, they would have to build a complex underground architecture."

As they arrived on Earth, they quickly chose to locate in a semi-wilderness region to avoid being discovered too soon. They found a hill near the small town of Digne in the south of France and dug themselves a home there. During their first days on Earth, the UMMO aliens were extremely anxious, expecting immediate attack from Earth's inhabitants. They feared having to rush out from their underground dwellings and flee if their presence was somehow made known to the nearby earthlings.

Another UMMO base was located in Australia, near the town of Adelaide. One of the UMMO people attempted to drive a car in their new home Down Under and died in an accident. The aliens are said to be "hemeralopic," meaning they have impaired vision during the daytime, so they live essentially during the night. In the day, they simply sleep, like owls.

One of the statements from the UMMO aliens about their relationship with earthlings involves the idea that the human life form is spread throughout the universe and is not the sole province of humankind on this planet. The UMMO aliens obviously blend in with normal human beings to the extent that they can put letters in the mail or at least hire earthlings to do it for them. But their grip on this planet might be much stronger than that.

ALIEN STRONGHOLDS ON EARTH!

Chapter Seven
WE ARE AMONGST TRUE COSMIC FRIENDS!

Paola Harris is an Italian-American photojournalist and investigative reporter who has worked for many years conducting interviews with military and government officials about their UFO knowledge and experiences. Harris says she takes a very "nuts-and-bolts" approach to the subject. She was an assistant to Dr. J. Allen Hynek of "Project Blue Book" fame and interviewed Colonel Philip Corso, a military insider who went public with claims of back-engineered alien technology. Corso told her at one point that the military wasn't worried about crashed ships or gray aliens but instead feared the idea of "some of these people walking in-between the halls of the Pentagon" - in other words, human-looking aliens.

Harris says it is rare for her to investigate cases of claimed contact with extraterrestrials, but she felt so compelled by the evidence for a case in Italy that she decided it needed further scrutiny. The case features human-looking aliens and is touted as an incredible story of mass contact between humans and aliens. Normally, people thought the contactees were a small group. But in 1956, there was a contact case involving hundreds of people. Several of them came forward and told their story to the late Italian researcher and author Stefano Breccia, from whom Harris received most of her information on Friend Ship.

The eyewitnesses told Breccia that the beings spoke perfect Italian. The beings explained that the Earth had been created for a positive purpose and that man was turning everything into evil. The level of human morality is

ALIEN STRONGHOLDS ON EARTH!

considerably lower than that of the aliens, who had come to ensure that the situation with mortal man didn't get completely out of control. The beings had not come to conquer but instead emphasized that all things required love and respect and that everything should be done in accordance with those principles. The ETs were familiar with Earth's history and its differing religions.

They had already been on Earth for many years, they told Breccia, living at secret bases in various places on the planet. They preferred not to reveal themselves publicly because people weren't ready for open contact. Breccia himself met many of the aliens, some of them very tall, including one alien who was 15 feet tall and was photographed towering over some trees in the background. The aliens were given the name "W-56s," because the year they revealed themselves to their communal followers was 1956. They sometimes communicated telepathically and at other times through crystal radio sets. The W-56s are a confederation of different people coming from throughout the known universe. Earth holds a mystical appeal to them since it is one of a tiny number of planets on which conscious life exists.

Some of the occupants were said to be upward of 15 feet tall in the Friend Ship case.

Having established a base in Pascara, Italy, the W-56s asked for help from the humans, requesting industrial quantities of fruit and vegetables of all kinds. After taking delivery of a truckload of vegetables, the truck driver was lured away by human beings to have coffee, at which point the aliens teleported the goods off the truck. The driver was surprised to return and find the truck was already empty.

Harris says that there were similar human/alien communal bases in Germany, Chile and Russia in the 1950s. Jealousy and competition soon

ALIEN STRONGHOLDS ON EARTH!

erupted, and the beings admonished the humans to "stay united." The W-56s also revealed the existence of an enormous undersea base in the depths of the Adriatic, almost in contact with the continental shelf. Many smaller bases are located closer to the surface. Meanwhile, topside, according to Breccia, "Our friends are living inside small bases or plainly within our environment. As far as I know, all of them are humanlike, with only minor differences, height among them."

There are bases near Pascara on the Adriatic Coast, which are difficult for Breccia to describe because of technology we don't understand. But there are no fixed entries into them. When necessary, a passageway is opened, and then closed, and everything goes back to the "status quo." One large base had a ceiling 300 meters high, and sometimes it rained inside the base.

"A lot of our Friends are living among us," Breccia said, "interacting at ease with our society, having Earth identities."

The Friend Ship beings were said to have set up a stronghold deep beneath this Italian castle.

INTERVIEW WITH PRIMARY WITNESS

Painter Gaspare de Lame, living on the shore of Lake Como, Italy, is one of the most important and influential witnesses and protagonists of the Friend

ALIEN STRONGHOLDS ON EARTH!

Ship case. Ivan Ceri conducted the following interview with de Lama in May 2010.

The interview was picked up by https://exonews.org/

IVAN CERI - When were you involved for the first time with the Friend Ship [Amicizia] case?

GASPARE DE LAMA - It started in 1960, between 1960 and 1961, in a very banal way, because I saw pictures made by [Bruno] Ghibaudi in a weekly magazine of about three flying objects that appeared on the coast of Pescara [Italy]. One was very strange. The picture was very nice and I thought that it could be real, because one object was really peculiar, while the other two were classic saucer-shaped.

UFOs were photographed on many occasions in association with the Friend Ship humanoids.

So I wrote to him a few lines, congratulating him and adding something like I hope that those beings help. After 2-3 days, the time for the magazine to receive the letter, I received a phone call from Ghibaudi, telling me that my letter was chosen among the many they received (he was using the plural) and he asked for an appointment.

He arrived in the evening - I had a group of friends, with whom I was sharing sightings information and field research, analyzing the different

ALIEN STRONGHOLDS ON EARTH!

cases, selecting hoaxes, from real ones - and I invited this group, too. He told about the things directly, without mentioning names (like Bruno Sammaciccia), he told about the W-56s, the bases, everything, and we were a little surprised.

Then, at the end of the evening, while we were going down the stairs, someone said: Are there any of the group still here? We were told, in fact, only one remained of that group, Paolo Torre, and all the others left. And after a couple of times that I have seen Ghibaudi, one evening he arrived with Bruno, and then my story began. I started to know a little more; the phenomena lasted for five years.

Bruno was a charismatic man, fascinating, with culture, he could speak very well, a passionate man, from the south. He was leading me slowly, nicely, through the events, the phenomena. I owe everything to Bruno. I still feel him in my heart, even if in the end he was tired, stressed. This story made two people go crazy. It's not an easy story. I also had some difficulty in dealing with it. One needs to be really balanced. The other world: know it, but we would like to be there. This world here: it is too unbearable, and so you live somehow in between, but after a while you get used to it and you manage it. Humans, who have a normal nervous system, can get used to everything. I imagine that the ones who had experiences even deeper than mine, had some stress, and Bruno also had a responsibility.

The first encounter was through objects teleportation. Film reels were materializing in the air and falling down to the ground

IC - Film reels of movies?

GL - Yes, movies that we then would watch or audio reels, with sometimes a greeting or sometimes some direction of things to do.

Then there were those control nuclei of the apartment, there was blue lightning, two to three meters long, with a diameter of 20-30 centimeters, light blue. They would pop up close to us without hitting us. They were renewing the nuclei of the apartment. Once every 20 days or so we would see those phenomena, because the nuclei needed to be renewed (updated?).

Then Bruno asked me to buy a little radio, he put it on the table and after two to three minutes a blue flame came out of it, half a meter high and he then said now it is ready. I always carried the little radio with me. Sometimes an ET member of the Friend Ship case or other members would speak through it. It would switch on by itself. Bruno would tell me to change the radio frequencies

ALIEN STRONGHOLDS ON EARTH!

and I would change them, but the voices would still be there. I even tried to put another radio close to it, tuned on Milan, both radios were tuned on Milan, but suddenly mine would switch into the voice of Sigir, while the other was still tuned on Milan.

Then, one day, Bruno told me "They want to give you a present," choose a place. So I have chosen a place close to Milan and we went there and we made a movie of the disc that I showed you before, and also photos. I then sent my photographic film to be developed and then we went home and we watched the movie.

Then a lot of funny things happened. I remember that in five years I have seen seven to eight times other discs after a call for an appointment, also small, bright, in the night, in the sky. One was moving in a particular way, doing like a theater, an exhibition. I saw many things.

IC - Did you have a direct encounter with one of the W-56s?

GL - No, I didn't meet any. Also, because it was a dangerous time, they couldn't get out of their bases. They were about three meters tall, so it wasn't so easy. Well, some were smaller. But it wasn't safe to go out. Only once they showed up on a hill, about 300 meters from the house of Bruno in Pescara, but I wasn't there. In the group we were about ten people. There was a judge, an economist, and a lawyer, and they saw them on that hill, saying hello.

Some of the aliens were short, under 3 feet, while others towered over the witnesses.

Bruno told us once that on that hill, that summer something would happen, and indeed it happened, they were there. They took pictures of them, there were some sea pines, and they were leaning towards these pines and were saying hello, I arrived just after that, and we went there afterwards to take measurements,

ALIEN STRONGHOLDS ON EARTH!

and we measured that he was four meters tall. They took pictures of them and we all went to the photographer to develop the roll of film.

On one occasion my wife was also there. We were at Bruno's home, and there was my little radio. We were a group of 10-12 people and we were sitting randomly. And Sigir started to talk from the radio. He said hello to everyone, following the order of our position. He could probably see us.

IC - How was he speaking, using good Italian?

GL Yes, good Italian, the Italian was perfect for all members, but Sigir, when he was greeting, he was saying greetings to everyone using an Abruzzo slang.

IC - They were imitating the dialect?

GL - Yes, they were imitating the dialect, and sometimes Dimpietro [an extraterrestrial] said "Gaspare, change your thoughts," because I was thinking about something not really good.

IC - With which one of the W-56s did you get on better? Which did you enjoy more? At least their voices.

GL - Sigir had a powerful voice, I liked Gallarate.

IC Why?

GL - Because first of all, he was one of the youngest. We called him Gallarate, because the first time that he arrived on Earth he saw Gallarate [name of a town, translator note] and he said "How beautiful is Gallarate," so we called him with this name. And one day there was the transmission of a radio quiz between two towns, Gallarate and Frosinone, and Gallarate was rooting (supporting) for Gallarate. And we laughed and I liked him because he was a little different from the others; he was more similar to us. But I liked them all.

Dimpietro did blame me twice, he was sweet but he was also very straight.

IC - Why did he blame you?

GL - Because I was thinking about something that shouldn't be thought. I was thinking about nervous things.

At the beginning, humans are doubtful. Doubt is part of an intelligent mind. Otherwise we would be too naïve. You can have strong doubts that disturb you or you can have light doubts that are only worries. But then, in the long term, from their voices and from their vibrations, you become trustful.

ALIEN STRONGHOLDS ON EARTH!

After all, the word "trust" exists. You can find it on the dictionary, so we should use it. At a certain point you have to trust someone. With doubt you can always question everything, endlessly, but trust came spontaneously. They make you feel it. It's like when you fell in love with your wife, it was enough, her word of love, and you trusted her. You didn't put her through a lie detector. You feel it. If we don't feel trust, it's our fault. You need more trust than faith, you could leave out faith, but trust is more important. Faith is too high, trust you can give it to a friend. Friendship is important. You can also not believe in God, but be loving. I know some atheists that are wonderful people. Trust is for me the most important thing.

I think that the differences were caused by different ideologies, Bruno once explained to me. There are things that we don't know about them (life values, laws, ethic, technology, science), so we cannot understand their different intentions.

To give me an example he said: Imagine a solar system that is disharmonic, that disturbs that side of the galaxy. Well, some civilizations, let's say the CTR [the enemies of the W-56s, translator note]. With their technology, they can cancel it, destroy it and therefore improve the harmony of that side of the galaxy. The W-56s would do different. In their ideology they think that if nature has created this solar system, one can try to reduce the damage while also respecting the nature of things. Of course the CTR would destroy the planet only if it was not inhabited, but they would interfere anyway in the nature of cosmos, while the W-56s would respect it, even if it disturbs.

This is a principle that develops also on ethics, on values. This doesn't mean that the CTR are bad. If they didn't destroy their own civilization it means that they love each other, they love their wives, their pets, but they have ideologies that are cooler and straight science could be their God. While for the W-56s, God is Love.

IC - Why do you think that those beings, that are so evolved, needed your logistic help?

GL - Yes, they needed water. For us, it was a minor effort, Bruno went to a friend who had barrels, he borrowed them, we filled them with tap water, we hired a van and we drove up there. Sometimes they would ask other material, rarely, four times in five years, it happened that you were asked for some material, and Bruno would organize it.

ALIEN STRONGHOLDS ON EARTH!

But I have a personal idea about this, I could be also wrong, but this is my idea: since they needed Uredda (love energy) to survive, they needed a certain quantity of it (if we want to put it in market words) but we didn't give it to them, because, we were not in harmony between us.

Let's say, I don't give you love, I don't give you friendship and so you jump in a river and, even if you can swim, you shout for help, to see if I give you my hand. So I have to help you and I give you my hand and so you receive my love energy that you need. So these demands for material could be a game to indirectly ask for uredda. But this is my idea. I told it to [Stefano] Breccia and he listened to me and said it could really be like this.

IC - Do you think that they have definitely left the planet, after 1978, after their defeat?

GL -- Well, I left in 1965, so I didn't live the last events. I hope not. I think not, because if they have this duty in regard to Planet Earth, they shouldn't be stopped by the failure of ten run-down people. I think, I hope that they are still around. They certainly are still around, but we as a group, on the uredda love energy aspect, we failed. We are not here doing heroics, saying victory, victory. No, no, we failed, which is worse.

One of many amazing photographs taken of the W-56s flying saucers.

ALIEN STRONGHOLDS ON EARTH!

IC - What did the W-56s give you, spiritually speaking? How did they change your vision about life?

GL - They made me understand that a better world is not utopia, because they exist. We are what we are, we are getting worse, while knowing that they exist and that they live in a wonderful way, and they are wonderful, makes you realize that it is not a utopia. So it is something, to live in a cosmos where there are goals that we could access.

Sometimes I was asking about God, once they answered me, "Look, Gaspare, think that we are here like a military party, not like a missionary one." We then understood, me and my wife, that we were asking things to which they could not answer, because we would have understood them on our own, through our spiritual evolution. We met Osho and this also helped us. So I received a lot from their way of speaking, from their presence.

IC -- Why, according to you, did the W-56s project fail, if it failed?

GL - Well, WE failed. Because of that uredda love energy, they called it uredda, it was an energy, like the one when there is a negative pole and a positive pole, quanta and tachyons, that uredda was the energy of love. A love that we should have shared between us in the group and toward them. Toward them it was easy. Among the group, we are what we are. After five years it was broken.

So they needed this uredda, which they collected in their instruments in the bases, defense devices or others, I don't know. And when they didn't receive this "fuel" (let's call it like this) the thing ended. They had to go, but I think, and it seems so, that they knew it very well, but they had to make this experience.

The interview was translated by Anissa Rahni. It is rough in parts, in particular where local slang words are used which are difficult to rephrase into English.

ALIEN STRONGHOLDS ON EARTH!

SECTION THREE

THE DESERT – ALIEN HOT SPOTS

Even if you don't spot a UFO or come across a concealed alien base, the desert is a wonderfully enchanting place. I know some people who upon their first visit never want to leave and end up moving or retiring to a real "hot spot" such as the Mojave Desert. But there is plenty of UFO activity to boot. Witness the following dramatic report – with stunning photo – http://www.section51-ufo.com/

"In December 2017 a Chandler, Arizona resident was photographing the moon when they noticed something far more spectacular in their camera, a UFO! Fortunately they submitted testimony and multiple photos of the UFO to MUFON."

"I witnessed the object hover," the witness/photographer said. "It's difficult to gauge the distance or size. It was black and circular or spherical. I didn't hear any noise. My husband was driving and the kids in the back seat also saw it. I immediately started recording because we often see strange things in the skies while driving the 347 and I never seem to get my phone out in time. Finally I have clear video! Hopefully some day we will have answers to what is going on in the sky over Maricopa."

So now let's take a closer look to see what the desert sands hold in store for us.

ALIEN STRONGHOLDS ON EARTH!

Chapter Eight
FROM THE DESERT SANDS CAULDRONS OF MAGIC WILL FLOW
By Regan Lee

EDITOR'S NOTE: There is something truly magical about the desert. The number of mystical experiences that people have in such locations - look at the pyramids of Egypt going back thousands of years! - is astronomical. I have been to Death Valley, Joshua Tree and the area around Kingman, Arizona, where the saucers fly on a regular basis and have done so since the late 1940's. Regan Lee is both a UFO eyewitness and a writer on her own UFO-related sightings and experiences and is quite a historian. She has the desert all figured out as far as its connection with alien bases and why the "Space Brothers" may have chosen the vicinity of Joshua Tree as one of their major strongholds. Regan's writing is poetic and relevant to our overall conversation.

* * * * * * * * * *

Many of the contactee experiences with extraterrestrials took place in the American deserts. The deserts as a place of mystical meetings with spirits from other realms is a setting known the world over. The desert has been the stage for other worldly encounters with Jinns, Space Visitors, Mary, religious deities and entities, and Dana Howard's meetings with the alien entity Diane was no exception to this idea of the desert as spiritual landscape.

As Diane said to Howard of this potent and ethereal location: "From the desert sands, cauldrons of magic will spring." It is in these silent and open

ALIEN STRONGHOLDS ON EARTH!

settings of the California deserts in the Yucca Valley that contactee Dana Howard met with the beautiful and wise Space Sister Diane, who called to Dana as other Space Visitors called to other contactees at the time. This is the same location where Giant Rock lives; home for George Van Tassel and, for a time, a place for all those to gather who had encountered peaceful extraterrestrials who wanted to share their knowledge with humanity.

UFO contactee Dana Howard.

During these meetings in the sacred desert setting, Diane shared with Howard eclectic discourses on the coming changes for Earth and humanity. These conversations followed much of the typical Space Brother and Sister message, which included warnings - no matter how lovingly or gently said - for humanity to get it together to better meet the intense challenges soon to come: dramatic climate changes, structural changes to Earth's geography, changes to the world economy and society's infrastructures. And last but not least, massive changes on a spiritual level. Diane's words, like many of the "aliens" during the contactee era, were words of love as well as warnings. Reading "Over the Threshold" today, which was written in 1957, is eerily prophetic, considering the climate changes, pole shifts, and economic fiascos we're currently experiencing.

ALIEN STRONGHOLDS ON EARTH!

Diane-She Came From Venus, by Dana Howard, and Why We are Here, By Gloria Lee.
Published By Inner Light/ Global Communications.

The pull of the desert was a strong one for Dana, and called to her in profound ways. The setting of the desert underscores the mythic qualities of Dana Howard's experiences. There is something quietly mysterious about the desert; a perfect place to meet visitors from other realms. The desert is an isolated area of course, where such esoteric meetings can take place without detection or interruption. Dana Howard saw the desert as sacred; calling the desert a "holy altar." A perfect place, this holy setting, for Howard to meet with her muse, her mentor, her personal astral guide.

Dana wrote that the desert was her "favorite retreat," a place where she could "seek seclusion." It is in the desert that our world intersects with other realms normally undetected. Diane explains the power of the desert to Dana: "Our deserts are the recognized last frontiers of hope. Out where the veil is thin ... (humanity can) readily be nursed back to health again." Somehow, some manifestation of an "other" came through that veil to communicate with Dana. It's possible the wide open areas of the desert, remote and fairly unbothered, act as portals between worlds. Someone once told me to "think about the sand" in relation to the desert setting and contactee encounters. What is the sand made of? Silica, crystals, quartz. Crystals are transmitters; they hold and impart information. It's not a coincidence humans have been using quartz crystals in not only technological ways but esoteric ways as well. As Venusian Diane tells Dana:

"The deserts are the storehouses of the Earth's precious minerals. Those who love the desert love it with a passion they cannot explain. At night there is an endless tune from the melodies of nature - voices and sounds from the

ALIEN STRONGHOLDS ON EARTH!

desert's own soul . . . brilliant by day with its billions of granules of golden sand, by night the spacious filament alive with twinkling stars."

SPIRITUALIZED ENERGY OF THE DESERT

The desert setting as a heavenly meeting space for alien visitors (whether that alien literally comes from Venus, or comes forth from another realm) was a powerful one for Howard. The desert, for Howard, was "in one's blood," and while she found the desert safe, peaceful and inspiring, she was also aware of the "desert violence" at times. Yet the desert always remained sacred: "But, with it all, when the desert was in one's blood, it was there forever."

The spiritual aspect of these meetings, while similar to many of the contactee encounters, seems to have been dramatically potent for Dana Howard. The very desert itself was "alive with spiritualized energy," seemingly acting as a magnet, pulling Diane from the ether onto the desert floor. Dana describes how Diane sometimes seemed to slowly dematerialize; sinking "into the Earth," or where her "presence was fading rapidly . . . to sink back into the sandy earth" once more.

It might be tempting to have an easy and glib response to stories like Dana Howard's - that she spent too much time in the desert sun. After all, what ridiculous stories!!! Meetings with a female Venusian named Diane; stories of subterranean demons; turning thought forms into physical reality; the secrets of remaining young; flying saucers - clearly the ranting of a kook, some could say. There were certainly shady aspects to many of the contactee episodes, and yet, even with the often goofy circus-type aura surrounding the contactee phenomena, synchronicities, UFO sightings, and other anomalous events occurred enough to make it difficult to dismiss these encounters outright. Add to this mix of mystically life-changing shifts with the bizarre claims and ridiculous antics of both contactees and the aliens is the fact that the government was interested in contactees.

Many of the contactees had some kind of military connection, and it's possible the desert setting was a convenient one for military psy-ops manipulations. We can't say for certain if Howard was some sort of shadow government mind control experiment or not. There were others who also saw the entity Diane, some independently of Dana. Witnesses saw flying saucers in the desert in the context of Howard's experiences. Like other contactee stories, which are often ludicrous on the surface, there are also things that aren't so easy to dismiss outright.

Too many "coincidences" occur, too many experiences, including independent witness accounts of UFO sightings, to entirely reject the contactee experiences, including Dana Howard's. In some ways, Dana Howard's meetings with Diane can be compared to BVM appearances. Like the figure Mary in Marian apparitions, Diane refers to Dana as "my daughter" numerous times. Howard describes Diane's "exquisite perfumes" and Diane's words were both warnings and urgings for humanity to reach a higher level of vibration, to work on compassion and self-knowledge.

Howard was aware of the traditional religious aspects of the desert as a sacred place. The Yucca Valley is home to Desert Christ Park, where a collection of statues based on Biblical holy figures silently witness numerous visitors throughout the year. Dana meets Diane here as well, where the message of a universal creed is preached, and the power of the desert is once again stressed. "It is ever in the sacred areas you will find the spiritual treasures. All of God's children seek the seclusion of the wilderness in days of stress . . . The shrines of the Earth serve as a focal point in consciousness . . ."

It's possible that Diane was of the same energy as the energy that gives us Marian apparitions and other "high strangeness" encounters (and not literally a "Venusian" at all). Something very powerful happened to Dana

ALIEN STRONGHOLDS ON EARTH!

Howard in the magical California deserts that stirred her creatively and spiritually. In fact, Diane, whoever or whatever she was, seemed deeply connected to Nature. Dana Howard's first meeting with Diane was in 1939 in the woods; as she wrote in her book "Diane: She Came From Venus"(1956): "My vision was directed to a gnarled old tree overlooking the antediluvian hills. Leaning casually against the grotesque trunk was a woman being of unsurpassed loveliness. Her head was radiant with a crown of fire, strands of golden hair cascading gently over her beautiful, slightly olive-tinted shoulders. The strange mystic light flooding her dark, prophetic eyes added a wishful something to all her other charms . . ."

Nature spirit, Venusian, Mary, a Trickster - Diane was a vivid energy that others besides Dana Howard also experienced in the desert "altars in the wilderness" where "cauldrons of magic" did spring forth, and, whatever the force was that was Diane, compelled Dana Howard to share with us.

Regan Lee

SUGGESTED READING

UP RAINBOW HILL

OVER THE THRESHOLD

SECRETS OF DEATH VALLEY

http://orangeorb.blogspot.com

http://reganleeufo.blogspot.com

ALIEN STRONGHOLDS ON EARTH!

Chapter Nine
MOJAVE BY STARLIGHT
By Diane Tessman

EDITOR'S NOTE: Although Diane has lived in a variety of "high energy" places both in the U.S. and overseas, nothing mesmerized her more than when she lived in the Mojave Desert, which she described as a place that is "exotically beautiful," allowing her the freedom and tranquility to experience many spiritual events which she than offered to the students of her Mystic Life Church. Now in Iowa living on the same property where she had her original contact with the space being Tibus, Diane recalls her days in and around Joshua Tree.

* * * * * * * * * *

Introduction: I treasure the years I lived in the Mojave Desert of California, and the many spiritual events and lessons offered to me by this exotically beautiful, mystical area. I sat at the base of Giant Rock and channeled powerful energies and messages; I witnessed strange lights in the dark desert skies; and I witnessed the ghost of a small boy sobbing beneath a Joshua tree. The High Desert has a pervasive presence of gold-scarlet sunsets, sweltering heat, and abundant paranormal, mystical, and spiritual vibrations. Yes, the Mojave herself is a great consciousness, a spirit who holds her secrets close but who delights in beckoning us to try to discover her mysteries! No wonder extraterrestrials and other dimensional beings love the Mojave too!

ALIEN STRONGHOLDS ON EARTH!

The foliage around Joshua Tree is unique to the Mojave Desert.

It was a clear, cold night in California's Mojave Desert, and I had never been closer to the stars. Nowhere else on Planet Earth do the stars shine and twinkle so brightly. The sky stretched overhead like a mystical black blanket with shining crystals everywhere.

Two friends and I had driven into the Joshua Tree National Monument to go UFO hunting. The Monument is a national treasure in the magnificent high desert. Incredible rock formations and bizarrely-shaped Joshua trees dot the desert landscape. It is all very alien and yet so richly of the Earth.

The three of us sat huddled under a blanket for about an hour and then decided to go home because of the cold. As we headed for the car, a large, brilliant, white light raced across the sky. Just as we struggled to tell each other it must have been a meteorite, it raced back in the opposite direction, stopping overhead for a second. It hovered just long enough for us to see smaller red, yellow, and blue lights in a circular pattern while its brilliant light, which illuminated the whole object, remained incandescent white.

Suddenly, it zoomed away, over the horizon from whence it came. We felt we had just witnessed something utterly incredible and otherworldly. We were speechless for a few moments, and then we couldn't stop talking about

ALIEN STRONGHOLDS ON EARTH!

what we had just seen. I will never forget that UFO sighting which the Mojave Desert offered us that cold, starry night.

It is fact: The Mojave Desert never fails to provide us with chilling phantoms, mysterious ghosts, and unexplained hauntings. It also offers us unidentified starships overhead and alien encounters under the watchful eyes of monster rock formations. It tells us stories of Coyote Man and the dreaded Chupacabra, and it even sings of "Hotel California," where you can check out anytime you want but you can never leave.

When I lived near the town of Joshua Tree, California, I felt I was undergoing an intense two-year education in all things mysterious and alien. I could feel the ghosts at Giant Rock, that gigantic, enigmatic boulder a few miles from Landers, a village which suffered a devastating earthquake in the early 1990s.

The ghostly phantoms at Giant Rock were mostly Native American in "feel" and once I heard their flutes playing in the desert wind. Also, there was the spirit of George van Tassel.

In the 1950s and 1960s, tens of thousands of people streamed into Landers, blocking the highways for miles around. On they went to the flying saucer Mecca of Giant Rock, gathering with George van Tassel. At several of those gatherings, it is said that van Tassel, at will, summoned his extraterrestrial friends, who appeared overhead. Many people felt the alien contact and followed van Tassel's enlightened, brilliant teachings.

In 1951, his friends from Venus astrally transported van Tassel aboard their giant star ship and introduced him to "The Council of Seven Lights." The Council told him to build a

A UFO appears over the Giant Rock UFO convention held in the desert sands of the Mojave.
Photo by Michael X Barton

ALIEN STRONGHOLDS ON EARTH!

structure in that energized area of California's high desert; they promised that this building would extend human life and help humans become enlightened.

Built according to the precise directions and requirements of van Tassel's alien friends, The Integratron still offers mind-blowing acoustics and experiences of an almost psychedelic nature.

I recently reread George van Tassel's book, "The Council of Seven Lights," and was amazed at the cosmic knowledge in its pages. It is a book which reflects not only metaphysical wisdom but which also delves into quantum physics within a spiritual format. Van Tassel was a genuine contactee of great experience and wisdom.

In 1995 and 1996, my daughter and I traveled almost daily to Giant Rock from our home in the town of Joshua Tree. We wandered around it; we meditated beside it. In the harsh sunlight of the desert day, the white quartz which composes Giant Rock gleamed and glistened. We tried to figure out how that huge boulder came to stand alone in the desert. There were no other boulders like it anywhere around. Did the Giant Rock roll across the desert from one of those hillsides miles away during an earthquake? Or did it come from the sky?

Giant Rock sometimes made us sad; there was ugly graffiti scrawled all over it. Hundreds of dirt bikes and motorcycles had wrecked the environment around it. There was also the infamous crack at the bottom caused by bonfires. The crack seemed to lead to a cave beneath the boulder. Rumor had it that a Nazi fugitive had hidden in this cave.

And so it was not surprising when, several years later, enigmatic Giant Rock suddenly split in half. When it did so, I had already moved to Iowa, but I remembered how sad the giant boulder itself seemed to be. No one respected it or seemed to remember the universal light work which had gone on around its domain. Giant Rock was a phenomenon of Mother Nature and perhaps a gift from outer space, and all humans could do now was to scrawl ugly words on it, scraping away the environment with their noisy bikes. One theory says that the vibrations from motorcycles helped split the mighty rock.

The tragedy of Giant Rock leads me to an insight on the mystical energy of California's Mojave Desert: This unique quantum energy can be used for enlightenment and goodness, or it can be used negatively.

The Manson Family's Spahn Ranch was in the Mojave.

ALIEN STRONGHOLDS ON EARTH!

It has long been joked that bodies murdered in Los Angeles end up in a hole in the Mojave.

The ghost of a rock musician who is said to have overdosed in the 1970s haunts the only motel in the town of Joshua Tree.

Yes, I do remember a feeling of panic sometimes in that hot desert sun, a feeling that the spirits there were restless. Coming home one noon, I saw a small child sitting under the Joshua tree across the road. The child was crying softly. I rushed over, only to have the child dematerialize.

My daughter witnessed a tribe of "restless spirits" one dark desert night as they seemed to be picking leaves off of one of the trees in our yard. She said they seemed confused and unhappy.

I researched various paranormal happenings for a video I did about Giant Rock and the Mojave. I traveled into Joshua Tree Monument to find the precise rock formation into which a teenage couple is said to have disappeared. I had just enjoyed the film "Picnic at Hanging Rock," which is the account of young girls on a picnic in Australia who disappeared without a trace into a mysterious rock formation.

Sand as far as Diane Tessman can see.

ALIEN STRONGHOLDS ON EARTH!

This particular formation in Joshua Tree National Monument is actually two formations, standing right next to each other. Between them is a narrow "doorway" through which one can squeeze. Apparently the teenage couple went through the doorway and was never seen again. Their friends hurried through the same doorway minutes later, searching for them. Was there a dimensional portal which opened precisely as they went through, and which then closed again?

Mother Earth has given the Mojave Desert very unique and dynamic energies which give rise to endless paranormal events as well as beckoning visitors from other worlds and dimensions. As far as I am concerned, and others may differ, I believe there have been more UFO sightings in the Mojave than any other area on Earth.

* * * * * * * * *

Diane's website: www.earthchangeprediction.com

Order online or directly from Diane: dianetessman0@gmail.com

Books

EARTH CHANGES BIBLE

THE TRANSFORMATION

UFO AGENDA

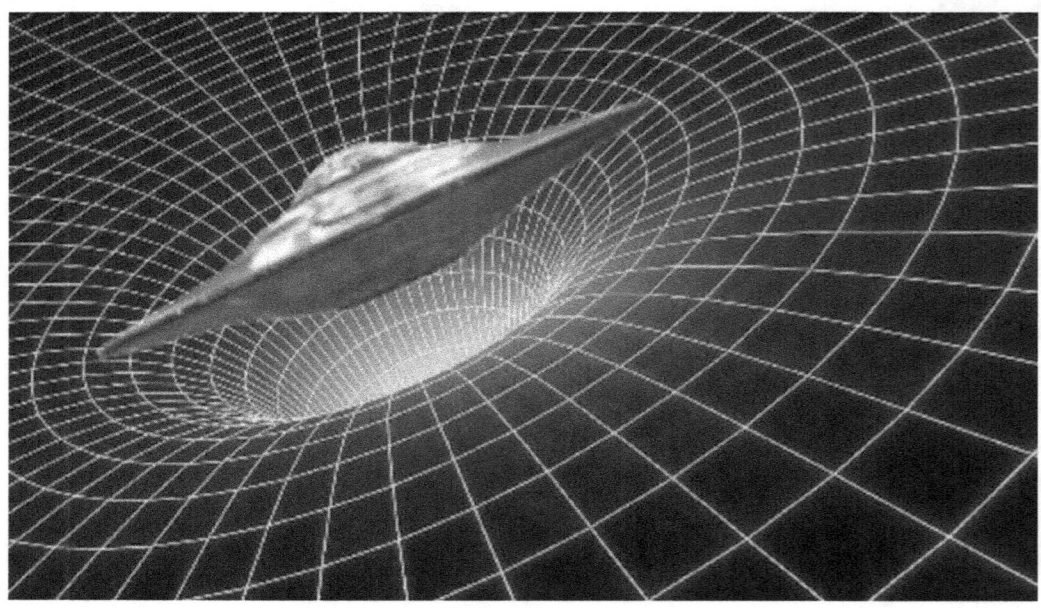

ALIEN STRONGHOLDS ON EARTH!

Chapter Ten
MIDNIGHT MADNESS IN THE DESERT
By Timothy Green Beckley

Author Tim Beckley wonders if a UFO will soon come down in Death Valley?

I had never seen anything like the sky at night out in Joshua Tree, California. I was off the beaten path a long way from Palm Springs where I had dug into one of the local resorts.

For my trip I had rented a convertible and, boy, am I glad I did. With the roof down it was possible to catch a breeze even though the temperature had been over a hundred a few hours ago, and was still probably hovering around 85 or so. But the warmth of the desert was nothing compared to the sky overhead. As the city and its mega lights vanished behind me the stars came out big and bright. They were dazzling. There was, I thought, a heaven for sure, and it had disguised itself as the Milky Way. We even had a UFO convention in Palm Springs in the 1990s. Cinema bigwig Robert Wise, who directed the "Day the Earth Stood Still," was our keynote speaker and all the contactees still living showed up to receive outstanding

ALIEN STRONGHOLDS ON EARTH!

achievement awards, including members of George Van Tassel's extended family.

Kesha (born 1987, Kesha Rose Sebert) is among a new generation of pop stars. I have to admit I am not familiar with her music, but now I am inspired enough to give her songs a listen - mainly because the musical trendsetter says she had a UFO experience in the desert.

There is no other place like Joshua Tree in the Mojave as far as UFO sightings and encounters - Yes! I said encounters - go. There is a magical sense about this place, as Regan Lee and Diane Tessman will soon tell us. But to get back to Kesha, who says she was totally sober at the time. The singer, songwriter, actress and rapper was so inspired by her experience that she describes it in a song on her album "Rainbow":

SPACESHIP

I always said when I'm gone, when I'm dead

Don't lay me down with the dirt on my head

You won't need a shovel, you don't need a cold headstone

You don't need to cry, I'm gon' be going home

I'm waiting for my spaceship to come back to me

It's coming back for me

I don't really care if you believe it's coming back for me, yeah

I been living in a lonesome galaxy

But in my dreams, I see them come 'n rescue me

Look up in the sky and there they'll be

I bet you'll think of me then

You're gonna say, "Ooh, look at that, oh yeah, yeah"

Damn, if it ain't true

They're coming back for me, they're coming back for me, yeah

I knew from the start I don't belong in these parts

There's too much hate, there's too much hurt for this heart

Lord knows...

Kesha's story first came out on the Zoch Song Show (it's on YouTube) and she was deadly serious about what she saw.

ALIEN STRONGHOLDS ON EARTH!

Pop star Kesha's life changed after a UFO encounter.

"I was in Joshua Tree, totally sober, let me preface - completely fucking sober - I think people would be like, 'She was on acid or something!' Well I wasn't. I was on nothing. I was just a lady in the desert. I looked up in the sky and there were a bunch of spaceships.

"I swear to God there was five to seven, and I don't know why I didn't like try to take a picture of it. I just looked at it. I was sitting on a rock and I was like, 'What the hell is that?' I was trying to figure it out, and then they went away. And then they came back.

The highly respected trade publication "Billboard" picked up on the story and featured it, pointing out how her single "Praying" was trending toward the top of the chart.

The pop star went on to say that "they came back in a different formation" than the one they were in previously. "I was like, 'Those are fucking aliens.' They were spaceships!"

"Fans might recall," Billboard notes, "that [previously] she hinted at this happening: 'UFOs are real. I have seen them. Not playing,' she wrote at the time."

ALIEN STRONGHOLDS ON EARTH!

That sighting wound up being a defining moment that partly influenced the theme of Rainbow. In her chat with the radio show host, Kesha also talked at length about her new single and evolving as both an artist and a person.

"I just feel like a totally different artist - and not in a good or bad way," the singer, who is now at a different point in life in her thirties, said. "I had a great time. The first record was super fun, and that's where I was at. This is where I am now."

Right on, girl. You tell 'em.

SUGGESTED READING

SECRETS OF DEATH VALLEY edited by Tim Beckley

Tim Beckley catches a hot breeze in the desert.

ALIEN STRONGHOLDS ON EARTH!

Chapter Eleven
HAUNTED DESERTS: UFOS IN THE EMPTINESS
By Scott Corrales

EDITOR'S NOTE: I have known Scott Corrales going back several decades. He is your man to see in the Hispanic community for up-to-date UFO activity. He was a vital contributor to our family of magazines, "UFO Universe," "UFO Files," and "Unsolved UFO Sightings." A prolific writer and investigator of UFO and paranormal events in the Hispanic communities worldwide, he is one of the most respected names in the global world of UFOlogy, with contacts in South and Central America, Mexico, Spain and the Caribbean. The Institute of Hispanic Ufology was established in October of 1998 with the appearance of the first issue of Inexplicata. The organization currently has representatives and contributing editors in over a dozen Spanish-speaking countries.

His research into sightings and hair raising encounters with the Chupacabras are the inspiration for this publisher's fascination with the lust for blood by the Ultra-terrestrials. He is also a contributor to the "Dark Side of UFOlogy Trilogy," which includes "Alien Blood Lust," "UFO Hostilities," and "Screwed By the Aliens."

****

Many years ago I wrote an article for *FATE* magazine about lost civilizations in our planet's desert areas - regions that may have once been suitable for large, organized communities, even cities, but which had

ALIEN STRONGHOLDS ON EARTH!

succumbed to erosion and were now simply uninhabitable. Even in the Sahara Desert we find the ruins of Roman settlements in desert oases, otherwise hospitable locations that settlers had to abandon due to a proliferation of scorpions, for example.

They may be the repository of lost civilizations, but it can also be said that our desert regions appear to be teeming with something else - unusual happenings that fall under the loose mantle of UFO phenomena, in the strictest sense. Are these luminous manifestations the residual energy of the peoples who once occupied this region, reduced to flickering lights in the dark? Perhaps even manifestations of the spirits of the empty lands that kept them in abject terror during the long desert nights? Or are we more inclined to think in terms of extraterrestrial visitors availing themselves of these hostile, recondite areas to shelter their spacecraft and operating bases on our small blue marble?

Deserts are most often haunted and attract UFOs like bears to honey.

ALIEN STRONGHOLDS ON EARTH!

Colombia's La Tatacoa desert is one of these locations, nestled in the heart of the mountains. The first report we have of its existence comes from Gonzalo Jimenez de Quesada, one of the lesser-known Conquistadors, entrusted with the mission of "reaching the Kingdom of Perú by following the course of Magdalena River, demanding gold from local natives to finance the expedition." Easier said than done, as the explorer traversed some of the most astonishing badlands in the South American continent, known as the "valley of sorrows" due to the overwhelming presence of rattlesnakes. Later researchers would find in La Tatacoa a startling deposit of Pleistocene fossil remains.

The odd geographical feature has also become known for its constant UFO sightings. A woman named Orfanda Soto, a permanent resident of this forsaken location, claims having seen these spectacular lights from her farm. "On two separate instances," Orfanda told journalists from Colombia's Huila Extra website, "me and my family have witnessed flashing lights and objects shaped like Chinese hats flying directly overhead. The light emitted by these UFOs is tremendous. It can even go straight through rock surfaces."

Expanding on her UFO sightings in this desert region, Mrs. Soto told listeners of Colombia's NCN Radio that fifteen years ago she and her family were gathered around seven o'clock in the evening when a "flying saucer" staged an appearance. The shock caused a pregnant woman present at the gathering to lose consciousness. The object made a noise similar to that of an airliner "as it takes off," according to her description. Orfanda Soto made it clear that these things do not frighten her, nor is she worried about being abducted by one of the objects. On the contrary, she would like one of the nocturnal visitors to carry someone away "in order to make sure that we're really dealing with flying saucers."

The prevalence of these lights led to the creation - at a cost of five million Colombian pesos and fifteen truckloads of stone - of a platform that has been dubbed an "ovnipuerto" (UFOport), but is more correctly described as a place where people gather to obtain healing from earth energies. It has been a success with the contactee set, who assure that only "those who manage to tune into the vibratory frequency to be found within the five concentric stone circles will be able to contact the higher goals of other worlds," whatever that means. There are suggestions that a Sasquatch-type creature may also live in the area: El Mohán, described as a monstrous, hairy humanoid.

As we head deeper into South America, we come to the better known salt deserts of Chile and Bolivia. The Atacama Desert is notorious for being one of the driest places on Earth, although abnormal weather conditions - such as the event in the year 2015 - have caused it to become covered in desert flowers, despite receiving less than half an inch of rain in a twelve month period.

Archaeologist Juan Schobinger has written in his "Prehistory in the Americas" (NY: M.E. Sharpe, 2000) that Chile faces one of the richest seas in the world and is backed by one of its most forbidding deserts. The dryness of the salt desert, where rainfall is measured in inches per century, made it ideal for preserving cultural artifacts such as baskets, textiles and even food.

It also preserved something darker - the rituals of forgotten shamans who would bury sacrifices deep in the desert for the "gods" to feast upon. The sacrifices would be held at night and the victim, usually a llama or a dog, left out. At daybreak, the ancient medicine men would return to the site to insure that the gods - the meandering lights of the desert - had accepted the offering. The carcass would be utterly exsanguinated and a puncture mark could usually be found somewhere on the body, which was then transported back to the primitive settlement to be consumed by the community. Subsequently, evidence of this communion between man and his deities was buried under a cairn known as an apachetca, a tangible link of the trade between ancient man and supernatural forces. It is easy to dismiss this as the savagery of ancient man until we remember that the books of the Pentateuch mentioned that the blood of the sacrifice belonged to the godhead. Contemporary thinkers of the paranormal like Salvador Freixedo have written at length about this curious aspect of the human worship (Defendámonos de los dioses, Spain: Quintá, 1985).

The first contemporary UFO account from this part of the world dates back to the year 1868, when a local newspaper, El Constituyente, reported on a strange event in the Copiapó Valley. The news item, dated November 14 of that year, reports: "Yesterday, around five o'clock in the afternoon, the time when work is over at the mine, all of the workers were gathered together, expecting our evening meal, and we saw a giant bird flying through the air, having taken it at first to be a cloud. As the object came closer, we were

ALIEN STRONGHOLDS ON EARTH!

rightly startled, realizing that it was an unknown flying entity, perhaps even the Djinn from The Arabian Nights. Flying a short distance over our heads, we became aware of the odd structure of its body. Its large wings were covered in dark feathers, the monster's head resembled that of a lobster (or locust), while its body only displayed glittering scales that sounded like metal as the strange animal pulled away." A compelling description, but of a cryptid or an unknown vehicle?

Centuries later, miners toiling in the same copper mines as those of the 19th century took a spectacular video of something bearing no relation to anything in The Arabian Nights. In 2013, a survey team photographed an apparently cylindrical object resting on one of the nearby mountainsides. Voices captured on the tape can be heard to say that "no one would believe this is actually happening" as the large object flew across the skies. A corroborating photograph from the Cerro Negro region was also taken in 2013 by workers of the Grupo CAP mining concern.

Perhaps even more startling than these events was the alleged CE-3 involving Argelio Araya, a desert hermit who witnessed an enormous "spaceship" disgorging its crew complement of so-called gray aliens. The terrified loner braved the distance that separated him from the local police station, where he was met by senior warrant officer Claudio Ramirez, who documented the event and ordered a search of the landing area where the object and its occupants had been reported.

In March 2005, local newspaper El Chañarcillo reported that a blackout in the city of Copiapó had supposedly been caused by two unknown objects flying at high speed over the city, submerging the community into stygian gloom between eight and nine o'clock in the evening on the third of March of that year. The story gained traction in spite of the usual denials from the area power utility, the Empresa Eléctrica de Atacama, particularly when a witness stepped forward to tell his story. Gonzalo Delgado told the newspaper that he was returning to the city along the Cuesta de Cardone when he saw how the two objects in question "crossed the sky at high speed, and when I turned around to look at the city, I realized it had vanished. That leads me to believe that it was at the time that the power failure occurred. Two trucks were also coming down the road at the same time, whose drivers could have also seen the phenomenon."

* * * * * * * * * *

ALIEN STRONGHOLDS ON EARTH!

ENIGMAS IN EMPTY PLACES - OUR HAUNTED DESERTS

One does not immediately associate the concept of deserts with Brazil. Our mental images of the South American giant immediately take us to the jungle greenery of the Amazon or to the bright pleasures of Rio de Janeiro. However, the South American superpower also includes extensive coastal deserts - complete with sand dunes - in the northern region of Maranhao, once known to be the wealthiest part of this Portuguese possession (so wealthy, in fact, that a Portuguese monarch was willing to abdicate his crown as long he was able to keep control over Maranhao). Located between the Mangueira and Parnaíba deserts, the vast sand dunes are contained within the Lencois Maranhenses National Park and aerial photography shows the sand encroaching on the surrounding vegetation, like a stain of white ink on a green tablecloth. This is not surprising, as the Maranhao dunes stand a staggering thirty meters tall and are a source of humidity that attracts all manner of wildlife to it.

The sand dunes of Maranhao are also the home of highly unusual paranormal phenomena. In 1997, researchers Pablo Villarubia and Carlos Alberto Martins crossed the desert to visit remote communities and interview locals about their brushes with the unknown. The people who somehow wrest a living out of this harsh land speak freely of a recurrent luminous phenomenon known as "the caburé," or even more picturesquely as "the phantom Jeep." Unlike tales involving phantom cars like the terrifying Haitian zobop, the ghost Jeep of the Maranhao dunes is seen where no vehicles usually drive; some claim having been blinded by the intense blueness of its headlights, which can illuminate the surroundings like daylight. One man interviewed by Villarubia and Martins was out deer-hunting when the ethereal vehicle made a beeline toward him, scaring him out of his wits and making him believe that he was about to be run over in the wilderness. Unable to move, he saw the phantom Jeep vanish into thin air before it struck him. The "phantom Jeep" may also have a Mexican cousin: the Carro de Banda reported in Durango's Zone of Silence since the 1920s.

However, the caburé isn't the only light in the Maranhao. Carlos Araújo, born and raised in the area, told researchers that he was hunting deer among the scrub when he came across a cigar-shaped light suspended in the air, looking like "the burning tip of a cigarette" and less than a hundred meters from where he stood in the darkness. Calling out to the object, thinking it

ALIEN STRONGHOLDS ON EARTH!

might belong to a fellow hunter, the cigar shaped light did something completely unexpected: it changed shape, elongating up, down and sideways into the shape of a cross. Believing that it was a sign of God, Araújo dropped to his knees in fervent prayer as the cross turned to the same blue color associated with the phantom Jeep's headlights.

Yet these experiences are hardly new. As far back as the 1930's, ethnographers were collecting stories in the area about strange goings-on that were quickly filed under "folklore." Author José Carvalho reported that fishermen along the Mangueiras River were used to seeing objects best described as brightly lit phantom boats that caused riverboat captains to panic and veer off course before a collision could occur.

But lights aside, the area contains even more compelling mysteries, such as the abandoned city of Tutóia, believed by 19th century archeologist Ludwig Schwennhagen to be a Phoenician fortified trading post in the manner of similar trading posts found along the Red Sea during the Hellenistic Age. It was believed that further proof of the Phoenician presence in northwestern Brazil could perhaps be found not in this desert-girt city but in the swamps and bogs along the shores of the Pinaré River.

SALT DESERTS OF THE SOUTH

In February 2001, residents of the northern Chilean town of Calama - located in the vicinity of the country's northern salt deserts - claimed having seen a "caravan of UFOs" in the Salar de Atacama, one of the driest spots on Earth. A strange silvery sphere had been causing a great deal of consternation among locals, but it wasn't until February 24 at 8:30 pm that Adolfo Trigo, a young resident of the outlying village of San Rafael, claimed having seen a UFO taking off from one of the village's quarters. The object, he would later tell the Diario de Calama newspaper, was a "fish-tailed cylinder with a phosphorescent green front, an electric blue middle and a violet-hued tail."

Trigo was spellbound as the multicolored object made a full turn in the air before rising into the night sky at full speed. But what makes Trigo's account unique is that he did not see the object lose itself among the stars, as is often described in UFO sightings, but rather "disappear into a doorway in the sky."

ALIEN STRONGHOLDS ON EARTH!

You might think that the desert before you is empty, but a UFO base could be hiding anywhere.

Others would become witnesses to this latest desert mystery. Weeks later, Gustavo Glade would become a witness to UFOs while traveling by truck along Cuesta El Diablo on the southernmost reaches of the Atacama Desert. The driver, accompanied by five other passengers, was able to see a sequence of bright rectangular lights that appeared to be flying in tandem. It looked, in his own words, "like seeing a train riding through space," a description corroborated by the others aboard his vehicle. However, the same peculiarity as in the Trigo sighting was noticed: the heavenly convoy did not fly away or shoot up into space - it seemed to enter into a cloud or "dimensional doorway" through which it vanished completely. Glade's sighting lasted a total of eighteen to twenty seconds and the objects involved were no more than a dozen, flying in an upward direction, which discarded the suggested possibility that the driver and his passengers had seen a meteor.

The UFO phenomenon's interest in Chile is mirrored by the U.S. military's interest in both the country and the phenomenon. According to journalist Cristián Riffo (www.ovnivision.cl), a Col. Hubert Brandon prepared a dossier on the anomalous activity in this country in 1965. This Defense

ALIEN STRONGHOLDS ON EARTH!

Intelligence Agency (DIA) dossier documents UFO sightings and encounters reported by trained professionals, including the September 1965 encounter of an LAN Chile airliner piloted by Marcelo Cisternas over the city of Arica, in which a zig-zagging object buzzed the aircraft for a number of minutes.

Months before the Trigo and Glade sightings, researcher Jaime Ferrer of the Calama UFO Center managed to collect a compelling account from the desert community of Chiu-Chiu which took place in October 2000. A man named Gonzalo, owner of a hard candy factory in the area and who distributed his product personally to the local towns, told Ferrer the following story: he had been driving some forty kilometers along the road when he saw a bright light the size of the full moon which appeared to be coming in for a landing. However, the bright object was actually suspended in mid-air.

Gonzalo pulled his delivery van over, turned off the headlights and lowered the driver side window for a better look. To his astonishment, the object "exploded" and vanished, scattering three lights - red, yellow and blue - in separate directions. What truly astonished him, he told Ferrer, was that no sooner had the lights scattered, he could hear a helicopter taking off in the darkness, although he couldn't see it. The helicopter kicked up a dust storm and Gonzalo noticed "a powerful ultraviolet light" aimed at the ground. Three wheeled vehicles, which he took to be Jeeps or 4x4s, followed the helicopter's beam and lost themselves in the desert. Does this serve as proof that the Chilean military is as interested in UFOs as it ever was, despite strenuous protestations that it keeps no files on the phenomenon?

****

DEATH LURKS IN THE SAND

Spanish author Miguel Seguí, writing in Año Cero magazine, mentions a conversation he held with Tunisian camel driver Mohamed Charaa regarding the perils of the northern reaches of the Sahara desert. In the vicinity of the town of Gafsa, said Charaa, the truly unlucky ran the risk of coming across monstrously large snakes known as taguerga which measure up to four meters in length and whose poison is lethal. In the late 1950s, desert nomads spoke of giant snakes that devoured their goats and sheep; when one specimen decided to help itself to a young camel at a desert campsite, the nomads decided that no matter how much they loathed the idea of doing so, it was necessary to appeal to the colonial authorities for help.

ALIEN STRONGHOLDS ON EARTH!

It was thus, according to Seguí, that a French army detachment was sent to investigate from the vicinity of Beni Ounif. It wasn't long before these romanticized desert warriors came across the largest snake they had ever seen - so large that their Enfield rifles were unable to fell it. The soldiers had to resort to a heavy machine gun to slay the beast, which measured a nightmarish 20 meters long - very nearly 90 feet.

Although the serpent's skin was preserved for a while, the political turmoil of the times and the withdrawal of French forces from the area caused all traces of the spectacular find to be lost.

Seguí was able to determine, however, that a year earlier, a native auxiliary had been attacked by a giant snake measuring anywhere between fourteen and fifteen feet. The skin of this desert beast had indeed been preserved and seen by many, but was ultimately sold for forty-five thousand Francs to a private collector. The notable characteristic of this monster snake is that it appears to be able to "jump up" to bite a human or camel in the head, and has a singular characteristic: what appears to be a crest of long hairs on its head, which also have horns.

Years would go by before another case was reported. It wasn't until 1967, during the construction of a massive dam in southern Morocco, that bulldozer operator Hamza Rahmani saw a seven long serpent engaging in a singular activity - eating its way through the construction site's entire supply of engine grease. Using his bulldozer's blade, Rahmani was able to kill the creature, which measured a little over nine meters long and had a "mane" of hair running along its head. According to Seguí, the construction project was bedeviled by the creatures, with a ten meter long one - complete with twisted horns - being seen the following year, and a twelve to fifteen meter one reported two years later. While even the most open-minded may scoff at these measurements and call them overblown, the author reminds us that eighteen-meter long snakes were common during the Pleistocene era in South America.

But stranger things than giant snakes can be found in the world's deserts. Ing. Marco Reynoso of Mexico's defunct Fundación Cosmos A.C. describes a case involving a group of teenagers during the months of December '89/January '90 as they traveled to visit a series of caves located in Cerro Pajarito, in the Mexican state of Chihuahua on the road leading to the Paquimé archaeological site. According to Alvaro Villareal, one of the witnesses, they found two dead, three-point deer and one doe on their path.

ALIEN STRONGHOLDS ON EARTH!

The animal's carcasses were not rigid and the eyes had been eaten by ants. Three perforations, spaced at three centimeters, were on their necks, forming a triangle. Footprints similar to those of a puma were seen in the area.

When the group entered into one of the caves, they heard squealing sounds and smelled an odor of burned wood; standing on an outcropping 15 meters away was an entity resembling the one described as the "Chupacabras," which advanced toward them. Seized by panic, one of the would-be speleologists drew his pistol and fired an entire clip at the creature, which was impervious to the hail of bullets. The group ran out of the cave, uncertain if the creature was dead or not. They also claim having encountered a thin, metallic green entity standing some 80 centimeters, which they took to be an "extraterrestrial." Drawings were subsequently made of both creatures. It is worth noting that the deserts of Northern Mexico have also been the locale for many encounters and sightings of winged creatures best described as "gargoyles" or even "Birdmen" (see "Return of the Birdmen" by Scott Corrales, FATE October 1998).

CONCLUSION

The desert is a place of great beauty, but also of danger. It is the place where animals and insects inimical to human life dwell and also the place seekers go to find hidden wisdom and revelations. Traditionally the "deserted places" were shunned by the ancients, who believed that the gods of the ruined cities in the desert reverted into angry demons, having no one to worship them. Tanith Lee, one of Great Britain's finest authors of sword and sorcery, writes a compelling account of a band of desert travelers who entertain a stranger by their campfire. Who should it turn out to be but the demon king, come to the surface to listen to the chorused voices of his "children," the desert predators? H.P. Lovecraft, whose visions disturb our sleep to this very day, had the "Mad Arab" Abd Alhazred title the fearsome Necronomicon "Al Azif" - supposedly the sound made by nocturnal desert insects who are, in fact, evil spirits.

But so much for the worlds created by our gifted fantasists. What wonders - and horrors - do the world's deserts hold for us?

* * * * * * * * * *

ALIEN STRONGHOLDS ON EARTH!

HOSTILITIES IN THE BRAZILIAN DESERT

When 16th century Portuguese explorers reached the northwestern corner of Brazil, they were faced with a surreal landscape - impossibly blue-green waters and enormous dunes of white sand. Accustomed to the sands of North Africa, they promptly referred to the area as Ceará (the Sahara Desert, or Saara in Portuguese, although this etymology has been challenged). Its spectacular dunes aside, this semi-arid region of caatinga-type vegetation has also been a hotbed of UFO sightings, something that can be said for the entire Brazilian northeast.

A UFO "invasion" allegedly occurred on March 3, 1996, when a still-unexplained blackout plunged the community into darkness at 6:45 p.m., and 26 UFOs cruised through the skies unmolested. Wellington Santos, director of EPUG (Equipo Pesquisa Ufologica Guarabira), observed that "the UFO situation in Guarabira is one of a kind in Brazil and the whole world, since never have there been so many collective sightings involving people of all ages, sexes and occupations, having repeated sightings over a long period of time."

Massive cigar-shaped craft flew over the region of 23 cities. According to EPUG's report, a farmer went out in the middle of the night to fire a shotgun-blast at one of the smaller discoidal craft which came closer to the ground than their putative "motherships." His hostile gesture was duly reciprocated by the UFO, which aimed a beam of light at the assailant, inflicting third-degree burns. In Mamamguape, fifty-five miles from Joao Pessoa, one of the cigar-shaped objects (known locally as charutos) reportedly fired a gas weapon against a hapless man who was running away from it. On October 14th, three hundred Guarabirans witnessed another UFO invasion, which included a massive craft reportedly as big as a twenty-floor building. "Had this been a southern city," Santos noted ruefully, "journalists would be raining out of the sky."

In 2015, the town of Santa Quitería in Ceará would face a similar wave of hostile UFOs. Car and motorcycle drivers would complain of being chased in the dark of the night by strange fiery objects along the stretch of road linking communities in this remote region, prompting some to leave their cars at home and use rail transportation instead to cover the distances involved. The A Voz de Santa Quitería news portal (www.avozdesantaquiteria.com.br) presents the following quote from an anonymous local driver: "I was on my

ALIEN STRONGHOLDS ON EARTH!

motorcycle with my wife, heading for my parents' home. Suddenly, a reddish light approached us. We felt a wave of powerful heat, prompting me to head into the bushes and get off the motorcycle. We were very frightened by that thing. We decided it was probably the device that chases people to suck their blood. Once the lighted vanished, we resumed our journey to my parents' house."

The news portal adds another case from the same region. A married couple motoring along the road leading to Trapiá was confronted by a shining object "engaged in making pirouettes" over the treetops. They were so taken aback that they wondered if it was prudent to continue their trip, but the bizarre craft - if craft it was - made the decision for them by flying off into the darkness. Reporters advised their readers to avoid taking any violent action or retaliation against the objects, "since we are uncertain as to how they might react."

The town of Almecegas - a sandy fishing community of two hundred souls, whose homes are sheltered by languid palm trees against a cloudless blue sky - has also become a UFO hotspot. A place that looks peaceful and inviting in the light of day becomes an island of fear in darkness, as its residents look to the sky for signs of abnormal lights. Fishermen have narrowly escaped from the strange objects when their boats are offshore at night - a situation reminiscent of the infamous Ilha de Colares attacks of the '70s, involving the mechanical "chupas."

Prof. Humberto Sales is responsible for most of the research being conducted in this remote area. He writes: "Stories like this are striking, because even one such isolated case would suffice to prompt us to look into the apparitions at Riacho de Meio, the location where the bulk of the sightings occur." Another reported case involved bikers on their way back from the locality of Aprazível. As they rode along, a powerful light appeared, flying low over their heads, causing one biker to fall off his motorcycle out of sheer panic.

****

MYSTERIES OF THE MEXICAN DESERT

On July 11, 1970 the world turned its attention from the ongoing lunar exploration missions and worldwide political crises to focus on a relatively small region of the deserts of northern Mexico.

ALIEN STRONGHOLDS ON EARTH!

An Athena V-123 rocket launched from Utah's Green River missile base went astray and landed in Mexico's Bolsón de Mapimí, a desert region covering roughly forty-seven thousand square miles of the states of Coahuila and Chihuahua and considered the southern reach of the Chihuahua Desert. The rocket, originally aimed at the White Sands range, somehow deviated twelve hundred kilometers to land in the so-called "Zone of Silence," or vértice de trino, as it is also called in Spanish, due to the fact that it occupies the place where the states of Durango, Coahuila and Chihuahua come together.

Quick diplomacy by the Nixon Administration averted an incident between the neighboring countries. Some Mexican sources, however, questioned the nature of the "accident" and suspected the Athena misfire could have been a deliberate effort by the U.S. aimed at exploring the mysterious area. American communiqués stated that the rocket's payload contained Cobalt-60 in an airtight container that would have almost certainly survived the impact, but a gargantuan effort was made not only to recover the payload, but also to remove and containerize supposedly "irradiated" soil to be returned across the border. Nearly seven hundred U.S. and Mexican personnel combed the desert for a month, collecting all manner of specimens.

The Mapimí Silent Zone is the popular name for a desert patch near the Bolsón de Mapimí in Durango, Mexico, overlapping the Mapimí Biosphere Reserve. It is the subject of an urban myth that claims it is an area where radio signals and any type of communications cannot be received.

ALIEN STRONGHOLDS ON EARTH!

UFO researcher Santiago García, the undisputed expert on the subject, believed the U.S. had left behind a remotely guided vehicle, perhaps similar to the Soviet Lunakhod, that would remain idle during the day and operate in the cooler desert night. García was of the opinion that this putative probe was looking for uranium deposits, but keeping an eye out for more interesting phenomena was not out of the question.

In 1975, a businessman known only as "Mister Wong" was making milk deliveries along an established route one night. When he came to the village of Nuevo Delicias, he was blinded by a tremendous light ahead on a narrow desert road. Wong's eyes adjusted to the sudden flash, and he was startled to see a saucer-shaped object hurtling toward him. He promptly began rolling up his truck's windows, as if doing so could save him from a certain impact with the unknown object.

The incoming object, however, avoided the truck with ease, flying overhead, turning around, and returning whence it came at low altitude, vanishing into the darkness. Wong, who was accompanied by his wife at the time, noted that the object made a shrill noise "like that of an old blender." He was more fearful of the possible collision than of the strange object itself, since according to his testimony, the local ranchers and truck drivers were quite accustomed to seeing these strange objects, which landed at a rocky outcrop at a location known as Cuatrociénagas in the state of Coahuila, where it was possible to find evidence of their landings in the desert sands.

Wong conveyed all this information to researcher García, who would find it corroborated by an even more incredible event. In early 1976, Jesús Berlanga approached the UFOlogist with a series of photographs purportedly showing a UFO landing less than two hundred feet away from Berlanga's father, who was exploring the promontory known as Cerro del Imán (Magnet Hill), when he came across the glowing, hat-shaped object. As though startled by the human's presence, the object rose into the air with a thunderous roar, allowing young Jesús and the other members of the expedition to see it.

ALIEN STRONGHOLDS ON EARTH!

SUGGESTED READING

ALIEN BLOOD LUST

UFO HOSTILITIES

SCREWED BY THE ALIENS

http://inexplicata.blogspot.com/

Scott Corrales leads the way in the global investigation of strange UFO encounters in Hispanic nations.

ALIEN STRONGHOLDS ON EARTH!

Latin America has been a hotbed of unusual UFO activity for decades.

ALIEN STRONGHOLDS ON EARTH!

SECTION FOUR

UFO or cloud over Mount Rainier? Courtesy Committee For Skeptical Inquiry.

GO TELL IT ON THE MOUNTAINS

People have been known to disappear as they approach the top of a mountain.

An entire series of books – the "411" series – has been based on stories of those who have vanished under the strangest of circumstances.

Mist-ridden phantoms are said to roam at the highest of elevations.

Bigfoot has often been encountered in the Himalayan Mountains.

UFOs come and go out of the deepest caves with complete freedom.

To stay ahead of the game, one has to be truly adventurous and put on their hiking boots. It's no task for a softy. First, you have to know where to look, but you also have to have finely attuned intuition working on your behalf.

The first modern sightings of flying saucers was a fleet of nine gleaming objects flying between the peaks of the Cascade Mountains. Kenneth Arnold was the pilot who saw them and gave them their name. Mount Rainier has always been the scene of much UFO activity – it's possible that there is a time warp that leads inside the mountain.

Chapter Twelve
HIGH IN THE ANDES
By Timothy Green Beckley & Joshua Shapiro

The Peruvian Andes are a "hot spot" both for international tourism as well as being a place steeped in unexplainable phenomena.

The Andes has attracted UFOs like a magnet for centuries - as long as written and verbal records have existed!

The locals see them coming and going into the mountainous regions almost as if they own the place - and just maybe they do!

I am going to make a pitch right off the bat for one of my favorite books. It's one that we have published and contains 200 pages of material directly related to the topic of Peruvian mysteries. The primary author of "Secret of the Andes and the Golden Sun Disc of Mu" is Brother Philip - a pen name used by George Hunt Williamson, an early UFO contactee - especially when he is writing about his South American travels. Originally published in 1961, our new edition was edited by myself with the luxury of additional material by Joshua Shapiro, John J. Robinson, Harold T. Wilkins, Charles A Silva and Brent Raynes.

In my introduction, "The Andes Land of Enchantment and Home of the Sun Disc," I point out that when we think of the Peruvian Andes we think of Indiana Jones, actress Shirley MacLaine, Machu Picchu and the Nazca Lines. All of these things are part and parcel of a wondrous land that too many of us seem so far removed from in our everyday lives. But yet, there is all this and a

ALIEN STRONGHOLDS ON EARTH!

lot more than meets the inner eye, as we shall see as we "invade" the realm of the Incan Empire.

Brother Philip went in search of a mystical kingdom few outsiders know about, only to return eventually to a distant, uncivilized world full of greed, crime and corruption. His spiritual exploits and the knowledge he gained has had a lasting impact since his story was described so eloquently in this collector's edition, which ties together into a tight knot the existence of the "lost continents" of Lemuria and Atlantis and their UFO connection. This book details the extraordinary spiritual adventures of Brother Philip in a lofty ashram high above the world, out of sight of prying eyes who would like to capture the Sun Disc for less than benevolent purposes. It is a fascinating story of good versus evil that is all the more relevant in today's highly charged world of political and social divisiveness.

Brother Philip, aka George Hunt Williamson, has kept alive the many mystical legends of the Andes.

ALIEN STRONGHOLDS ON EARTH!

HIDDEN MONASTERY HIGH IN ANDES HOSTS SUN DISC

"The Golden Sun Disc of Mu," the ashram's greatest treasure, we are told by Philip, "was not made of ordinary gold, but was transmuted gold and unusual in its qualities in that it was a translucent metal similar, evidently, to the 'metal you can almost look through' of the UFOs. Held by ropes of pure gold in a shrine in the greatest Temple of the Divine Light of the Motherland of Mu, the gigantic Golden Disc of the Sun was placed on an altar, which was a pillar carved out of solid stone. There blazed the eternal White Light of the crystalline Maxin Flame, the Divine Limitless Light of Creation.

After the destruction of Mu, the Sun Disc eventually found its way to Lake Titicaca.

"About 30,000 B.C., the Maxin Light went out on the altar because of the evil of some of the priest-scientists of Mu. The Sun Disc remained in its shrine, however, until the time of the final destruction and submergence of 10-12,000 B.C. The Disc eventually found its way to Lake Titicaca and was placed in a subterranean temple of the Monastery of the Brotherhood of the Seven Rays. Here it was used not only by the students of life daily but also by the Masters and Saints from the Mystery Schools throughout the world so that they might be teleported back and forth to sit in Council or to partake of some Transmission Ceremony.

"When the spiritually advanced Incas came to Peru they placed the Disc of the Sun in a specially constructed Garden of Gold where it will remain until the day 'when man is spiritually ready' to receive it and use it once again. On that day the Golden Disc will be taken out of its subterranean chamber and placed high above the Monastery of the Brotherhood. For many miles the pilgrims of the New Dawn will see it once again reflecting the glorious rays of the Sun. Coming from it will be an undeniable tone of purest harmony that will bring many followers of light up the foot-worn path to the ancient gate of the

ALIEN STRONGHOLDS ON EARTH!

Brotherhood of the Seven Rays and they shall enter the Valley of the Blue Moon for fellowship."

Those into poetic, "New Age," verbosity will doubtlessly appreciate such a tantalizing tale easily conjuring up larger than life images that a great producer like pioneering filmmaker Cecil B. DeMille might bring to the screen of such a lost temple and its hordes of praying monks whose sole purpose is that of protectors of the golden sun disc. We can all but imagine the sky above the monastery being filled with flying vehicles of one type or another, such as are depicted in scenes from the 1936 cinema classic, "H.G. Well's The Shape of Things to Come." We of the "nuts and bolts" crowd might enjoy a good ancient astronauts story from time to time, but mostly we like our Terra Firma to be a bit more firm-a when it comes to closing in on possible alien bases that might still exist today, much less centuries upon centuries upon eons ago.

That's not to say that there might not be something to Brother Philip's "psychic conjurations" as I prefer to call such visions. My longtime friend, crystal skull aficionado Joshua Shapiro, thinks highly of Philip, aka George Hunt Williamson.

"I (Joshua) first heard of George Hunt Williamson while traveling on faith in 1981 and discovered another one of his books, 'Other Tongues, Other Flesh,' which discussed the 'Wanderers' and other information related to how man came to the Earth and links with ETs and cosmic forces. As a result of this book, I discovered that I could be a 'Wanderer' as I went through a shift in consciousness. Furthermore I had a brief contact with George Hunt Williamson when he answered a letter in 1984 in which he gave encouragement to continue my spiritual work."

And continue it he has!

Joshua Shapiro has been involved with the crystal skulls since 1983 when he saw one made out of amethyst in northern California ("Ami"). He felt such a strong connection with this artifact that since that time he has devoted his life and resources to sharing the best information he can about these crystalline skulls with people all over the world and the future role they will play in helping our planet achieve global peace.

As a self-admitted "Wanderer," Josh points out that he has had an opportunity to privately visit with a number of the best known crystal skulls, including: the controversial "Mitchell-Hedges Crystal Skull of Love"; "The ET

ALIEN STRONGHOLDS ON EARTH!

Skull;" the "British Museum Crystal Skull;' "Synergy," and "Ami," among many others. In 2011, Joshua and his divine life partner Katrina Head released the first book, "Journeys of the Crystal Skull Explorers - The Travelogue Series," with "Travelogue #1, Mexico 2009." Then in late 2012 and early 2013, "Travelogue #2. Search for the Blue Skull in Peru" was released, and in 2018 a revised and updated version came out. That same year, Joshua released his first paranormal novel working with his British co-author Karen Tucker entitled, "Journey into the Unknown and Back Again, Book #1," a small booklet about his contact with the ancient amethyst crystal skull "Ami" and also a revised edition of the "Explorers," as a free crystal skull e-book.

PERU - LAND OF UFOS

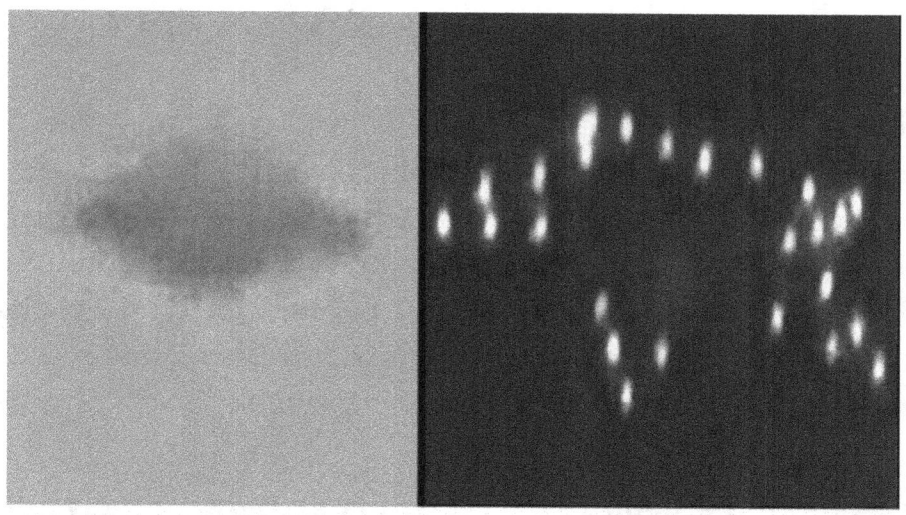

The Andes is a magical place to see a UFO and encounter ET forces, many claim.

Though written a number of years back, Joshua still welcomes all to travel to Peru for the UFO experience of their lives. Alien Bases? Pretty much for damn sure, to hear him tell it!

In order to keep on topic, we have edited out some of the more touristy information, which you can freely find online or in a library. We mainly wanted to zero in on the UFO-ET connection, both modern and historical, of this wonderful land that has so continued to enchant our literary host.

The places Joshua visited include Lima, Nazca, Ica, Cusco, Lake Titicaca and probably the most famous spot, Machu Picchu. Located at an altitude of 8000 feet above sea level high in the Andes, it is a 15th century Incan citadel which most archaeologists believe was constructed as an estate for the Incan

ALIEN STRONGHOLDS ON EARTH!

emperor Pachacut. Machu Picchu was built in the classical Inca style, with polished stoned walls. Its three primary structures are the Intihuatana, the Temple of the Sun, and the Room of the Three Windows. Most of the outlying buildings have been reconstructed in order to give tourists a better idea of how they originally appeared. There are two ways to get there: walk "uphill" along the Incan trail from the nearest town (a real pilgrimage) or by train. Many believe it to be a sacred site and Joshua has even gone there to energize his crystal skulls.

* * * * * * * * * *

Greetings, dear readers and fellow UFO enthusiasts. My name is Joshua Shapiro, your typical Aquarian networker turned world explorer (of course, since I am an Aries). In this article I would like to share with you some of my experiences and intuitive insights from my two recent trips to legendary Peru, the land of the Incas and more!

My first trip was in December of 1989 and was done solo. I organized this excursion with my friend Peter Schneider, who is from Switzerland and has lived in Peru for several years. Peter is the owner of Peru Mystic Tours in Lima, Peru, which is a tour agency interested in the more metaphysical aspects of Peru. The second trip was last September with my then fiancée, Vera, from Brazil (the tour organizer) and 50 other Brazilians. So I discovered I had different experiences when I traveled only with a guide or a whole group of people.

I think one of the main reasons Peru is so paranormally noteworthy is because there are many ancient ruins that remain in good condition. Some of these ruins are very mysterious and there are powerful energy vortexes connected to them. If you talk with the Peruvians, I found that approximately fifty percent of them either had a UFO experience or knew of a person who did. And also, just as the controversy is being raised here in the U.S., some of these people have had a pleasant contact and others have not. In the more rural areas, UFOs are accepted as real and nothing extraordinary. The legends and traditions of the Inca are very strong in Peru. Although, their present religious beliefs and ceremonials usually combine the Catholic teachings brought by the Spanish with the Indian heritage.

Pacha Mac is a large complex of temples about an hour away from Lima. Like all the ruins in Peru, it is composed of large stones and has a temple of the Sun, a temple of the Moon and a temple for the Women. I visited this site in

ALIEN STRONGHOLDS ON EARTH!

my second trip and participated with the Brazilian group in a powerful meditation in one of the main temples. To me, I sensed a presence of a spirit that was very grateful for us activating its energy force. What one must remember is that many of these sites are much more than what we only perceive with our physical eyes. There are powerful energies one can feel if they are sensitive (which I believe we all are in our own way). Also, it depends on if one has a Past Life Connection with these places as well. When I was with the group from Brazil, I watched many people go through dramatic cleansings of deep seated emotions; either weeping, having their body shake fiercely or feeling utter peace and joy. Lastly, we were told that Pacha Mac was a school to teach the wonders of the universe to the Indians. It is a beautiful place, near the Pacific Ocean.

Another place near Lima, which I was unable to visit but has a strong connection with UFOs, including many sightings, is called Chilca.

Joshua in meditation with Portal de Luz against a sacred stone in Machu Picchu.

ALIEN STRONGHOLDS ON EARTH!

About fifteen years ago, Sixto Paz and a group of other young people went to this area and made telepathic contact with some extraterrestrials who claimed to be based on Ganamede, a moon of Jupiter, bur originate from the Orion system. Eventually they formed the RAMA Mission Group, one of the most well-known UFO groups in Peru. Later, Sixto went back to Chilca and on one occasion saw a domed structure in the desert. An ET type being motioned to him to come to the dome, and, after defeating his fear, he entered this structure.

The structure was very tiny from the outside but very large on the inside, similar to the time-space dimensionality demonstrated in the British series called "Dr. Who" (are you a Whovian?). Sixto was teleported onboard a space craft and taken in suspended animation to this moon of Jupiter where he saw Crystal Cities. They held him in suspended animation because his physical body was not prepared to handle the hyper-dimensional jump to travel to Ganamede. When I met Sixto in the San Francisco area, I recognized that he was a contactee because through his meetings with the ETs, they have energetically charged his body. His group teaches many Peruvians spiritual messages, meditation and yoga-type techniques. I attended one of his meetings in Lima (didn't understand much of course) but there were over 2,000 people there who were very religious but still seeking answers to life which conventional and religious teachings do not provide. In March of 1989, the ETs told Sixto they would appear for the media and did so. I have seen a brief video showing the crafts moving in the sky with their lights blinking. The final piece of evidence that Sixto is having this special contact was when he was asked to leave this country by our government when he traveled here in 1989.

Another sacred area close to Lima is called Marcahuasi. For my friend Peter Schneider, this is one of the most powerful places in Peru. Again, I have been unable to go there yet, but one of the famous 1950s UFO researchers, George Hunt Williamson, talks about this place in his book "Road in the Sky." In addition to the many reports of UFOs sighted here, there are these gigantic stone faces of people, from many different races of man (some which do not exist in Peru) as well as many varieties of animals from around the world. Mr. Williamson felt that these shapes in the stone were left by the Els (sometimes called the Elohim) who existed on our Earth millions of years ago and eventually evolved beyond the physical plane of existence. Marcahuasi is about 12,000 feet above sea level, and there are groups of Indians that still

ALIEN STRONGHOLDS ON EARTH!

live there, telling of its legends. This is definitely one place I plan to go. Also, Peter showed us the cover of a Peruvian magazine that featured an extraterrestrial standing on one of the mountains in this site, waving. The person who took this picture never saw this being.

Of course, everyone has heard of the Plains of Nazca (lineas de Nazca). This is the place where one sees many figures drawn perfectly in the ground but can only be seen from the air. Since we have only had aircraft since the early part of this century, and these figures were unknown before then (contemporarily speaking), then who did this? And besides, there are some shapes in the ground which have no connection with anything we understand and many patterns of lines which make no sense.

The first time I flew over Nazca (you take these small propeller planes but be careful because the pilots weave them this way and that), I was surprised that I didn't feel much energy from the area. However, last September, when we arrived at our hotel, not far from the plains, I began to receive a telepathic communication from an extraterrestrial. I did a meditation with my girlfriend to share this energy, and she had a vision of how the figures were created. She saw what looked like spacecraft flying over the plains of Nazca with a light beam emanating from the craft and literally carving the figure in the ground. You cannot see these figures if you stand next to them on the ground. With my computer background, I understand how they could program the figure into the computer and let the computer guide the laser beam.

Some of the figures you see include several bird or Phoenix symbols, a dog, a whale, a monkey, a smooth (landing type) of trapezoidal shape (two of them) and of course the Space Man, who is carved on the side of one of the mountains nearby. I also met a local man who said that an archaeologist had just uncovered the remains of people who lived in this area that was carbon 14 dated to be at least 4,000 years old and that these patterns were here before the Inca. The Peruvian Government loves this site because it is a great tourist attraction but offers no interest to try to research it to understand it.

About 120 miles north of Nazca is the city of Ica. In Ica there is a very good museum which has many Inca artifacts. On some of the pottery it looks like drawings of extraterrestrials that are made with antenna-looking handles. Also they have skulls which are pointed toward the back, which the Inca did with their children when they were born for some religious purpose.

ALIEN STRONGHOLDS ON EARTH!

However, the most interesting thing in Ica is the engraved stones found in a nearby cave. In the downtown area of the city, Dr. Javier Cabrera has been studying these stones for many years and has a museum with over 11,000 stones.

The engraved stones of Ica depict scenes of an advanced race of man, who dealt with dinosaurs and did heart transplants. From scientific tests on the stones, Dr. Cabrera believes that they are a history book of a race of man that came from the Pleiades about one million years ago. In modern archaeological fields and scientific studies, they of course believe that we are the most advanced race of man that has ever existed on earth. I believe that there have been many advanced civilizations in our past, such as in Atlantis or Lemuria, but that the Earth has gone through many cleansings in which either man destroyed this world or else it was subjected to natural disasters or polar shifts. When I was in presence of these stones, I felt they were very authentic and further proof of possible contact with an extraterrestrial race. The stones also show a configuration of continents on the Earth that no longer exists, pyramids, other types of animals, spaceships, etc... So, if you go to Peru, you probably want to go see Dr. Cabrera.

Another place which most people are familiar with is Cusco. Cusco is said to be the capitol of the Inca and if I was going to live in Peru, I would probably live there. Cusco is about 12,000 feet high and is in the Andes, totally surrounded by a valley of mountains. I think there are about 350,000 people who live there and most of their homes are an adobe type structure. In Cusco you really see the typical Peruvian customs you expect. There are many old churches and buildings from the time of the Spanish and most of the people seem to have Indian blood. Here you will hear the Peruvian music with their flutes and drums.

Near Cusco are many ruins, above the city in the hills. The ones I went to included Sacsayhuaman, Tambo Machi, Kenko and the Temple of the Moon. The place where I had the strongest connection with as well as a strong sensing of an ET connection was Sacsayhuaman. In this place are very large stones, irregularly shaped, which are fit together perfectly with no space between them. In my mind, it would be impossible for as primitive a culture as the Inca to have made this structure. Sacsayhuaman (sounds like "sexy woman," but its purpose is far from that) is comprised of three sets of stone walls in the shape of a serpent. At various points in the wall it juts out at a 45-

degree angle. There are doors and steps, and the doors are very tall. Above this set of walls is another set of stones in the shape of an astrological wheel where many special ceremonies were held. Each June, the local people reenact some of the sacred Inca ceremonies in the field near the stone walls.

Again George Hunt Williamson felt that the Els were responsible for the creation of this place. Both times I visited there, I felt that tall beings were involved as well. I had two personal visions, one was that at one time, you could step through the doors here and be teleported to another location. The second was seeing a tall being (in spirit) step through the wall to greet me. Another woman in the Brazilian group said she received a telepathic communication from ETs while in this area, heard music which another woman heard, and knew she needed to come back.

Lastly, while we were doing a group meditation in the astrological wheel, I saw many UFO-type clouds (UFOs ionize the air with their electromagnetic force fields and create a cloud around themselves so as to not create panic and fear amongst the people. A sensitive can feel the energy of the cloud as being different, like it is more alive or there is a weight or something within it. By the way, we see many of these types of clouds here in the Las Vegas area. Okay, back to the narrative) above us. I brought with me a conch shell that a Native American Indian had carved a hole in so I could blow the shell (sounds like a horn). He told me they use this shell in their purification ceremonies. During our meditation, I blew the conch shell in the four directions from the center of our group circle and then held it up into the sky. A woman in our group saw a Gold Light come down upon me from above (I don't see things, I usually feel energy or am more intuitive) and then this light touched each person in the circle. For me, this place is very special and there is no doubt in my mind that it was built by a very spiritually advanced race of people, whether native to the Earth or not.

THE CRYSTAL SKULLS

Now, as some of you know, I am a co-author of a book on the Crystal Skulls (human-sized and shaped skulls made from quartz crystals found in ancient ruins in Mexico and Central America and possibly in Northern South America). To me, there is a strong connection with the Crystal Skulls and the UFOs and I believe the skulls are another strong piece of evidence which shows the existence for UFOs. Anyway, there were three temples I felt guided

ALIEN STRONGHOLDS ON EARTH!

to go in Macchu Picchu (in my second trip) and do a meditation with three pictures of the famous Mitchell-Hedges Crystal Skull.

Each of these temples were composed of the more advanced type of stones. I went with Vera and two other members of our group to the Temple of the Sun, the Temple of the Three Windows and the Pyramidal Temple housing the sacred stone called Enti Hutono (approximate spelling). After each meditation I finished by blowing the conch sell. At the Temple of the Sun, I felt as if one of the skull pictures became alive as if that crystal skull was fully present. Afterwards, because I went so deep in meditation, it took me awhile to come back to Earth because the energy was so strong inside of me. When we did the meditation near Enti Ontono, I felt the presence of ETs all around us. It was like in the movie "Ghost," where they were standing right next to us. Also, I received a telepathic message (I would have forgotten this if it hadn't been recorded on video) from them.

A few other notes about Macchu Picchu from this last trip. One day while we were there we saw a large rainbow. It was quite beautiful. Usually, when one sees a picture of the ruins, you see a particular mountain in the background. The name of this mountain is called Huanu Picchu (small Macchu Picchu). I have always felt an energy connection with this place, especially toward the base, as one perceives it when you are actually in the ruins. Sometimes I would see UFO-type clouds over this mountain. And thus, I decided that I must climb to the top of Huana Picchu using the trail. And by the way, there are ruins on top of this mountain. Well, I was disappointed, because, when I got to the top, I didn't feel any special energy, although the view was spectacular. Nevertheless, I strongly sense that there is some kind of UFO base within this mountain.

Lastly, our guide, Edwin Flores, told us that in 1987, during the Harmonic Convergence, they had a meditation here with over 700 people. There are some closed windows in some of the structures which, when you place your head inside, will create a spectacular resonance of sound. So these people did an "om" in the windows and the people living below the ruins said they could feel the mountain and the ground shake for some time. Interesting huh?

For myself, even more powerful than Macchu Picchu was a ruin in between there and Cusco called Olyantytambo. You know, after you have seen several ruins, the patterns of the buildings are similar, and so it is with

ALIEN STRONGHOLDS ON EARTH!

Olyantytambo. As with most ruins, you see a stone structure with steps and many tiers, high up in the mountains. From the base of the structure you basically see the same small stone patterns. However, as one nears the top, off to your left, you see stones like in Sacsayhuaman, closed windows and two doors which lead further up. Above this area is the Temple of the Sun (each ruin usually has a Temple of the Sun and a Temple of the Moon) which contains a third type of stone that is very finely done, large and has a pinkish tinge to it. It was here, in the Temple of the Sun, where I had one of my strongest experience (Dec., 1989).

For a reason I didn't understand, when I first went to this temple, I felt this eagerness to just run up the hill to go see it (without really knowing what I would find). I sensed from the stones that this place was at least 100,000 years old and I had a vision of a vast temple of which only a few stones remain now. The major part of the Temple consists of six tall stones with a narrow strip of stone in between. On the large stones were protuberances of sacred Inca animals (serpent, puma, etc.) and on another stone was engraved a pattern of four sets of nine square shaped steps. My guide said each of these stones is like a book and shares the history of the people. While I was meditating in this area I received a telepathic contact (I sensed of a Pleiadian nature) and felt as if a computer was under my feet. All around me it felt as if I was in a time-space energy field and I became oblivious to everything else with a peaceful feeling enveloping me. In my vision, I saw spacecraft or flying ships carrying the huge stones to build this temple. I saw in the valley below thousands of people participating with the priests of the temple in a sacred ceremony. Lastly, I told my tour guide to look in the sky directly above us and a cloud would appear, manifested by a UFO that was there from another dimension. And, indeed, the cloud appeared (sort of like the legend of the great American baseball player Babe Ruth pointing to where he would hit a home run). Then I heard them say goodbye and it disappeared. To me, this was one of my homes in Peru. When I returned to the U.S., my co-author Sandra Bowen, who is a very good sensitive, asked me where I was on this day, because she had psychically connected with me. When she saw my video of this place, she confirmed that it was the location she experienced.

Olyantytambo and the general surrounding area has a special energy. Even in my second trip there, when we did a meditation at our hotel, trying to contact the ETs, I saw many stars flashing multi-colored lights and moving. My

ALIEN STRONGHOLDS ON EARTH!

girlfriend went into a trance and had a direct contact with them. But again, I am sensing more of a Pleiadian presence here.

Lastly, I would like to discuss the area near Lake Titicaca. I became interested in this area when I read a book by Brother Philip (actually George Hunt Williamson) called "Secret of the Andes." In this book he describes a secret brotherhood in this area where there is a special school for those on the spiritual path. Actually Brother Philip, according to Williamson, is the head of this school, which was started during the time of Lemuria. So, with my natural Aries curiosity, I wanted to go there and find out.

Lake Titicaca is even higher than Cusco. The Lake itself is very large and there are many islands within it. The large Peruvian city which is on the shore is called Puno, and this is where one stays. I know many of you have seen the derbies the women wear in Peru (which they got from the British, when they were there) and this is the case in Puno. Some of the local people have villages on the reed islands and, in our last trip, we were able to go on one of their reed boats, which were very sturdy and comfortable.

I asked our navigator if he ever saw UFOs in this area, and he said it is a common thing. Many people claim they have seen UFOs come in and go out of the water. Another friend told me that Jacques Cousteau once went in a submarine there to see what is under the water and was so shocked by what he saw that he has never spoken about this. My tour guide said the local people believe the Golden Sun Disc of the Inca is buried here. I think of all the places in Peru I visited, I saw more UFO-type clouds here than everywhere else. Also, all the islands in the lake have stone terrace structures everywhere. The question I asked myself is, where did they get all these stones?

On my first trip to this area, my guide took me to some of the ruins near the Lake. One place was called Kutimbo. It is an ancient village on top of a hill. In this area, one can see many other hills with totally flat surfaces on top, somewhat similar to Devil's Tower in Wyoming (ala "Close Encounters"). Also in this site as well as the Puno area are many tower-like structures which they call Chulpas. Some of the Chulpas are made with more detailed and precisely cut stone blocks and others are more primitive. They have found mummies in these structures and the archaeologist believe they are like burial tombs.

In another site in this region, called Stilistani, there are many Chulpas that also border a small lake where the island in the lake has a flat top surface

ALIEN STRONGHOLDS ON EARTH!

as well. My intuitive sensing was that there was a UFO base under this island. Also my guide said that the Inca had the Sun Disc here for a time. Lastly, I showed my guide a UFO type cloud in the sky here and he felt that it was one too. This cloud disappeared and then in the same shape and size reappeared in another location in the sky. I had never seen this before so I made sure I got a photograph of it which I show in my slide presentation.

I was able to spend one night on one of the islands in Lake Titicaca called Amantini. My guide had a friend there who offered us his hospitality and some food I have never tasted before. The people here seem to be very religious; there is a heavy overtone of Christianity and the women wear black scarfs. There are two temples on this island but my most interesting experience was after we finished exploring. When we came down from the ruins, I saw a perfectly shaped UFO with a dome on top in a cloud hanging over the lake. So I grabbed my camera to get a picture of it, but this cloud did not appear in my slide, although people who have viewed the slide feel UFOs were in some of the other clouds near that one. I saw this cloud again on my second visit to the island also, but it vanished very quickly.

My guide knew a local shaman and I received a spiritual reading from him. The shaman used cocoa leaves. What he would do is use a leaf to represent me or a situation and then would spontaneously throw other leaves over them. After studying each leaf for its qualities - whether it was perfectly formed or folded - he would understand the situation in question. Many of the things he said came to pass for me (for example, he said I would not marry an American but a Peruvian - he probably was seeing Vera, as one of our strongest past life connections was in Peru. Please see our story in "Angels of Love" for more information about this most unusual connection). But the most important thing we discussed after the reading was the underground tunnels. In my second trip he took me to a spot (now covered over) where he claimed there was a tunnel that went from Lake Titicaca to Cusco (about 300-400 miles away) that he saw when he was a young boy. After we spoke about the tunnels, I went into an altered state, felt incredible energy around me and joy inside of me. I know I have a connection from a past time with these tunnels. I believe that a great deal of the knowledge of Atlantis was brought to Peru (possibly stored now in the tunnels) and in the forthcoming Aquarian Age is getting ready to come out.

ALIEN STRONGHOLDS ON EARTH!

Well, my friends, this is only a brief summary of what happened to me on my journeys into Peru. In all my studies and networking around UFOs, I find that Peru presents some of the strongest evidence for contacts with UFOs, including sightings that have happened in the past as well as those continuing to occur in the present time. I think that more research needs to be done here. I have also stayed and lectured in Brazil and had many people come up to me with stories about numerous UFO sightings there. So I firmly believe that South America has a key role to play in the emergence of the forthcoming prophesied Golden Age and that there is still incredible ancient wisdom yet to come forth and reveal itself.

Thank you and God Bless,

Joshua Shapiro

EDITOR'S NOTE: Joshua is happy to hear from you and can be found on Facebook as well as at his web site and through email.

Website: http://www.cse.crystalskullexplorers.com

Email: crystalskullexplorers@gmail.com

Macchu Picchu is a wonderful place to bring your crystals and energize them, as Joshua is doing with his crystal skulls.

ALIEN STRONGHOLDS ON EARTH!

Chapter Thirteen
THE MAGIC OF SEDONA'S RED ROCKS
By Timothy Green Beckley

Sedona is a great place to visit - especially if you spiritually inclined as well as looking to fawn over nature's beauty.

The air is clear, no pollution, and the entire city of just over ten thousand is surrounded by unique arrangements of red rocks which form such "palaces of the sky" as Bell Rock, Cathedral Rock and Boyton Canyon. The most wonderful sight would be to visit Sedona during a full moon and to see the moon hang in the heavens as a backdrop to one of these natural monuments. You can hike about freely during the day and touch the earth and pick up on the energy that the red rocks supposedly give off. A lot of tourists start out at the Red Rock State Park for an entire day's outing, but we suggest it's best to get off the "beaten track" if you want to experience the paranormal at its abnormal best.

The "New Agers" and mystical minded arrive by the droves to take part in vision quests, meditate with crystals and dream-catchers and, above all else, look for UFOs.

On a number of occasions, Tucson-based researcher and shutterbug Charla Gene has accompanied me to the "right spots" and introduced me to the "right people," so as to enhance any possible mind blowing experience I might entertain.

ALIEN STRONGHOLDS ON EARTH!

Tim Beckley strolls about near the red rocks of Sedona. Photo by Charla Gene.

UFO-wise it's been pretty much a bust - but synchronicities, well, that's another matter altogether.

Take the time - and I describe this in full detail in "The Mind Control Matrix of Philip K Dick and the Paranormal Synchronicities of Timothy Green Beckley" - I had spent a couple of days with former APRO librarian Allen Benz in Tucson, taking notes on what it was like to work for Jim and Coral Lorenzen's prestigious Aerial Phenomena Research Organization In its heyday. Founded in 1952, APRO was the first group to investigate seriously reports of humanoid crew members that were coming in from all over the world and needed translating and filing for comparison purposes. Benz had been selected by the Lorenzens to act as a go-between for the creators of the motion picture "Close Encounters of the Third Kind," the production of which was just getting underway. Allen answered all the questions posed by the filmmakers, turning them on to some seriously incredible reports. But it was Dr J. Allen Hynek who ended up being featured in the movie - smoking his pipe and all - and given the bulk of the credit, though it was the APRO librarian who had done the original leg work.

ALIEN STRONGHOLDS ON EARTH!

Following my visit with Benz, who now heads his own World UFO Group, Charla Gene and I headed down the road to Sedona without letting anyone know where we were going or even that we were headed out of town.

Before arriving in the city of Sedona proper, we stopped for a late brunch at the Coffee Pot Diner, near the Airport Vortex. The Coffee Pot is known for its menu of 103 types of omelets (Let me tell you, there is nothing like a peanut butter and pineapple omelet with a scoop of cottage cheese on top). After a Bloody Mary we headed back out into the parking lot and noticed that the vehicle parked right next to ours was sticking out of its space quite a bit. We couldn't help but notice the rear license plate. And this is where the incident gets really bizarre - in bold letters were four letters which spelled out APRO.

After socializing and interviewing Alan Benz, the former librarian for the long defunct Aerial Phenomena Research Organization (APRO), Beckley motored on to Sedona with associate Charla Gene. Upon leaving the Coffee Pot Cafe and returning to their vehicle, they noticed the "unusual nature" of the license plate on the rear of the car parked immediately next to them. The plate's initials spelled out APRO, an organization once based in Tucson which hasn't existed in over two decades. A mere coincidence? Not in Sedona, where synchronicities are an everyday occurrence.

ALIEN STRONGHOLDS ON EARTH!

Well, even though we had spent the previous day with the group's former librarian, the organization itself has not existed since at least 1988, with the passing of both Jim and Coral, who were the guiding lights of APRO, and its sole proprietors. According to Dr. John Harder, they had left word for their files to be burned and the group disbanded forever.

It was like a "ghost ship" -- or ghost automobile, in this case -- and parked right alongside us, a true synchronicity, and a really bizarre one at that. How did the masterminds of the Matrix know we would be stopping at the Coffee Pot? The trickster was more than active that day. And it's not like anyone knew what we were driving nor would it be likely that they could park in the space right next to us since the parking lot was full!

This is not the only synchronicity that has taken place at this locale. Judge for yourself what gives here by reading the book about Philip K Dick and my very odd "coincidences," to be clued in. Charla can vouch for all of this, as she was with me both times and can bear witness to the perplexities of being a UFO and paranormal pioneer.

THE BRADSHAW RANCH - ON THE EDGE OF FOREVER

Security specialist William Hamilton III, who spent many years investigating the UFO phenomena until he retired from active research a number of years ago, has every reason to believe Sedona is a UFO hot spot and has selected a number of areas which could house a UFO base, be it physical or existing on a parallel plane.

"There are UFOs and strange orbs of light that move through the back canyons, notably Long and Boynton Canyons. A mysterious military or para-military presence has been reported in Boynton Canyon, Secret Canyon and Sycamore Canyon. Back in 1991, I traveled to Sedona to visit a man who lived in Long Canyon. John was a caretaker on an old housing project. He had sighted a large boomerang traveling from the direction of Secret Canyon in the north to the edge of Sedona in the south. The remarkable thing about this very large vehicle was its attitude of flight: it was flying on end and leaving a sparkling trail!

"Strange, unmarked helicopters had been seen coming from the direction of Secret Canyon and flying south, the same direction as the boomerang flew. That day, when I was in one section of Long Canyon, I could hear the whooping blades of a helicopter behind the mountains to the north.

ALIEN STRONGHOLDS ON EARTH!

Shortly, an olive drab helicopter flew low over the trees after taking off from somewhere within the canyon. Once, a fellow investigator tried to hike back to Secret Canyon around one o'clock in the morning when he heard the whooping swish of helicopter blades. Attempting to follow the trail back into the canyon, he was stopped by a voice that emanated from a loudspeaker warning him to go no further. Thinking the speaker was there to ward off hunters, he proceeded further until he was stopped again, this time by a laser-targeting light moving around his chest. From the direction of the laser's source, he heard another voice telling him that he had entered a restricted area and that he was to turn around at once.

"Field investigator and researcher Tom Dongo has spent his last few years living in the Sedona area, interviewing witnesses and chasing UFO sightings, abductions and other paranormal phenomena as well as trying to track down the reports of a secret military presence in the canyons. He has written books on his findings. He kept searching for a focus for the phenomena and found three; one was on a 90-acre ranch off the Boynton Canyon back roads in an isolated canyon between Red Canyon and Loy Butte.

The nature of Tom Dongo's various experiences in Sedona are highly unusual, even for a UFO Repeater.

"Our friend Kim had moved to Sedona to raise her children and attend Northern Arizona University in Flagstaff. We introduced her to Tom and she started going on nightly sorties with Tom out to the ranch in this isolated canyon where all manner of things were happening. Tom always brought his camera loaded with 400 ASA film and a time exposure trigger. Kim brought her own camera. They would shoot one, two or three rolls of film, just pointing and shooting whenever they felt moved. The owners of the ranch are Bob and Linda Bradshaw. Bob was a freelance photographer as well as a rancher and his beautiful photos of Arizona landscapes have been published in books and magazines. Linda seems to be the contact point between worlds. Her experiences of the paranormal go back to childhood.

"My wife and I were invited to go out on a sortie and meet Linda. We gathered our cameras, video camera, binoculars and tri-field detector and headed north for Sedona on October 7, 1995. I was prepared to meet the unknown.

Large orange orb photographed at the base of the Bradshaw Ranch.

"We rendezvoused at Kim's house in Sedona. Tom arrived, bringing photographs that he had taken at the ranch. These photos mostly showed a variety of inexplicable light phenomena. In one photo, a randomly-laced trail of variously-colored light hovered over the ground. Other photos showed light streaks, orbs, and, in a few cases, structured objects. Tom did not see most of these lights and orbs, but they registered clearly on his film. I was eager to travel out to the ranch site before sunset so I could get a look at the surrounding terrain.

"We traveled in two vehicles, Tom in his van and the rest of us in Kim's trans-sport van. We piled jackets and cameras in the back. The road was rough and rocky in places and riding in the van gave me the feeling of riding in a nineteenth-century stagecoach. The last mile or two along the ranch road was the roughest surface we had yet encountered. We managed to arrive as the sun was setting, and I could still get a good daylight view of the property. The main house and two other buildings sat squarely at the bottom of a little valley surrounded by trees and bushes. We were far away from city noise. Linda and her dogs came out to greet us as we disembarked from the vans, making us feel welcome and invited. We went into a well-decorated house that had all of the accouterments one would expect to find in an urban house and sat around the kitchen table. Linda served us coffee and handed us a

ALIEN STRONGHOLDS ON EARTH!

large photo album filled with the strange pictures of paranormal light phenomena. The sheer number of such photos was remarkable. Others have taken similar photos, but not in such quantity. Linda told us parts of her story as we sat looking through her fascinating photo album.

"Linda tells us that she has experienced strange phenomena all her life, but, after moving onto the ranch, the frequency and strangeness of the experiences increased. One night while she and her husband were sitting in the kitchen they heard a noise that sounded like shattering glass come from inside their kitchen space, but nothing was seen and no shards of glass were ever found. She has heard footsteps both outside and inside the house when nobody could be seen. To further compound the mysterious events, some unknown agency would lift her camera at night and snap pictures around various parts of the house. One picture showed the light over the kitchen table, yet the area surrounding the light was completely dark! Another picture taken by the unknown agent showed the yard as seen through one of the kitchen windows, but it wasn't quite the same yard, as a portion of the scene seemed blocked off by a mysterious illuminated border.

"As it was getting darker and a full moon was rising in the east, we decided to gather our coats and equipment and go for a walk around the property. Linda first took us to the horse corral. There were many nights when her horses were spooked by something that left tracks in the dirt. These large three-toed tracks were not identifiable as belonging to any of the known wildlife in the canyons. Linda indicated a trail that we could walk toward an old Western movie set that had been erected some time ago. She said that we would find more tracks as we walked into the Old West town. Most of the buildings were just facades. Linda said we should look for the tracks of Big Girl, a Bigfoot that both she and her son had seen on occasion and which had left evidence of its presence at nearby locations.

"I was told that if I tripped my camera flash in the dark that I would see that the air was filled with an unusual sparkling energy. I deliberately flashed my camera in the dark while looking through the viewfinder, and, indeed, I could see glowing particles filling the air. Seeking a conventional explanation for this spectacle, I surmised that particles of dust must be suspended in the air, and that my flash simply reflected off these numerous particles of dust. But, as I continued the experiment, I noticed that the glittering particles did not move around as I have seen dust move but rather seemed to be suspended or frozen in the air.

"As we continued walking, I noticed from time to time that a tiny light would flicker on in distant bushes then extinguish. I asked Tom about this and he said that he noticed this on all of his frequent excursions out there. They appeared to be like the fireflies I used to watch at my uncle's house on Long Island when I was a young boy. But fireflies were not known in Arizona.

"Tom kept looking around the horizon for the lights of UFOs. He claims that the frequency of UFO sightings over the canyons had picked up lately. He then proceeded to pull night-vision binoculars out of his pack to scan the horizon more closely for signs of movement. I could see a number of aircraft lights off in the distance to the south and east of us. When we came to the movie set we turned our flashlights on the ground and could make out some unusual tracks. One track looked exactly like those I had seen published of alleged Bigfoot tracks. I photographed it. Other tracks were of the large three-toed variety akin to those made by large birds or small dinosaurs.

"At the end of the trail sat a platform made into a gallows. It was an ominous sight to greet in the light of the full moon. The women climbed the stairs to sit on the

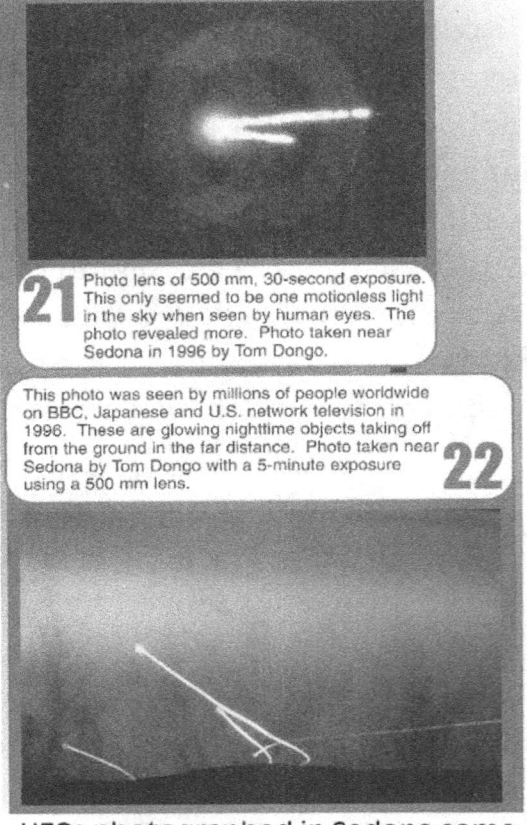

21 Photo lens of 500 mm, 30-second exposure. This only seemed to be one motionless light in the sky when seen by human eyes. The photo revealed more. Photo taken near Sedona in 1996 by Tom Dongo.

22 This photo was seen by millions of people worldwide on BBC, Japanese and U.S. network television in 1996. These are glowing nighttime objects taking off from the ground in the far distance. Photo taken near Sedona by Tom Dongo with a 5-minute exposure using a 500 mm lens.

UFOs photographed in Sedona come in all shapes and sizes and are creating their own unconventional flight paths.

platform followed by one of Linda's dogs. Tom and I walked around, scanning the horizon for any faint movement. The air was still and silent. Occasionally, Tom would raise his camera and shoot on a seeming whim. When the camera flashed, I could see the strange glitter in the air, but nothing else seemed out of place or mysterious.

"After standing around for a half hour or so, we headed back to the ranch. When we all got cozy in the kitchen, Linda served coffee and I started to ask more questions. Linda told me about her son Victor's experiences.

ALIEN STRONGHOLDS ON EARTH!

Victor had taken a hike back in the canyons one day and stumbled upon some white trucks and men in white suits. One flat-bed truck carried a wingless craft on its bed. Victor felt that he was being observed. He had his video cam at the ready and was scanning the scene below his position when he thought he heard a noise in the bushes behind him. When he turned to look, he saw a creature peering back at him and then ducking out of sight. This creature looked like a typical gray alien. On another hiking expedition into the canyons, he had become lost. He was walking in one place in daylight; then he found himself in an unknown location and it was suddenly night!

Tom Dongo's book, "Merging Dimensions," contains some of the most stunning photographic images taken of unknown aerial objects in and around Sedona.

"Tom had also seen a creature, but it was right near the ranch. One night while Kim and Linda were talking, he saw a small humanoid in a brown suit dash across the field near the juniper tree. The dogs gave chase, barking and running after the entity. As it neared the fence line, it seemed to vanish into thin air, and the dogs quite suddenly gave up the chase. Tom had never seen anything like this and was startled after the entity vanished from sight.

"Linda gave me a copy of the book that she and Tom had published, titled 'Merging Dimensions.' It is replete with dozens of photos. Unfortunately, the photos are reproduced in black and white and one misses seeing some of the startling colors that are visible in the original photos. Each of them are accumulating more anomalous photos every week. Anomalies have also appeared on some of Kim's photos.

"Pamela and I went back to the ranch for a second visit on December 7, 1995. The night was even colder than the first night's visit. After nightfall, the stars sparkled like jewels. Tom set his camera up on a tripod with a timer attached to the camera to get long exposure photos of distant moving lights. Tom and Linda had been seeing 'a ship' that would characteristically pop up behind some far hills to the south and west. Pamela had loaded her camera

ALIEN STRONGHOLDS ON EARTH!

with 400 ASA film. We did see some unusual moving lights that night, but they seemed too far off to classify them as UFOs. Sky-watching is a game that involves a lot of patience.

"During a break in our watch, I went inside to get warm and convinced Linda to show me the video that Victor had pieced together from several different shoots around the canyon. This fifteen to twenty-minute video was shot in daylight and darkness. On it I saw some of the most peculiar 'things' flitting around near the ground. One segment focused on a low-flying airplane which was blocked out by a brilliant orb of light that flew across the plane's path. The video was compelling. Very strange things were happening on this ranch.

"I kept asking Linda for details about the photograph of the window or gateway taken near the juniper tree. She had only seen a bright rectangle of light, yet the developed photo looks like a window into another world. Unless Tom, Linda and now Kim were in collusion on a magnificent hoax, I would have to think that the photos are untampered with and show what they purport to show. While it is true that they have not been subject to expert analysis, it still leads one to speculate about the happenings on the Bradshaw Ranch."

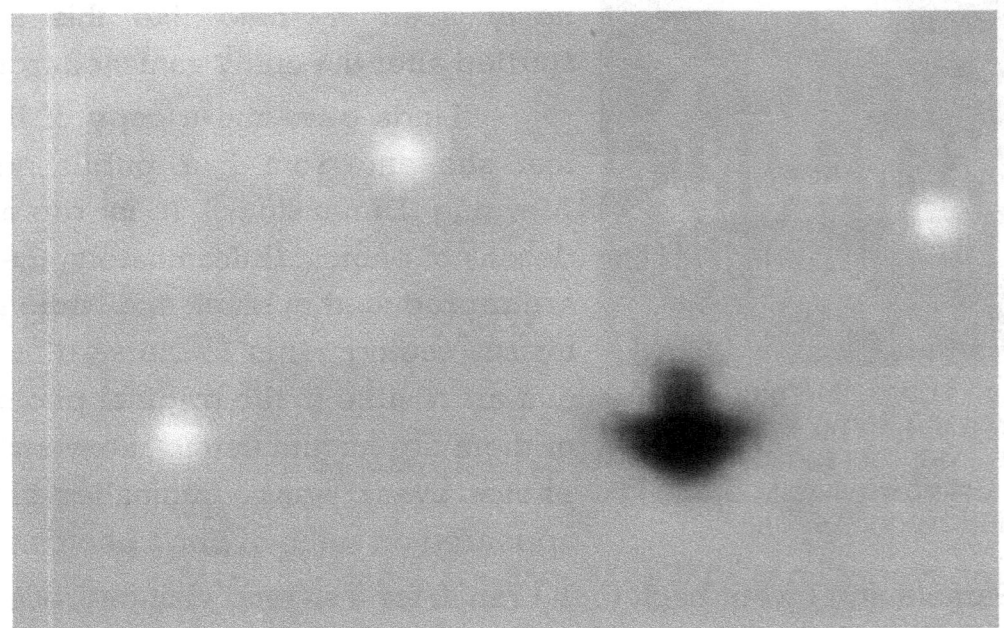

Three UFOs meandering about over Sedona on an unknown mission.

Continuing with his report, Hamilton says he has reached the conclusion that there are three significant elements to the events on the Bradshaw ranch: "1) The Gateway Window; 2) the ever-present orbs; and 3) the sparkling energy in the air. The presence of humanoid entities, mysterious craft and mysterious animals seemed tied into the elements offering clues to the mysterious world that was intersecting our familiar world in this remote canyon beyond Sedona.

"Looking at the Gateway photo reveals a number of things. The scene inside the window area is in daylight. A structure that looks exactly like a telephone pole with the cross struts and insulators is on the right. A third of the way down from the top of the window one can see a dark oval object that looks like a flying saucer. At the bottom left corner is a jumble of indistinct objects that could be foliage or even a humanoid figure. What is even stranger is an embossed area to the left of the phone pole that looks like a light, round object with projecting lines and the number 39 raised up to the right of the round object. There are two photos of the window taken in rapid succession before the window closed down. There are no telephone poles on the ranch property and there are certainly none stuck in the ground next to the juniper tree. If one wanted to come up with a hoax scenario, it would have to involve snapping a picture in daylight and superimposing it over a picture taken at night in another location."

Concludes Hamilton: "Some UFOs may be someone else's spacecraft from an extra-solar planet in our Milky Way galaxy, but some UFOs may be visiting us from points of space that cannot be seen. I remember a conversation that I had with my informant, Charlie, about objects that had completely disappeared from the surface of the Earth, some of which he acknowledged were known about and others that were classified as military secrets. According to Charlie, not all UFOs come to Earth from outer space. Some tunnel here from another space-time dimension. He told me that some of the recovered crashed discs had a unit that we called a "trans-spatial resonator." These resonators could open portals and allow the craft to pass from one dimension to another. Maybe Charlie is telling the truth. After visiting the ranch on the edge of forever, I not only think of Sagan's billions and billions of stars but also the possible billions and billions of universes that are out there somewhere."

Linda sold the ranch and now lives in Montana. I moved from Arizona.

Bill Hamilton Executive Director (Retired) Skywatch International, Inc.

ALIEN STRONGHOLDS ON EARTH!

TOM DONGO - A UFO REPEATER

One would be hard pressed to find an "ordinary" explanation for this disc in the sky. Photo by Tom Dongo.

Some people have the uncanny ability to spot UFOs on a repeated basis. To clarify what I mean I suggest you pick up a copy of "UFO Repeaters – The Camera Doesn't Lie!" Tom Dongo is your go-to-see man if you ever want to have a UFO experience around Sedona, though he may be hard to find these days, being in semi seclusion after running his skywatch tours around the city for many years. A million tourists a year visit Sedona. Naturally, not all come for UFO activities, or even to climb the red rocks, the town being a recognized hub for art, Native American jewelry and all around culture in the Southwest.

If you go to my YouTube Channel - Mr. UFO's Secret Files - and watch the video "Invisible Aliens 'Invade' Town - Underground Bases Exposed," (it has gotten over 25,000 views) you will get an agreeable, pleasant view of the town's supernatural underpinnings as experienced by a gentlemen who seems to be trailed by all that is unexplained and decisively strange.

Tom Dongo runs the ultimate and most illuminating jeep tour of Sedona. He knows the continuum of this place like the back of his hand as well as its incredible geology. And, if you want to go on a UFO Sky-Watch, you've picked the person who knows his alien lore - from the location of possible underground bases to secret canyons where UFOs have been known to hide.

On a recent visit to Sedona, when Tom came to where I was staying, he didn't arrive empty handed. Under his arm he had two hefty photo albums, the kind with glossy pockets that you can place 8.5x11 prints in for protection so

ALIEN STRONGHOLDS ON EARTH!

that they don't get fingerprints all over them or have drinks spilled on the one-of-a-kind pictures.

Seated on the couch, my associate Charla Gené and I bombarded Tom with questions for an hour or more as he thumbed through the albums, selecting prime photos to show us which offer "irrefutable" proof that Sedona is "up there" when it comes to high-strangeness UFO cases. There were orange orbs, entities that showed up in pictures when they were not visible to the human eye and weird machines nestled back among the red rocks like something out of a science-fiction backyard. Sedona is known for its various vortexes, including one near the post office and one located on the road to the small community airport. Here again is an instance where the UFO shenanigans seem at least partially to do with a specific locale - i.e., Sedona a known portal or UFO "window area" - but are centered on one or possibly a number of UFO Repeaters as the primary impetus.

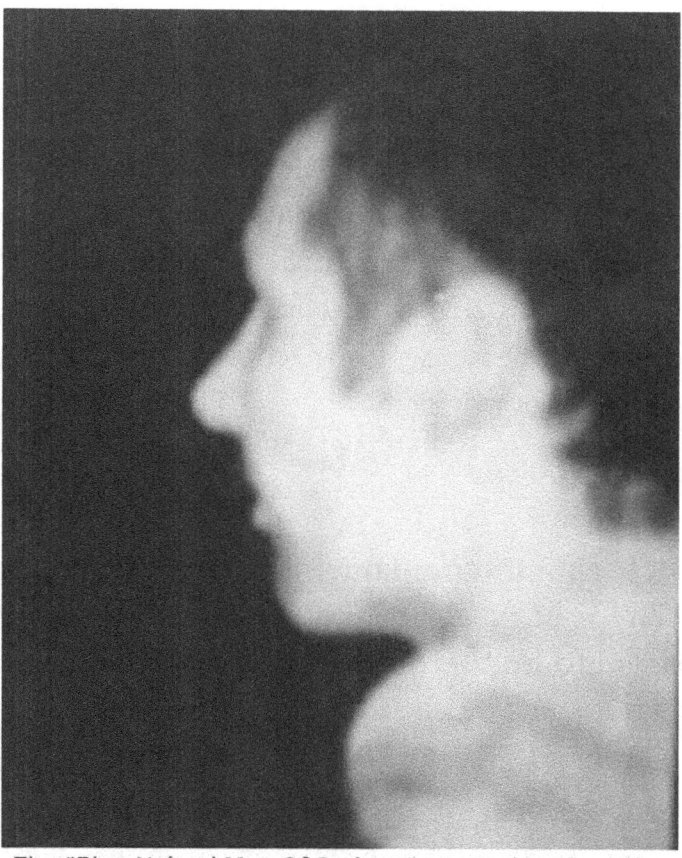

The "Blue Haired Man Of Sedona" was not seen at the time the photo was taken. Noted Tom Dongo: "Linda (Bradshaw) and I were standing side-by-side when she took the Blue Haired Man photograph. We were the only ones in the vicinity."

Tom Dongo would certainly fit that category as he waxes on about the topic philosophically. "I find the whole subject of UFOs and ETs, as well as anything connected to that subject, to be absolutely fascinating - even some of the attributes of the phenomenon viewed by some with a measure of fear and loathing or even terror. I think the reason for the fear is, in part, that many people fail entirely to grasp the actual magnitude of the presence of alien beings here on our planet.

"I feel that the existence alone of these ET entities, as well as the almost inconceivable technology and mental abilities they must possess, is an

ALIEN STRONGHOLDS ON EARTH!

opportunity for us to learn from them. It is a chance for us to break away finally from the railroad track-like rut we have been in for so long. Look, for example, at some of our social, economic and religious belief patterns. Some, if not all of them, should have been tossed in the junk pile decades ago. Worst of all, like obedient sheep, the common man has been manipulated into position by greedy and power-hungry individuals for thousands of years.

"This is a good chance to make a new start - a clean, fresh start. Will it take something like bizarre-looking space aliens to jolt humanity out of our subservient, materialistic lethargy? Humanity surely needs to begin to work cooperatively together to create heaven on earth and to preserve what was given us to cherish."

WHY TOM DONGO?

But the fundamental, unanswered question remains - why Tom Dongo? Why, out of all the honorable folks living in and around Sedona, would he seem to be the main focal point for all these strange occurrences? He admits that he isn't quite sure.

"A hundred times I have said - why me? This stuff has been going on for over 25 years now, and I have written six popular books regarding many of these inexplicable occurrences. Why is it that I have such strange paranormal happenings around me, sometimes on a continuous basis? I don't understand it. I don't have a clue. I have had many borderline-psychotic explanations from, usually, well-meaning people as to the reason behind this activity. Such as: Recently, I did a presentation at Sedona MUFON. There were about a hundred people in the room. I noticed while showing some UFO-type slides that a number of people were acting very uneasy in the audience. It wasn't until after my talk that someone told me that two blue, basketball-sized spheres of light with little lightning bolt flashes in them came through a high window and were sitting about five feet above my head. Then another sphere came out of one of the first two and flashed across the room. At that, the three of them blinked out and did not return. This sort of thing has been going on for a long time now. Maybe I will never know why!"

* * * * * * * * *

ALIEN STRONGHOLDS ON EARTH!

And maybe none of us will - but we can almost guarantee that we haven't seen the last of unexplained UFO phenomena in and around the red rocks of Sedona. You can bet your Venus-bound Mother Ship on that!

Editors Note: All photos except those taken by Charla Gene in this chapter are from the Tom Dongo Collection. Copyright by the individual photographers.

SUGGESTED READING

BOOKS BY TOM DONGO - AVAILABLE FROM AMAZON.COM

MERGING DIMENSIONS: THE OPENING PORTALS OF SEDONA

UNSEEN BEINGS, UNSEEN WORLDS

EVERYTHING YOU WANTED TO KNOW ABOUT SEDONA IN A NUTSHELL

MYSTERIOUS SEDONA

MYSTERIES OF SEDONA: NEW AGE FRONTIER

MERGING DIMENSIONS

Website: www.TomDongo.com

Gloria Reiser took this strange photo in Boynton Canyon in 1990. Behind her is a "machine" that looks like something out of a bad sci-fi movie. "Kronos" comes to mind.

ALIEN STRONGHOLDS ON EARTH!

Could this be an Ultra-terrestrial in the middle of shape shifting?

Paola Harris' group has met with Antarel on Shasta (see YouTube) producing this celestial visitors collage.

ALIEN STRONGHOLDS ON EARTH!

Chapter Fourteen
AIN'T NO MOUNTAIN HIGH ENOUGH
By Timothy Green Beckley

Being a certified explorer and not an armchair investigator would probably enable you to uncover suspected alien bases more easily. You need to be able to climb, tunnel down and slink through the thickest of undergrowth, be it along the Amazon or somewhere less exotic near your own home town.

A prime example could be found by tuning into the Travel Channel's "Destination Truth," hosted by Josh Gates, who heads a team of paranormal juggernauts traveling the globe in search of the supernatural. They hunt down monsters hiding in darkened South American caves, vampires in a supposedly haunted Transylvania castle, and UFOs that have made a nest for themselves in some remote locale that humans are not supposed to know about. Along the way they interview terrified witnesses, search for physical evidence and research the history of the area they are venturing into.

It's probably something the average person will never get to do. I have gone out personally on a number of adventurous treks but, not being physically fit, I have not climbed Mount Everest looking for the Abominable Snowman or put on scuba gear to confront the Loch Ness Monster face to face.

I can however lead you in the right direction should you wish to venture out to places that are a bit more accessible, though you still have to be inclined to wear a good pair of hiking boots to traverse little locomotive paths

ALIEN STRONGHOLDS ON EARTH!

or hug the side of a rugged - bushes, shrubs, jagged rocks - incline on the way to a predetermined apex.

MOUNT SHASTA - HOME OF THE ANCIENTS

UFOs over snow-covered Mt. Shasta.

I find it very strange that upon occasion people disappear off the face of the earth. One of the places this seems to happen from time to time is on Mount Shasta in northern California. I wouldn't worry too much if I were you, as this is so rare. And perhaps - just perhaps - some of these people actually wanted to vanish into what is said to be an entrance way or vortex to the Inner Earth, inhabited by the ancient masters who are said to never grow old (maybe they will teach you the secrets of longevity).

If you go back to California's newspaper archives over a century and a half, you will find news reports written by journalists with no ax to grind when it comes to this most beloved mysterious spot. Located in a community of just about 4,000, the pleasing locale attracts thousands of tourists every year who arrive to trail blaze up the multitude of paths that lead to Mount Shasta's picturesque summit.

ALIEN STRONGHOLDS ON EARTH!

They also come to meditate, sky watch for UFOs, say a telepathic hello to a friendly cryptid like Bigfoot, or pay their respects to the ageless spiritual masters such as Count St. Germain, the man who is said to "live forever." They also come to poke and probe the many crevices toward the top of the mount for an entrance to the Inner Earth, in particular the underground city of Telos, which is located beneath Shasta, be it in a physical form or existing in another dimension or on the astral plane. Those "in the know" claim that Telos is part of a vast underground system with geological roots dating back to the lost Lemurian Empire, a "super civilization" located in the Pacific region in our planet's most remote past.

This is thought to be an alien base like no other - lots of ultra-terrestrials from all over the place to keep you on your toes. You just need to learn how to avoid the despots.

Visitors by the droves come to Mount Shasta to meet the master Count Saint Germain, if he should appear.

STUMBLING INTO A STRANGE AND ANCIENT WORLD

Historically, credit is said to go to prospector J.C. Brown, a British national who came to Mount Shasta around 1900 and a few years later supposedly discovered a lost city beneath the mountain while in the employment of the Lord Cowdray Mining Company of England. Hired to prospect for gold, he hit "pay dirt" in a sense when he discovered a cave which sloped downward for eleven miles. He found an underground village there filled with valuable objects, such as golden shields and mummies, some

ALIEN STRONGHOLDS ON EARTH!

being ten to twelve feet tall. Three decades went by and eventually a certain John C. Root organized an exploration team out of Stockton, California. Eighty people were on the team, but the day they were to be sent up the mountainside, Brown vanished and was never heard from again. And since no one possessed any maps as to where the cave entrance was located, the venture was scrapped.

Others have tried over the years to locate the "booty room," as it has been nicknamed, but have been unsuccessful in their quest. So all that wealth goes unclaimed, perhaps being guarded by underground dwellers who are often said to prevent surface dwellers from entering their cherished abode.

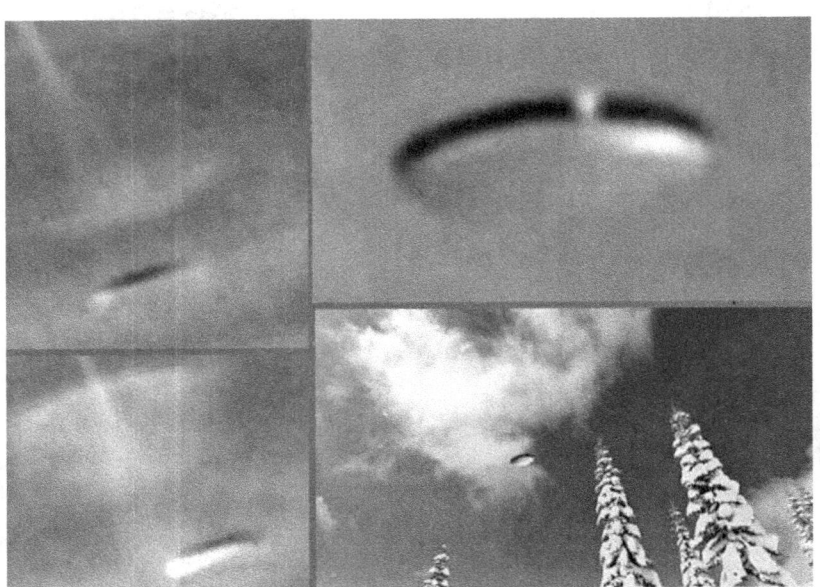
UFOs hidden in clouds?

Located in close proximity to the Oregon border near the southern end of the Cascade Range in Siskiyou County and reaching an elevation of 14,180 feet, Mount Shasta is a potentially active volcano which last erupted in 1786. In order to access this mystical marvel of nature, visitors are apt to set up shop in any of the numerous motels or bed-and-breakfasts that dot the towns of Shasta and nearby Weed. They will undoubtedly stop in at one of the metaphysical bookstores like Soul Connections to get their bearings, perhaps purchase a crystal that has drawn itself to them or to network with others coming into the area for the first time, just like they are doing.

Some locals, as a suspected interloper may quickly find out, shy as far away as they can from discussing anything odd they may have seen or heard, feeling it attracts the wrong kind of tourist who come more for spiritual relief than to contribute to the economy. Instead of chowing down at a fancy restaurant they might, it is felt, want to head off to places like the local Buddhist monastery Shasta Abby, the "I Am" Pageant of the Angels, sponsored by the Saint Germain Foundation, or attend a private screening of

ALIEN STRONGHOLDS ON EARTH!

"Dreams Awake." Written, produced and directed by Jerry Alden Deal, it is in essence the first feature film in a newly emerging cinematographic category known broadly as Transformational Media to be shot on location in and around Mount Shasta.

Over the years, I have been told of some incredible experiences that have transformed the lives of individuals both visiting and living in the vicinity of the mountain. There is, of course, Saint Germain, who pops up in the tree-lined areas, extending bits of philosophy and prophecy to those who wish to stop briefly and listen before he vanishes before their eyes.

And let's not forget that one of the classics of the occult book industry is a channeled volume "A Dweller On Two Planets," that was transmitted through a teenager in the period around 1900 while he was working as a cattle herder on his father's ranch skirting the mountain slopes. It was this work passed on by reincarnated souls from Atlantis and the cosmos that first turned actress Shirley MacLaine onto UFOs and New Age philosophy. We have our own edition of the book, edited by Sean Casteel, for those who wish to peruse this further. Check out "Mysteries of Mount Shasta."

My friend, the late Bleu Ocean, who was the percussionist who arranged Pink Floyd's highly rated drum sequence on their classic 1979 album, "The Wall," told me that as a Native American child growing up around Mount Shasta he and his friends and family heard the sounds of Bigfoot and were often confronted by a little race of beings who would throw stones at the indigenous natives. Bleu told me that UFO sightings were a dime a dozen among tribal members, many of whom considered the land to be sacred.

In the old days, passengers on a train going by would often notice strange lights on the side of the mountain. There is ample evidence that something strange is going on around - and perhaps inside - Mount Shasta.

One blogger in contemporary times insists that the whole area is a UFO hot spot.

"Regular sightings are reported, and several pieces of footage have made their way online, claiming to show strange cosmic craft vanishing into some kind of portal in the skies of the mountain.

"There are also equally regular sightings of strange creatures with glowing red eyes that lurk in the cave systems around the vast base and woodlands of the mountain. One particular story from recent times was that of a three-year-old boy who went missing for five hours while camping with his

ALIEN STRONGHOLDS ON EARTH!

grandparents. He was eventually found safe and well. However, he would tell a strange and unsettling tale shortly after the incident.

"He claimed that a 'robot Grandma' had taken him into the caves and into a room 'full of guns and spiders.' Furthermore, the robot Grandma claimed that he had been placed into his mother's womb by beings from outer space."

Though I haven't seen her in many years, an old friend, Hana Spitzer, told me that a UFO restored her husband's lost sight when they were visiting the mountain with a friend. And a local columnist for the "Shasta Herald" stated in 2008 that a group of five people had claimed to have witnessed a jellyfish-like craft that hovered noiselessly over neighboring McCloud with what appeared to be "a fire raging inside it."

A regular guest on our "Exploring the Bizarre" podcast, Canadian UFO expert Grant Cameron told cohost Tim Swartz and myself on the air that entire groups directed by Paola Harris were gathering along the tree-lined slopes to visit with interdimensional beings who sort of popped in and out of our reality.

You can find the episode on our YouTube channel, "Mr. UFO's Secret Files." Grant's web site is likewise worth visiting - www.presidentialufo.com

I would have to say that Mount Shasta is indeed an "A-1" UFO base prospect.

SUGGESTED READING

MYSTERIES OF MOUNT SHASTA by Timothy Beckley

UFO base monitor - courtesy Dreamtime movie.

ALIEN STRONGHOLDS ON EARTH!

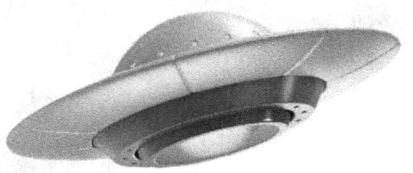

Chapter Fifteen
MIND CONTROL, REPTILIANS AND THE SUPERSTITION MOUNTAINS
By Timothy Green Beckley

One place you should really stay as far away from as possible is Arizona's Superstition Mountains. True, there are all sorts of stories which maintain that vast tunnels containing millions of dollars in hidden treasure, left by the Spanish and protected by the Indians, are available for the "lucky" treasure hunter, but so far there have been so many strange deaths – murders, actually

– and disappearances in the Superstition Mountain range that you're better off alive and poor, rather than dead and potentially rich. Here is a rather hair-raising rundown of some of the weird events which have taken place in the Superstitions over the course of many years. Some of the base activity is above ground - other activity goes on below the surface. How deep? We really can't say for certain.

There is a dark element, indeed, about this area. Mind-controlling aspects of the paranormal are evident. We know from past research that the Ultra-terrestrials are capable of a mental hold on us if they are so determined.

* * * * * * * * * *

A few years back I was on the History Channel's "UFO Hunters" show, hosted by Bill Birnes. One of the researchers I traveled with was reptilian "mastermind" John Rhodes, who has been chasing after serpent-like inner earth beings who have massive headquarters underground throughout the Southwest. He told me that the Superstition Mountains in particular concerned him because of all the negative UFO related events in the area.

ALIEN STRONGHOLDS ON EARTH!

Seen here with Bill Birnes, host of "UFO Hunters," Reptilian quartermaster John Rhodes says the scaly ones make their home in and around the Superstition Mountains, having burrowed underground.

I requested a description of the type of beings we should be on the lookout for and Rhodes provided me with this list of qualifying features.

www.reptoids.com

Beaded or scored skin like a lizard or serpent. The scales (scutes) are larger on broad areas such as the back and chest. The hands, face and other malleable areas of the body have small scales that allow finer flexing.

- A slightly large, slightly back sloping cranium (sometimes appearing conical) with two bony ridges that begin near the brow region of the forehead and extend backwards.

- Two slit or almond shaped eyes with either vertical or circular pupils (Vertical indicates adaptation to low light environments, circular to near surface or lighted environments.)

- Two ears (small holes) one on each side of their heads that may or may not be covered by thin scales.

ALIEN STRONGHOLDS ON EARTH!

- A flat and wide nose with a very little bridge area in between.
- Lipless mouths with varying dentition.
- Very muscular and trim torso with strong arms and legs.
- Four to 6 digits of each hand covered by fine scales.
- Tails that have been seen to be as long as four feet to as small as 18 inches. Some do not have tails at all, only a small bump at the base of the spine.

Independent verification of reptilian activity in the vicinity has come our way via Marcus Lowth, writing for Listverse.com

"The valleys around the Superstition Mountains in Arizona are popular with hikers. They are also popular, if you believe the reports, with reptilian humanoid creatures that like to abduct people and take them into their base deep within the mountains. One particular account, that of a woman known in the report only as 'Angie,' is particularly bizarre and harrowing. While enjoying a walk around the valleys, something she did regularly, Angie was suddenly confronted by a person in a strange mask trying to scare her. It was only when she realized the mask was actually a real face, and the person was some kind of strange reptile-like creature, that the fright turned to absolute terror, and she blacked out.

"The next thing she realized, she was sitting behind the wheel of her car, driving it toward her home, with no memory as to what happened. She would spend the next several days locked away in her apartment, scared and confused.

"It was only when she sought help through hypnotic regression did the encounter come back to her. She had come to in a strange cavern inside the mountain. She was surrounded by several of the reptilian creatures. She was on a table in the middle of the room, naked and tied down. As one of the beastly beings approached her, she blacked out again. Although the regression did not reveal it, Angie believed she was raped by the creature before being brought back to her car."

ENTERING AN UNDERGROUND BASE

There is a story about two unnamed prospectors seeking the motherlode who came across an opening on the side of the mountain near

ALIEN STRONGHOLDS ON EARTH!

Weaver's Needle and decided to venture downward. Soon they heard the sound of moaning. As they continued their journey deeper into the cavern, the moaning continued to grow louder and louder and the air became heavy with a sulfuric odor. After they had descended about a thousand feet, they came to a side drift with its mouth almost closed from a fall of rocks.

A short distance down this drift they stumbled over a pile of bones which they estimated to be the skeletons of a dozen or more persons. Searching around, they soon discovered various bits of broken Indian pottery. In the drift they neither saw the flashes nor heard the moans, but the poisonous air made them quite drowsy.

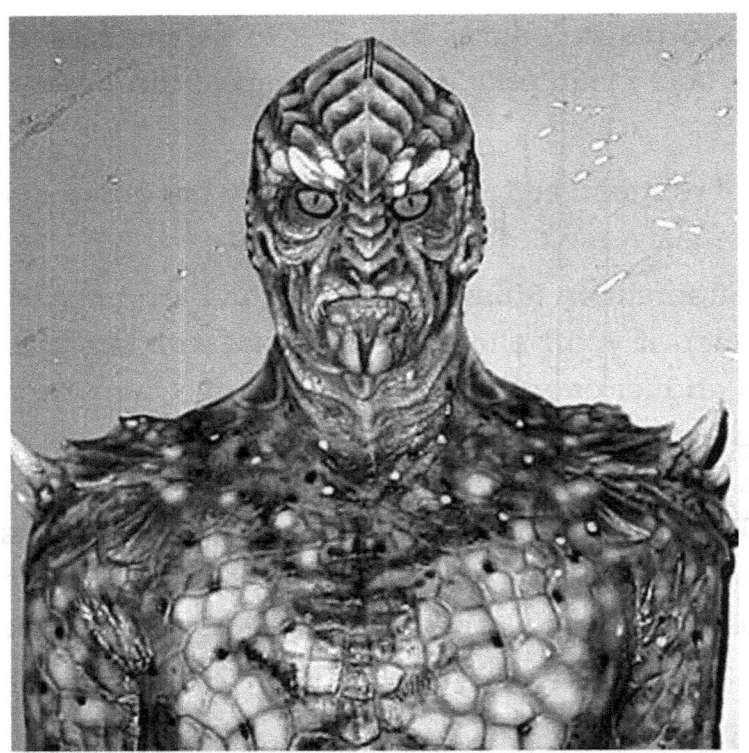

Reptilians could be guarding Alien Bases, a good reason to keep your distance.

Because of this situation they soon found it impossible to continue any further and thus they had to return to the surface. It is not known to this day if this entrance has ever been relocated by anyone else. Those who have dared brave the shadows of the Superstition Mountains say that there is something that puts evil in the minds of people who go into the mountains in search of the Lost Dutchman Mines!

Probably the richest treasure yet to be found by man is located somewhere within the bowels of the Earth in these mysterious mountains. In searching for this treasure, many people have been killed; many others have died of mysterious causes; while still others have met death at the hands of fellow prospectors who crave one of the Earth's greatest treasures - GOLD!

Indeed just what is it that makes men go stark raving mad upon the mountains that make up the great Superstition Range? Is it the bloodthirsty lust for this precious metal or something far more sinister and perhaps supernatural?

ALIEN STRONGHOLDS ON EARTH!

Benjamin M. Ferrira of Honolulu, Hawaii, told staff reporter Jack Karie of the Arizona Republic, while serving a sentence in jail for the killing of his gold-seeking partner on April 19, 1959 that:

"There is something that happens to the minds of people going into that mountain to look for gold. People just get started hating each other - first thing you know they're at each other's throats.

"It didn't make sense! There's something there on that mountain that makes men foolish. I know from experience - from a very sad experience - that mountain does things to the minds of men. At least I think I went completely nuts - one time I thought those canyon walls were moving in on me."

Some months later, in November, Laven Rowlee of Phoenix was shot to death by Ralph Thomas after a life and death struggle that took place just southeast of the famous Weaver's Needle, named for its discoverer Pauline Weaver. Mrs. Thomas asserted, according to a special report in the Arizona Republic, that Rowlee first approached the couple "jabbering something about us trying to kill him - he said my husband was an FBI agent. I really didn't understand what he was talking about. It sounded like a lot of gibberish."

After Rowlee attacked the couple, they somehow managed to grab his gun and overpower him. As the two proceeded to march Rowlee to a nearby prospector's camp, he screamed, "I've got another one." Thinking Rowlee meant a gun, Thomas fired and knocked Rowlee down with a shot from his own hand weapon.

Rowlee died a few hours later.

But the stories coming out of this area, from those who have seen the vast mountain range and know its innermost secrets, often reveal strange circumstances which refuse to be put to rest. Many of them could well be the product of overworked imaginations caused by the hot desert sun and the fearful winds that howl through the mountain passes like the sound of those from another world beckoning to those that dare set foot on its sacred ground.

In May of 1959, two dingy, dirty, sweaty prospectors told a strange story while visiting with an old time resident of the Phoenix area. They claimed that for several days they noticed what they at first thought to be several small children playing near and in a small creek which had water in it only during the early spring season. To find children so far from any desert dwelling or residential area puzzled the two. They were quite familiar with the many "strange" deaths that had occurred in this area and wisely felt that children had no business there. These small "children" appeared to be about five or six years old and would be seen in the same dry creek bed day after day as the prospectors went about their diggings. One day they decided to investigate and see what the children could possibly be doing in such an area. When they reached the creek bed they discovered, to their amazement, that the "children" had completely vanished but there, still very fresh in the sand, were footprints.

These prints appeared as MINIATURE DUPLICATES OF ENGINEER BOOTS. Although the miners returned to the same spot the next day, they reportedly never saw the "children" again. Other witnesses claim to have seen these little "children" at closer range and say they look more like men than children. Some ranchers, while on roundups in this same area, say that they could clearly see "little men," as they called them, on the tops of ridges and mountains of the Superstition range watching them. Not one of those present on the roundups would bother them but would only gaze silently at them as they went on about their work.

Many years ago, a teenage boy working with a large ranch concern on roundup was somehow lost from the rest of the crew and wandered about the area for several days without either water or food. This, as any prospector or treasure hunter worth his salt can tell you, is more often than not very fatal. He passed into a semi-conscious twilight between consciousness and unconsciousness.

During the time he was in this state he was aware of several little men around him giving him continued help and directions. They finally were able to lead him out of the range where he made it to Gobe, Arizona, a distance of about 50 miles from where he was lost. They did not give him either food or water, but somehow he had strength. He could not plainly make the people out and thus he was not sure whether they were "ghosts" or real entities. But he did manage to say a few words to them and they spoke in turn to him.

BRIAN SCOTT'S EXPERIENCES

At least four or five individuals have come forward to tell of their "wanderings" underground inside the Superstition UFO base. Two of these individuals I know of have lost their sanity, while the others have either had

ALIEN STRONGHOLDS ON EARTH!

nervous breakdowns or have vanished from their hometowns in order to go into seclusion. Only one man, Brian Scott, has publicly aired his story, and the UFOnauts he encountered at this base turned out to be rather deadly, as his home became haunted, his bedding caught on fire, and sometime later he became possessed by negative entities.

Before his encounter, Brian Scott had led a hardworking existence. It was while he was on vacation in March of 1971, not far from the famed Superstition Mountain range, that he was "beamed" onto a craft underground with a purplish light emanating from its underside. Inside the ship, he was taken to a "darkened compartment" where seven-foot-tall creatures "moved their hands over my body and disrobed me."

Scott described the UFOnauts as being "large - very bulky - but with two arms and two legs, like humans." In appearance, he admits they "gave me the willies," explaining that they had skin textures that were "a cross between an elephant, rhinoceros, and crocodile." As for their faces, "ears would start at the top of their head and run all the way down the whole side of their face, and they had an extra layer of what seemed to be hide, which covered them from approximately just below the chest to just below the knees. They also had a bit of an odor about the breath, which reminded me of dirty socks."

Subsequently, Brian claims four additional encounters with the identical group of aliens, plus meeting a being who is almost totally human in appearance and who calls himself "the host." Placed in a hypnotic trance by Dr. Alvin Lawson of California State University (Long Beach) Scott revealed in amazing detail how his hands and feet were up against one of the walls of the ship, spread-eagled, and he found it impossible to move. "In front of me," recalls Scott, "was this box-shaped thing - a machine. One of the creatures standing next to me made a couple of gestures with his hand and the machine began moving up, starting from my feet, to the top of my head, as if photographing my insides."

Scared to the breaking point, Scott urinated in his pants. "I thought I was going to die right then and there. A terrific pain was building in my head, like 10,000 migraine headaches all clumped into one. I tried to fight, but was held in place by some mysterious force. There was this one really big guy who seemed particularly interested in me. He placed his hand on my forehead and it felt like we were exchanging thoughts."

ALIEN STRONGHOLDS ON EARTH!

Since the day of his encounter, Scott says his brain has been functioning much faster than usual. While he possessed no formal technical training (nor was he a college graduate) prior to his experience, today the Garden Grove, California, resident is a highly paid draftsman, the ability having been "given" to him, he insists, by the creatures aboard the UFO.

Even more remarkable is the fact that Brian periodically falls into deep trances, during which time an entity that identifies itself solely as "Asta" speaks, giving technically advanced data not normally known to the contactee. Voice prints made by the Rohe Scientific Corporation and studied under the supervision of researchers from UCLA indicate that the voice patterns "could not technically have been made by a human being," but resemble the patterns made by a machine, perhaps a robot or computer.

Hair disheveled following a UFO encounter, Brian Scott was "beamed" onto a craft inside the Superstition Mountain Range.

Bizarre lights have also invaded the Scott home on numerous occasions, and the police were called at least once when Brian disappeared inside the house and could not be found by his wife, though he was dressed only in boxer shorts. Hours later he was found wandering in a daze in the back yard, supposedly after being brought back to Earth by the UFOnauts.

Research was conducted at the time by such groups as the then-prestigious Aerial Phenomena Research Organization, and Brian is convinced that "the beings who contacted me are preparing for what might turn out to be a mass landing on Earth, not too long in the future."

Brian moved about after his initial experience. He found himself and his family being constantly harassed by some form of invisible beings, most

ALIEN STRONGHOLDS ON EARTH!

likely those associated with his abductors. His home nearly burned down as a "spaceman" took over his body. One night the bedding caught on fire. A ball of light came from out of the floor and flew within a few inches of his head - and then it shot straight up and went right through the ceiling.

I investigated the case along with parapsychologist Barry Taff and author Brad Steiger. Scott became more paranoid as he began to receive some sort of communications from the ball through thoughts and pictures that were apparently transmitted directly into his mind.

One wonders if he later wished he had never had been abducted in the Superstition Mountains. UFO bases there are highly unpredictable.

Keep a safe distance!

SUGGESTED READING

MYSTERIES OF THE MOJAVE DESERT

Many felt that the famous Phoenix Lights were headquartered in the Superstition Mountains.

ALIEN STRONGHOLDS ON EARTH!

The valleys around the Superstition Mountains in Arizona are popular with hikers...and apparently also with visitors from other realms.

ALIEN STRONGHOLDS ON EARTH!

Chapter Sixteen
STAR CENTER OLYMPUS
Coordinating Our Journey Throughout Eternity With Their
Celestial Chariots Of Light
By Hercules Invictus

EDITOR'S NOTE: We have saved the "best" for last. Most of us have grown up enchanted by stories of the gods who live on Mount Olympus, said to be the site of the throne of Zeus. Yet we have been led to believe that this is all mythology, that the heavenly hosts never existed and that all the stories related are metaphorical. Yet the people of Greece, especially the older folks, consider this blasphemy. To them, the deities of the Mountain are "real," even if they possibly come and go from a parallel dimension. They are even said to come down and mate with humans (is that why Greek women are usually so beautiful?). And we're not talking eons ago, back in antiquity, but to this very day, says our associate "the great" Hercules. So get out your spyglasses or position a telescope at the base of Olympus and take a shot at seeing a UFO - as this may be one of the greatest alien bases on the face of the Earth.

* * * * * * * * * *

High atop Mount Olympus there is a portal which leads to a higher dimension, an ancient Heaven in which the most powerful personages of Greek Mythology happily dwell. This rift in space-time can sometimes be observed from the foot of the physical mountain and was understood by the aboriginal inhabitants of Northern Greece to be a glimpse into the Realm of

ALIEN STRONGHOLDS ON EARTH!

the Blessed Immortals who know no toil. These Celestials, whose spheres of influence extend far beyond our Earth, joyously partake of nectar and ambrosia while ceaselessly celebrating their exalted existence. From Mount Olympus they observe, guide and occasionally participate in the events unfolding in the Heavens above and on the Earth below. They walk among us freely, unrecognized in their human forms, and sometimes their visitations are accompanied by spheres of supernal brightness.

THE COSMIC PLAYGROUND

The gods of old - were they ancient astronauts?

The gods of old, though intimately involved with events on our Earth, are actually much older than our planet.

Theosophical lore, both ancient and modern, reveals that a number of the Olympians are actually Elohim (Creative Forces) from the farthest reaches of the Milky Way. They were invited here by Helios, our Solar Logos (Living Sun), and his twin flame Hestia (aka Vesta) to give shape to their Dream for our solar system. These beings, led by the Cosmic Hercules and his twin flame Athena (aka Amazonia) also established evolutionary paths through

ALIEN STRONGHOLDS ON EARTH!

which various life-streams could flow on their journey from Alpha (the Beginning) to Omega (the End). In the Theosophical writings the Alpha and Omega are opposite poles of the same paradoxical place, a location beyond Time and our limited comprehension of reality. The path to and fro is sometimes represented as a rainbow.

One of the few books dedicated to the investigation of UFOs and alien forces in ancient Greece and Italy.

The Heavenly nature of the Olympians is chronicled in the firmaments themselves. The planets of our solar system are named after the Roman designations for the Olympians: Venus (Aphrodite), Mercury (Hermes), Terra (Gaia), Mars (Ares), Jupiter (Zeus), Saturn (Kronos), Uranus (Ouranos), Neptune (Poseidon) and until recently Pluto (Hades). Most of our solar system's moons follow suit. Our sun and moon are rich in mythic associations and most of the constellations in our night sky immortalize personages, fabulous beasts and select artifacts from the Greco-Roman Myths.

The Elohim established various levels of spiritual activity in their creation through which the souls entrusted to their temporary care could descend and then re-ascend. They shaped incarnational vehicles befitting each level for themselves and for their charges. This process is reflected in the ancient accounts which relate that the Olympians are the get of Titans, who are in turn children of Heaven and Earth, and thus very much a part of our planet's unfolding evolution. Chaos came first, then the Protogenoi (Cosmic Forces), then the Titans (Primal Lords of Creation) and then the Gods of Olympus (the next and more refined generation of Titans). Hercules and Athena not only operate on all these levels simultaneously but have willingly chosen to descend and re-ascend as humans (and other terrestrial intelligences) countless times. Apollo and Poseidon also shared this fate (as a punishment however) according to the Myths.

ALIEN STRONGHOLDS ON EARTH!

Eros, an abstract being that emerged from Chaos in the beginning, later incarnated as a son of Aphrodite. Hercules was, among other things, an Idean Daktyl during the Age of the Titans. He protected the infant Zeus and was later turned into a lion by Kronos. During the reign of Zeus, Hercules incarnated as the son of his former charge and embraced the challenge of becoming Earth's greatest hero.

All of the Elohim involved with this project are still active in running it and often communicate with us through their chosen channels in the I AM Activity and other neo-Theosophical and Celestial endeavors focused on disseminating Cosmic Spirituality. They also communicate with individuals who embody fragments of their essence or serve their purposes in other ways. Hercules, Athena, Hermes, Zeus, Poseidon, Nike (aka Victory) and many other Olympians have affirmed through these communications that they are indeed the same beings whose symbolic adventures are recounted in our Mythologies and that they have been known by many names in diverse cultures throughout human history.

[In 1992 Inner Light Publications published a series of channeled Olympian communications in a slim volume called "Space Gods Speak."]

CELESTIALS: BEINGS OF LIGHT

The Olympians are multi-dimensional intelligences, radiant Beings of Light. This truth is preserved in Theosophy as well as the Bacchic cycle of the God of Wine. In the Myths the princess Semele, who was unknowingly having an affair with Zeus (and became pregnant thereby), is tricked by Hera (Zeus' divine wife and Queen of the Olympians) into asking her regal paramour to reveal himself in all his glory. Though he tried to persuade her to request another boon, the princess was insistent. Alas, the daughter of King Cadmus and Queen Harmonia did not survive the epiphany, but Zeus managed to save his unborn son Dionysus and later birth him from his thigh (as he had previously birthed Athena from his head).

From the surviving lore we know that the Deathless (Athanatoi), as the Olympians are sometimes referred to, are shape shifters who can easily assume the guise of animals and natural phenomena. Father Zeus alone manifested as a swan, two bulls, a cuckoo and a shower of rain during the course of his legendary seductions. The ferocity of storms were a reflection of the Sky Father's wrath. The activity of water mirrored Poseidon's moods.

ALIEN STRONGHOLDS ON EARTH!

They also enjoyed assuming the forms of humans and meddling in the affairs of mankind. Zeus and Hermes often posed as simple travelers to test how faithfully people were adhering to the hospitality laws they had established. Athena assumed the guise of Mentor, a friend of Odysseus, to guide young Telemachus during his father's long absence while embroiled in the Trojan War and its aftermath. Zeus appeared to Alcmene as her fiance Amphitryon while he was busy battling the Taphians. The Lord of Dark Clouds froze time to triple the duration of his visit. The product of their union was the Theban Hercules, destined to help the Olympians triumph in their prophesied war against the Giants.

The Olympians like to appear in ideal human forms, youthful and very fit. In the dawn of the contactee era, some of the blond haired UFOnauts identified themselves as Venusians. True to form they indulged in numerous amorous encounters with humans while teaching Space Age Theosophy. Nowadays they call themselves Pleiadians, a designation rich in Atlantean connotations. Due to their Scandinavian appearance and occasional Hyperborean names, many mortals call them Nordics. The divine twins Apollo and Artemis had a Hyperborean mother and often appeared as young and athletic blondes.

"Clouds" - or mothership - over Mount Olympus?

ALIEN STRONGHOLDS ON EARTH!

CELESTIAL CHARIOTS: ANCIENT

Although they can accomplish anything through the exercise of their divine imaginations, some Olympians prefer to express their artistry and mastery by working within the inherent limitations of mortal existence, which is ephemeral and framed by linear time.

Sometimes Chariots were employed by the Olympians in getting from place to place. These Chariots could appear as conveyances drawn by Celestial horses or as what we would now term UFOs. The Theban incarnation of Hercules stole (or borrowed at arrow-point) one of Helios' Sun Chariots to reach the Sunset Lands of the Red Island and/or the Garden of the Hesperides. In some accounts the vehicle is a "krater," a drinking vessel akin to a saucer.

Aside from Hercules and Helios, Apollo and Hyperion were also known for driving golden Sun-Chariots. Artemis, Diana and Selene drove silvery Moon-Chariots that were drawn by lions and other fabulous beasts.

CELESTIAL CHARIOTS: MODERN

In modern times some of the metaphysical systems that honor the reality of UFOs have clear associations with the Olympians as well. The Unarius Academy of Science, for instance, represents a vast spiritual organization of highly evolved beings, generically referred to as the Unarius Brothers, whose teachings were channeled by Ernest and Ruth Norman since the early 1950s and are now disseminated worldwide by the Academy, which is headquartered in El Cajon, California.

Echoes of the Olympians reverberate throughout the vast Unarius Cosmology.

The first inspired tome penned by Ernest L. Norman was titled The Elysium.

The five volumes of the Pulse of Creation series, which contain many of the Unariun core teachings, are titled:

- The Voice of Venus
- The Voice of Eros
- The Voice of Hermes
- The Voice of Orion
- The Voice of Muse, Elysium, Unarius

ALIEN STRONGHOLDS ON EARTH!

The Unarius Academy of Science - El Cajon, California.

Classical columns and Hellenic statuary grace the public areas of the Unarius building to honor the Golden Age of Greece.

And in the Unarius Academy of Science's Star Center, a mural commemorates fabled Atlantis, founded by Poseidon, at the apex of her glory. Poseidon was guided by Maitreya, a Space Brother in a UFO.

Aside from the personages and places mentioned above, such Hellenic luminaries as Anaxagoras, Pythagoras, Plato, Socrates and Herodotus can be encountered and interacted with through the application of Unariun spiritual practices.

These Olympian elements first drew my attention to Unarius, but the greater my exposure to this organization, the more impressed I've become at the depth and vastness of Unarius' cosmic vision, the positivity of their message and their dedication to continuing the work of their Founders.

Another venerable neo-Theosophical organization that embraces both Olympus and UFOs is Mark-Age.

ALIEN STRONGHOLDS ON EARTH!

Mark-Age was founded by Nada-Yolanda of the Sun (Pauline Sharpe) and El Morya (Charles Boyd Gentzel) at the dawn of the twentieth century's sixth decade.

The Mark-Age Revelations affirm that an Elder Race of Golden Giants once tread upon Gaia. They were the Titans of old and they birthed the human race during the Golden Age of their long and remarkable reign. It can truly be said that we are their descendants in this, the third dimension.

After the civil war that rent Heaven asunder (the Titanomachy) some of the combatants migrated to Neptune while others were exiled to Venus. Their human children remained here, stuck in a lower vibrational frequency.

The Golden Giants who remained, whom we know as the Olympians, guided our evolution and sought to free us, sometimes by incarnating among us as heroic or otherwise exceptional individuals. They taught us how to ascend to our lost estate through Apotheosis.

After the destruction of Atlantis, circumstances changed for the human race. Many of the Golden Giants had been freed and had evolved beyond the Earth. But alas, not all.

From MAPP to Aquarius Entry # 40: Gods and Goddesses in Mythology

"Some of the gods and goddesses of your mythology once lived on Earth and have evolved to Neptune. They have a sense of responsibility to the Earth, since they helped to create it. The entire mystery of your Atlantean civilization refers to these myths.

"Although our activities serve the I AM presence expressing itself through human individuation, our approach honors the legacy of 'the Elder race,' or the elect, who worked and lived and loved and made mistakes during those early times of settling the Earth."

The Legacy of the Founders of Mark-Age is preserved and their mission continued by Phillel of Motah (Philip J. Jacobs) and Robert H. Knapp, MD, co-Executive Directors of Mark-Age, Inc. The Mark-Age Revelations continue on Phillel's Motah Chronicles blog.

An emerging New Age spirituality that also acknowledges the role of the Olympians in our evolution and the existence of luminous Celestial vehicles (Seraphic transports) is the 6th Revelation, which sprang from a California couple's in-depth study of The Urantia Book. Michael and Dianne Dunkin, life-time seekers and servants of the Ancient Wisdom, launched this

ALIEN STRONGHOLDS ON EARTH!

movement at the direction of Celestial beings, many of whom revealed themselves to be the Gods and Goddesses of Greco-Roman Mythology. Though both can and do communicate with these Celestials, Dianne's abilities in this area are more developed. Prior to The Urantia Book their pilgrimage brought them to the Theosophical Society, Summit University, Rosicrucianism and oriental wisdom, especially Maitreya Great Dao. Though many of the Olympians interact with the Dunkins, Lord Maitreya has involved them in his Magisterial Mission and the Goddess Venus has charged them with heralding a worldwide Religion of Love. Michael is a Musician and Dianne is an Artist. They have launched a YouTube channel to share their journey and their message. At present they are compiling their writings into a book and host "The Magisterial Mission" podcast monthly on "Pride of Olympus."

A CALL TO ADVENTURE

Throughout my Mythic career I have issued many Calls to Adventure, and I will honor this custom by repeating it in the here and now to the readers of this epic anthology.

Mythic Astrology, Astro-Mythology, Theosophical channelings throughout the ages and the Myths themselves contain an invitation, and a warning.

The bulk of humanity is said to belong to one of the life-streams wending their way through our solar system's Cosmic Schoolhouse or Proving Grounds. Some souls however are older and are remnants of earlier evolutions.

The invitation, issued to the incarnate Ancients still among us, is to follow the Mythic Path that ultimately leads one back to the Heavens (Elysiums), and perhaps even beyond them to the Star Center on Mount Olympus itself. Psyche and Dionysus made it all the way back to Olympus. The Dioscouroi (Castor and Pollux), Orion and Perseus (along with his wife and in-laws) earned their own constellations in the night sky. The Theban Hercules managed to do both.

The warning is that if you're not truly worthy you will be cast back down to Earth and crash land quite dramatically. The sagas of Bellerophon, who sought to place himself in the company of the Immortals by riding Pegasus (who was indeed worthy and could freely travel back and forth to the Realm of the Gods), and Jason, who betrayed his divine purpose time and again, are

ALIEN STRONGHOLDS ON EARTH!

tutorials in what not to do. Jason's ship, the Argo, is immortalized in the firmaments, as is the Golden Fleece. Medea, his estranged wife, made it to Elysium despite her many crimes. Jason died homeless, destitute and drunk, crushed by the prow of the legendary vessel that made him famous, which he abandoned and allowed to rot on a nearby beach.

We will not repeat these errors, though we will doubtless make many new ones of our own during the next epic Argonaut Voyage. I sound the Horn of Summoning and now issue my Call to Adventure. Our Argo, our Vehicle of Light, will be the Pride of Olympus and our journey will hopefully return us to our soul's True Home.

The Pride of Olympus is our Merkaba, our Sun-Chariot, our Celestial Barge, the Wheels-Within-Wheels shamanic vehicle that facilitates our journeys to the Astral Realms of Gaia's World Tree.

The Pride of Olympus is our metaphorical vehicle for exploring various thematically related but seemingly different approaches concerned with explaining our human origins, guiding our human development and actualizing our maximal potential.

The Pride of Olympus supports all of humanity's efforts to transcend this world and venture forth into the great beyond, be they metaphysical, mechanical or even imaginal.

Like all Astral Conveyances, our Celestial Argo, the Pride of Olympus can and does assume many forms. At present it takes the form of a podcast on Blogtalkradio's Spiritual Unity Radio Network (SURN). The Cosmic spiritualities mentioned above, and several others, are actively involved in our exploration and offer much relevant lore, many keen insights and numerous spiritual tools that make our expedition easier.

PRIDE OF OLYMPUS INTRO:

Who am I?

What am I?

Where did I come from?

Why am I here?

Is there a purpose to all of this?

ALIEN STRONGHOLDS ON EARTH!

Join Hercules Invictus and the crew of the Pride of Olympus in seeking answers to these and other timeless questions while they serve Mount Olympus by safeguarding the Path of Mythic Ascension.

PRIDE OF OLYMPUS OUTRO:

Olympian Blessings on all who have joined us on our adventure.

Now go forth... and create a better world, one filled with Light and Love. On behalf of the Pride of Olympus and her crew, may your journeys be joyous!

Onwards!

© Hercules Invictus

SUGGESTED READING, GLOBAL COMMUNICATIONS BOOKS TO WHICH HERCULES HAS CONTRIBUTED:

UFO HOSTILITIES AND THE EVIL ALIEN AGENDA

SCREWED BY THE ALIENS: TRUE SEXUAL ENCOUNTERS WITH ETS

WEIRD WINGED WONDERS

THE MATRIX CONTROL SYSTEM OF PHILIP K. DICK AND THE PARANORMAL SYNCHRONICITIES OF TIMOTHY GREEN BECKLEY

HIDDEN TREASURES OF THE KNIGHTS TEMPLAR

Our one and only Hercules Invictus.

ALIEN STRONGHOLDS ON EARTH!

SECTION FIVE

UFO over the Great Pyramid – could this be for real?

PYRAMIDS AS ALIEN BASES

There is something exceedingly strange about the world's pyramids. When we think of these massive monuments to the gods, we are most often thinking about the pyramids of Egypt. But pyramids actually exist all over the world. South America, Central America, Australia, China and even in the United States. Those into the ancient alien theory have long believed that these stone structures may be linked the gods from on high. George Hunt Williamson, whose writing we discuss throughout this book, told us that there was actually a "hall of records" beneath the Great Pyramid of Giza. And others have gone on record as believing that there could even be a spaceship housed beneath the Sphinx eons ago, perhaps for someone's "great escape" in the future. Here we quote from Tablet 5 of "The Emerald Tablets of Thoth the Atlantean," interesting because of its mention of a spaceship beneath the Sphinx:

> *"Raised I to Light, the children of Khem.*
> *Deep 'neath the rocks I buried my spaceship,*

ALIEN STRONGHOLDS ON EARTH!

waiting the time when man might be free.

"Over the spaceship, erected a marker in the form of a lion yet like unto man.

There 'neath the image rests yet my spaceship, forth to be brought when need shall arise.

"Know ye, O, man, that far in the future, invaders shall come from out of the deep.

Then awake, ye who have wisdom. Bring forth my ship and conquer with ease.

Deep 'neath the image lies my secret. Search and find in the pyramid I built.

"Each to the other is the Keystone; each the gateway that leads into Life.

Follow the Key I leave behind me. Seek and the doorway to Life shall be thine.

Seek thou in my pyramid, deep in the passage that ends in a wall.

"Use thou the Key of the Seven, and open to thee the pathway will fall.

Now unto thee I have given my wisdom. Now unto thee I have given my way.

"Follow the pathway. Solve thou my secrets. Unto thee I have shown the way."

And while we are unable to explore beneath the Great Pyramid or the Sphinx, Carol Rodriguez and I did voyage to Mexico to see if we could find out anything about a possible alien base there.

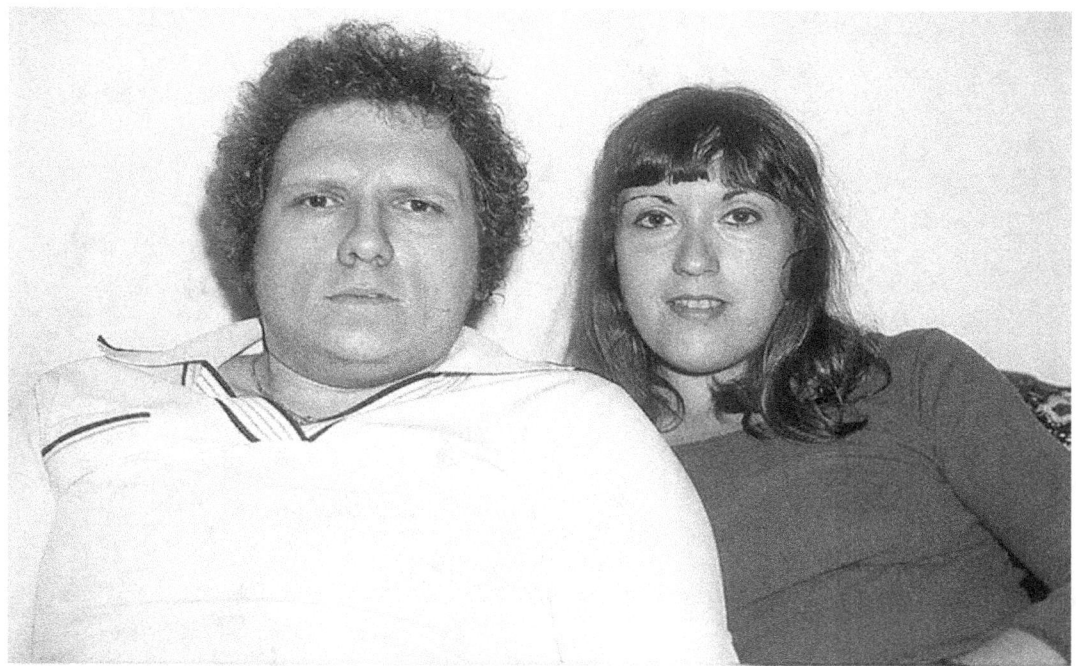

Tim and Carol seated on a couch at the NY School of Occult Arts and Science after giving a talk on their exploration of the pyramids of Mexico.

ALIEN STRONGHOLDS ON EARTH!

The sarcophagus lid of Pakal the Great - King of the Maya city-state of B'aakal, seems to portray the king as an astronaut flying a spaceship.

ALIEN STRONGHOLDS ON EARTH!

Chapter Seventeen
SEARCHING FOR "FLYING TORTILLA" BASES IN MEXICO: AN ON THE SPOT INVESTIGATION SOUTH OF THE BORDER
By Timothy Green Beckley and Carol Ann Rodriguez

Immediately upon leaving Merida, the capitol of the Yucatan, the jungle sprang up all around, threatening to swallow us up. As twilight approached, we winded our way through several tiny villages where thatched-roofed huts without electricity made up the majority of the dwellings.

From time to time, the Indian children, who still walk the streets barefooted, tried to sneak a peek into our van, but our only response was to kick up a cloud of dust into the air as we sped along the narrow dirt roads. From what we could see of the surroundings, it was becoming easier to accept the various stories we'd heard that flying saucer bases exist in the more remote sections of this beautiful, abundantly green, Mexican state. Before leaving the USA, we had been informed through our friendly space contacts that members of the "Ashtar Command" would be along to guide our journey - if not in a physical sense, at least psychically.

Over the past few months we'd repeatedly been told that the space people find the Yucatan to their liking, having established a foothold in the region centuries ago. Our source for this information is a personal friend who professes to have established a telepathic rapport with aliens. He is known to regularly engage in what is termed "space channeling," a process in which he goes into an altered state of consciousness and extraterrestrials actually take over his vocal cords and speak through him. From what he had told us,

ALIEN STRONGHOLDS ON EARTH!

supposedly the aliens who frequently landed there made contact with the early inhabitants of this area. In support of this theory, many of the legends of the Yucatan apparently do tell of superhuman gods who descended from the heavens and helped the natives develop a highly technical culture which included the practical use of astronomy and perhaps even space travel.

As we drove into the night, venturing further and further away from civilization, the stars began to twinkle above our heads with increasing brilliance, their presence seemingly having an eerie hypnotic effect of our mood. Using a bit of imagination - no doubt caused by the potential excitement of our adventure into what is still largely uncharted jungle - we began to see the stars as if they were in reality a flotilla of glittering spaceships piloted by golden-haired ancient astronauts, who almost assuredly visited Mexico during the distant past.

From time to time, our guide would utter a few words in Spanish. He indicated that we would arrive at Uxmal in time to view the nightly light and sound show that is put on for visitors who come from all over the world to marvel at the towering structures that still stand in honor of the gods Quetzalcoatl and Kulkulcan.

STRANGE FORMATIONS

As our gaze reached further out into the blackened cosmos in search of anything unusual (like a UFO!) that might be hidden among the stars and planets, we recalled that Mexico has always had a rich UFO-related history; not only throughout antiquity, but even in more recent times. Over the years, many exciting stories have passed through our hands involving face-to-face meetings with space beings south of the American border. Close encounters in Mexico are pretty common and are generally accepted by the populace - especially by those Mexicans who have not been educated in the big cities where such things as folklore and UFOs are treated as being nothing more than superstition. In fact, it was in Mexico where the first photographs were taken of an entire fleet of UFOs by no less an authority than a highly respected astronomer. That was nearly 100 years ago, but the account is still a thrilling one to relate.

Senor Jose A.Y. Bonilla, director of the observatory at Zacatecas, was looking through his telescope at 8 A.M. on the 12th of August, 1883, when he noticed a luminous body passing in front of the sun. The trained astronomer

ALIEN STRONGHOLDS ON EARTH!

was trying to observe sun spot activity from his observatory, located two miles above sea level. He said the object - "a dark form" - circled the sun, and it was then that he was able to capture its image on a photographic plate. A brief while later, Bonilla was shocked once again when additional objects of various shapes and sizes appeared in his telescope.

"I had not recovered from my surprise (from the first sighting) when the same phenomenon was repeated. And with such frequency that, in the space of two hours, I counted 283 bodies crossing the solar disc. Little by little, however, clouds hindered the observation. I could not resume the observation till the sun crossed the meridian, and then only for 40 additional minutes."

Later on that same day, he followed the activity of some 48 additional objects which traveled from north to south. The objects were black and would become luminous as they crossed in front of the sun. They passed in ones and twos and appeared to be round or "stretched out" like a cigar. On film, they took on an "irregular form." The following day, from 8 A.M. to nearly 10 o'clock, Bonilla saw a total of 116 more "mysterious bodies" from his observatory in Mexico.

MESSENGERS FROM THE STARS

The Yucatan is steeped in mystery as well as history. Nobody knows exactly when they were built or who really constructed them - there is no record to give clues, the Spanish conquerors made certain of that - but the pyramids of this region testify to the fact that an advanced culture once existed here. We do know that the Mayan and the Toltec natives worshipped feathered gods as well as the serpent, but elements of both these ancient cultures have sort of become intermingled over the centuries, and archeologists admit that they are still attempting to sort out the true nature of civilization as it once existed in early Mexico.

We do know that there are a number of strange correlations between the pyramids in Mexico and those in Egypt. For example, the dimensions of the base of the "Pyramid of the Sun" at Teotihucan are said to be exactly that of the Cheops pyramid, and its height is precisely half of the structure that sits near the Nile. We also know the Mayans DID possess more than the bare fundamentals of astronomy, going so far as to be able to calculate the rotation of Venus.

ALIEN STRONGHOLDS ON EARTH!

UFO over Mexico's Pyramid of the Sun, circa May 4, 2016.

Of course, the many legends of the Yucatan are even more interesting than what has positively been proven. For example, tradition has it that the main pyramid at Chichen-Itza was built directly over a "device" which once traveled across the frontiers of space. Supposedly, it was left behind by the ancient astronauts and will one day in the future fly again. Another belief is that a princess whose hair was as fair as the sun was buried in a secret tomb in the Pyramid of the Moon in Teotihucan. She is said to have come from the lunar surface, but died before she could return.

Taking these stories into consideration, it's no wonder that writers such as Erich von Daniken have had a field day when it comes to examining the stonework to be found on many of the structures which stand in this region. There are any number of "helmeted" gods etched on the temples and priests with lightning bolts (laser weapons?) shooting out of their hands and bodies.

And what about space travel?

Perhaps best known is a carving found on the lid of a Mayan sarcophagus which dates to around 680 A.D. The sarcophagus was discovered under a large pyramid at Palenque, Mexico, and, according to von Daniken, shows a priest seated at the controls of a rocket-like device shooting off flames. Says the leading authority on ancient astronauts: "Here sits a human being with the upper part of his body bent forward like a racing motorcyclist; today any child would identify this vehicle as a rocket. It is pointed in front, widens out and terminates at the tail in a darting flame. Our space traveler is not only bent forward tensely, he is also looking intensely at an apparatus hanging in front of his face," sort of a control panel, von Daniken asserts in a quite serious way.

ALIEN STRONGHOLDS ON EARTH!

DIRE WARNING FROM THE GODS

In addition to the Mayan traditions, the Aztecs made no bones about their belief in deities of a "higher order." In reality, it was their belief in such "gods" that caused their civilization eventually to come to ruin at the hands of the Spanish conquistadors. Passed down from generation to generation was a tale which told how the great "White God" who had visited their land and taught them much had gone away, but had promised to return one day. When the Aztecs saw the Spaniards with their white skin, they assumed it was their rightful legacy coming to pass. Their land was quickly overrun and their society totally raped of its culture.

Actually, one of the greatest UFO-oriented stories from this period involves Montezuma, the emperor of the Aztecs. The story is hardly known to outsiders, but it is a tale that has been passed from lip to lip among Mexicans for many centuries.

According to the legend, Montezuma was warned that his empire would soon be wiped from the face of the Earth. Thirteen years before Cortez arrived, Montezuma was paid a visit by the King of Texcoco, a neighboring kingdom. It was widely known that the King of Texcoco had sometime before made a pact with the gods which enabled him to see into the future.

The King of Texcoco told Montezuma the bad news, but said that, if Montezuma wanted to escape, they could go to a place where they would be safe. They would leave their temples behind and stay in the jungle where soon a chief known as Huemoc, who was thought to have been dead for 700 years, would come and transport them to Ciclaco, or "a house on the rabbit," which is interpreted as being the moon.

Apparently, Montezuma thought his friend had been bounced off one pyramid wall too many and went right on living it up as usual. He definitely had second thoughts a year later, when in 1509 a fair-skinned priest named Tzoncoztil, "the blonde one," observed a strange object in the air throughout the entire night. It looked like "an arrow made out of multicolored clouds," and apparently the priest believed it had great significance because he ran off to tell Montezuma of his vision the very first thing the next morning.

Somewhat disturbed by the appearance of this large "arrow" amidst the stars, the Aztec king decided to confer with the King of Texcoco to see if he couldn't get a clearer in his mind about what this apparition really meant. The King of nearby Texcoco had a logical explanation. He said this was Huemoc's

ALIEN STRONGHOLDS ON EARTH!

vehicle, which was waiting for Montezuma to finish his affairs of government and join him.

Time passed, and as in any era even the great must pass into spirit. Advancing in age, the King of Texcoco invited the nobles of his land to witness his death. Together they climbed a hill where the pyramid supposedly served as an observatory. After praying and meditating for several days, the king asked to be left alone. Adhering to their leader's last request, they left the hill immediately. Eventually, all signs of life's light were extinguished, and the servants climbed the hill to recover the king's body.

He was gone!

The King of Texcoco had vanished without a trace. It has been reported that Montezuma was so frightened and shocked by the disappearance of his ally that simulated mock funerals were conducted and the entire matter kept a closely guarded secret from everyone.

THE TALKING ROCK

We have it on good authority that Montezuma received several warnings to be on the lookout for those who would not be satisfied until they conquered his people.

To the south of where Montezuma established his empire, there was a most majestic rock which the ruler wanted very much to have as a center stone in his courtyard. Because of its tremendous size, he realized that it would take many men to cart it the required distance to his palace. In order to accomplish the deed, he ordered the mobilization of laborers from eight villages. Almost from the start they were frightened of the power this rock seemed to possess. At times it was so heavy that it broke cables, planks and anything being used to haul it. At other times it would become so light that four men could carry it without a great deal of effort.

Eventually the rock was brought to Montezuma and apparently he too became spooked by it. According to legend, the rock began to speak. It said that it did not want to stay in Mexico because a disaster was going to occur. Montezuma was stubborn and he threatened the laborers who would not fulfill their duty with death. The terrified workers took advantage of the moment when the stone was light and moved it on their own. They built a special bridge made out of cedar logs to be able to move it to the island which was the heart of the city. Halfway over the bridge the rock became heavy and the

ALIEN STRONGHOLDS ON EARTH!

bridge collapsed. Not even the divers were able to find it after that. Several days later it was found with its four corners cracked at the same exact spot where it had originally rested.

Montezuma must have gotten the fear of God thrown into him, as from then on he is said to have spent a good portion of his time scanning the sky from one of the terraces of his palace. One afternoon he saw a "white cloud" rise up into the sky. He knew it was a considerable distance away and this was confirmed the next day, when a farmer sought permission to see the King of Mexico to tell him the details of his unusual experience. The farmer said he had been tending his land near Coatepec when a "powerful eagle" grabbed him by the hair and lifted him high up into the air. He was put into a dark cave. Then someone took him by the hand and led him into a room where a great and powerful man greeted him and asked him to sit down.

The man gave the farmer flowers to smell and a pipe to smoke. Later he was told to look into space and he saw Montezuma asleep. Then the man ordered the farmer to burn the king on the thigh with his pipe. When Mexico's ruler did not even budge, the strange figure told the farmer that this was how oblivious Montezuma was to the potential loss of his kingdom. In a vision, the farmer supposedly saw by whom and by what means the loss was to occur. Before leaving, he was ordered to go to Montezuma and tell him what he had seen. Then the "eagle" returned him to the field from which he had been abducted.

After hearing the story, Montezuma was on the verge of hysterics. He had the man thrown into a dungeon which he had sealed with lime to guard the secret which had been entrusted to him. It was easy to prove that the farmer was not telling a tall tale. He had seen the "white cloud" and there was a burn on his thigh, which he didn't know how it had gotten there.

After that incident, just before sunset every evening, Montezuma was tortured by the vision of a large luminous pyramid. The people of his kingdom also saw it and were extremely frightened. Montezuma believed that it might mean one last offer of salvation made by Huemoc, but he didn't know what to do about it. He eventually decided to communicate with the gods.

To do this, he used information obtained from the King of Texcoco. Montezuma sent his ambassadors to the deep cave. No one today, supposedly, knows the whereabouts of this subterranean cave, but Montezuma's representative journeyed there, expecting to gain admission to

ALIEN STRONGHOLDS ON EARTH!

this chamber. However, the blind beings who were authorized to take the worthy before the gods twice refused admission to the king's men. The third time they were able to go before Huemoc, who ordered an eighty-day fast for the ruler of the land. Montezuma was not allowed to eat, drink alcohol, smoke tobacco or sleep with a woman.

Huemoc had promised that if Montezuma kept to this rigid fast in eighty days he would come to redeem the king.

There was great rejoicing in the palace. On the appointed night, there appeared in the sky a glowing "white cloud" that made the heavens as bright as day. Montezuma, along with a delegated party, went to where the object landed (and was supposed to land), when suddenly another object thrust forward, pushing the first one away. The second craft then positioned itself very close to the pyramid at Chapultepec. Montezuma and his group became frightened.

Meanwhile, the priest with the "blond hair" was sleeping in his residence nearby when he was awakened by a presence in his room. There stood an entity which told him, "Montezuma wants to escape, but his destiny has been decided. The master of the gods has ordered that he must face the tragic invasion along with the rest of the populace; for that reason, I have been sent to stop Huemoc from taking him. He refused to go when the time was right and now he must stay. Montezuma is nearby. Go and tell him he has been ordered to return to the palace."

The rest of the story is history. Montezuma was not "picked up" because he would not heed the original warning and too much time had elapsed in the interim. We can testify that the King of Mexico must have cursed the gods for their role in his plight. Along with the thousands of tourists in the past, his "revenge" was swift and highly uncomfortable for us, but the exciting time we had on our journey made it possible for us to take our minds off our minor stomach problems - at least from time to time.

A SPACEMAN SPEAKS TO US

As our van rumbled along in the dark, hitting just about every bump and crevice in creation, our minds momentarily flashed back to a series of exciting telepathic messages we had recently been receiving via our contactee friend from an entity known as Ashtar. Commander-in-Chief of the Free Federation of Planets, Ashtar, according to tradition, keeps tabs on all relevant activities

ALIEN STRONGHOLDS ON EARTH!

occurring on Earth from a gigantic space station orbiting near the planet Saturn. Part of his duties include communicating with select earthlings in an attempt to champion the cause of the Space Brothers who are concerned about our warlike activities and our childish behavior, and would like to see us develop further along on the spiritual path.

Ashtar's end-time predictions have been popularized in the book "Psychic and UFO Revelations in the Last Days," and he continues to beam down relevant messages on a regular basis, not only to our friend but to dozens of other contactees from far and wide.

Never one to forego a golden opportunity to speak out on a subject of particular interest to him, Ashtar made it known in plain and simple language that he approved of our sojourn. From his "conversations" he made us feel as if we were the real life counterparts of Indiana Jones and his beautiful sidekick Marion, about to embark on an expedition to uncover something as tremendously important as the lost Ark of the Covenant.

"Are you preparing for your visit to the Yucatan?" Ashtar asked point blank during a channeling session conducted some months before we were due to leave New York for Mexico. For centuries, Ashtar stated, the Yucatan has been a focal point for extraterrestrial activity, the site of the various pyramids in the Yucatan having been used as a waystation for alien visitors to our planet.

"The history of this part of your planet is dear to us," Ashtar declared. ""We go back thousands of years, to when this part of your globe was just being settled. We taught the natives much about astronomy, science, medicine, and controlling the weather. A great deal of what we taught them has since become part of the legends and the lore of their people." The spaceman confirmed beliefs we pretty much already held to be true.

In addition to the Yucatan being a space port, Ashtar said "There were also Egyptians here, as well as Atlanteans. They all shared information with the people, who were so friendly and intelligent that for many, many years their civilization flourished." Ashtar, backing up the ancient astronaut hypothesis, noted that the natives "built giant monuments out of stone to show their appreciation for what they had been taught. For many years the lived in peace and harmony, not only amongst themselves, but with their Masters, and with the universe."

ALIEN STRONGHOLDS ON EARTH!

Eventually this society crumbled when their culture literally went to the devil. "There were those who were in touch with the serpent race, who came and took over the area and slaughtered many of the Mayans and enslaved others. They overran the area because the land was so productive." But as always negativity begets negativity and the Creator showed his wrath.

According to Ashtar's version of history, there came a great rain and flood which covered the entire Earth. Spaceships hovered over the pyramids and lifted up those who deserved to be saved. The others thought they would be taken away too, but they were mistaken. They even went so far as to climb to the top of the pyramid at Uxmal, anticipating that the flood waters would never go that high. In the days that followed, they were swept away and drowned.

Time being a nonessential factor where they come from, Ashtar and his merry band of space travelers still hold that the Yucatan is sacred ground, and have indicated that, during the "final days" predicted by many, tremendous spaceships will land in this area and save the worthy.

"We will return and put on an (aerial) display for the people," Ashtar has said. "Some of the descendants of those who left with us are still living among us now. From time to time, we drop some of them down as they can easily pass on the street. They will help in the evacuation when the moment arrives."

During our communications with him, Ashtar has stated that artifacts from their visits in antiquity still exist in the Yucatan, going so far as to hint that we might find something of interest if we kept our eyes open.

"There are still some artifacts from our visitations left. There are so many things to be found there; things that your scientists have not yet discovered. There are tombs underneath the pyramids that haven't been found. They contain much information, some of it about Atlantis, some of it about space travel."

On another occasion, Ashtar proclaimed that many secrets remain hidden in the ruins to be deciphered by future archeologists. "There are secrets of telepathic communication, secrets of interplanetary travel, as well as the secret of levitation which helped to lift the stones of the pyramid into place."

Despite his overwhelming approval that we visit the Yucatan, he did add a stern warning: "Keep in mind that there are individuals who will go to

ALIEN STRONGHOLDS ON EARTH!

any length to hide the truth . . . Make sure you are not being followed. Go on this trip with the thought that this is a practice run for the evacuation (to take place later on) . . ."

Ashtar even threw in that eventually "the jungles will flourish and someday a new space port will be built there. But be careful," he reiterated, "and we shall see you soon," indicating (as he had done previously) that he or a representative under his direct command might present themselves to us so that we might experience a close encounter of our own.

Our hearts beat twice as rapidly as normal in anticipation of a physical contact with our friends from space in the Yucatan jungle. Will our fearless explorers discover UFO bases? Will Ashtar make an appearance? Find out in part two.

Homage paid to Tim and Carol's trip in search of an alien base in Mexico.
Art courtesy Carol Ann Rodriguez.

ALIEN STRONGHOLDS ON EARTH!

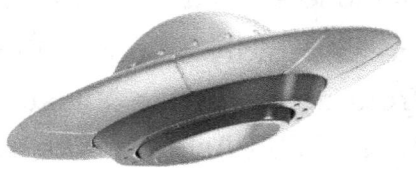

Chapter Eighteen
PART TWO: THE MEXICAN ADVENTURE CONTINUES

John Hart has spent many hours in the air. In addition to being a pilot, he is also an explorer who enjoys new challenges and looks forward to the next adventure. But when he first flew over the jungle in the state of Oaxaca (pronounced Wah-ha-ca), he couldn't believe his eyes. The ruins on the high mountain crest extend for 24 miles and are considered to be an archeological wonder. Exquisite gold works and intricate pieces of jewelry have been dug up in recent years, and, in addition, here can be found strange rock carvings which indicate that the early colonizers of this area knew a great deal about the rest of the world. There are, for example, drawings which depict giant apes to be found in Africa, and men with slanted eyes, indicating that a link has been made to China.

But what pilot John Hart saw from the air is even more astonishing, for, according to a clipping from the Port Chester, New York, newspaper, Hart observed what he feels may be a UFO base located in the dense jungle near these ruins. "On one occasion, I saw a brightly-lit spherical object hovering a few feet from the ground at the far edge of a small clearing. When it disappeared, it flew away at great speed." He added that UFOs have often been seen by natives, who take the appearance of these flying saucers pretty much for granted.

As we climbed the pyramid at Uxmal, it was easy for us to visualize how this area must have originally looked at the height of the Mayan civilization.

ALIEN STRONGHOLDS ON EARTH!

Here, all around us, stood towering monuments built in honor of the gods of antiquity who, according to local legend, descended from the clouds in glittering spaceships.

The night was warm and full of sounds as we listened to the stories of how the peaceful dwellers of this majestic site were taught much by those we believe to have been the ancient astronauts. Folklore has it that the grand Pyramid of the Magician was actually constructed in one night by the god Chac, who disguised himself as a dwarf. Chac had asked for the hand of the king's daughter, and was told that she would be his, but ONLY if he could put up a towering temple in the span of one night. Using occult powers of transmutation, levitation and laser beam technology, he accomplished this task with no difficulty.

Back in New York, before we began our trip, we had been told that we would not be alone, that our guide - though invisible to the eye under normal circumstances - would be the space being Ashtar, who, for many years, has regularly beamed messages down to Earth for the sake of all mankind. Naturally, since we couldn't see him, we felt it would be impossible to say for certain if he had come along for the ride. According to the various channeled communications we had been receiving, the space people are very fond of the Yucatan, having landed there over the centuries.

CHAUFFER CONVERSES WITH ALIENS

UFO contacts in Mexico are pretty common. In fact, in the first issue of "UFO REVIEW," we detailed the rather astounding experience of a Mexican doctor who insists that he actually gave a physical examination to an extraterrestrial who entered his office one afternoon.

Back in the summer of 1953, UFOs were just starting to receive wide attention when a Mexican chauffer came forward with a tale that was out of this world.

Salvador Villaneuva Medina had been hired by an American couple to drive them from Mexico City to Laredo, Texas. Salvador had picked up the couple outside their hotel early in the day and proceeded on the journey, which was to take them over some pretty rough roads.

Beyond the town of Valles, the chauffer began to experience problems with this auto, a 1952 Buick. It appeared as if the gears would not hold.

ALIEN STRONGHOLDS ON EARTH!

Realizing that he would not be able to go any further, Salvador pulled off the road and started to jack up the car. Sensing they would be of no help, the couple decided to hitch a ride to the nearest town.

Though it was getting darker by the minute, Salvador continued to tinker with the car. He believed that he would eventually locate the problem and be able to fix it. He was working under the Buick when he heard footsteps coming closer. Initially, he thought help had arrived, but upon crawling out from under the car, he realized his problems were definitely not over.

"A man with a very white face was standing before me. He was dressed in a one-piece garment of corduroy-like material which covered even his feet. It was tight at the ankles, cuff and neck, but was loose elsewhere, giving the appearance of being elastic. Around his waist he wore a thick belt about three inches wide of a bluish color. The strange thing about the belt was that it had holes in it, and the holes would light up little by little, as if they had electric lights inside. Under his arm was a helmet like those used by football players, but from the ear pieces ran fine wires. He had fine features and a penetrating look. He had no beard and his hair was fine, wavy, grey, and reached his shoulders. He seemed to stand about four feet tall and to weigh approximately 110 pounds."

Salvador said later that it was at this point that he became really nervous. "I was trembling. He asked me twice in correct Spanish what was wrong with the car. I could not answer because I was frightened and was watching him closely."

Finally, Salvador got hold of himself and asked if the man was some kind of aviator. "Yes, I am," the man stated, pointing off in the direction of a nearby field where a strange machine stood.

"But you are obviously not from Mexico," the puzzled chauffer noted. "Yes, that is correct," he was told. "I come from a place at much space," which is a literal translation of what the "aviator" said.

Salvador saw that the man was friendly and so he invited him into his car since it was almost pitch black outside.

"But just then his belt began to send out luminous flashes and I noticed a buzzing sound coming from it. He put on his helmet, raised his arm in a parting gesture and walked away toward a hill. At about 200 meters, I could see his belt twinkling like fireflies."

ALIEN STRONGHOLDS ON EARTH!

As time passed, Salvador began to get tired and so he decided to take a nap inside the car until morning, when he would go off to seek the services of a mechanic. "Later on I was aroused by knocks on the car window. I saw two people standing near the car and thought they were the American couple who had hired me. My surprise was great when I saw it was my aviator friend, but this time he was accompanied by a taller person but dressed in the same sort of uniform."

His curiosity aroused, Salvador invited the two men inside the parked Buick.

"I was very interested in learning where it was they came from, and so I asked the gentlemen if they were Europeans." Salvador was told that they came from a place a great distance further away than Europe. "The smaller of the men told me that in his place the towns cover everything. There were no uninhabited areas, and the streets were continuous. The people did not walk on the streets because they were metal and from them their vehicles took their power."

Continuing the conversation, Salvador then asked about what kind of food was eaten in the land where the men came from. "I was told that all the houses had little patios in the center where there is a garden and a well. They are able to produce all the food that is needed. He added that they did not have tall buildings and that in a street/block they had continuous buildings."

Salvador was told that on their world there were oceans and that their chief source of power was the rays of the sun - this years before we earthlings considered solar energy to be of any value. They also talked about government and said that poverty had long ago been wiped out, and that children were educated in a "certain zone" and were taught according to their physical and mental qualities. They added that their planet passed through the stage of development that we are currently in thousands of years ago. They also added that their world had suffered many wars and destructive retrogressions and that finally an agreement was reached between the different governments, so that what we call nations and countries disappeared "and we all became sons of the same world." Supposedly, a council of "wise men" was formed, all of whom had exceptional minds.

At dawn, their conversation completed, the two men excused themselves and started off down the road. Salvador followed them until they came to a ship which was ten meters in diameter and about half as high. "At a

ALIEN STRONGHOLDS ON EARTH!

signal a section of the ship opened and I could see certain things in the interior. My visitors invited me inside. At this I became panic stricken and turned and ran back to the car. A few minute later, I saw their ship rise slowly above the trees. It was oscillating and luminous with bluish rays around it. Then it took off and quickly disappeared in the direction of the rising sun."

Shortly after dawn, the American couple returned with a mechanic and the car was repaired. For a long while, Salvador kept his experience bottled up inside until eventually he broke down and told his wife. Months later, his account was the talk of Mexico, and pioneer researchers Bryant and Helen Reeve thought so highly of Salvador's story that they devoted an entire chapter to it in their classic UFO book, "Flying Saucer Pilgrimage."

PSYCHIC APPARITION AT UXMAL

As we sat on the ledge of one of the buildings that makes up the great complex of ancient structures that is known as Uxmal, we expected almost anything to happen. Though the night was pitch black, the various ruins were basked in colored lights that gave off strange illuminations. One could very easily imagine the long dead priests as they went about their magical rituals, which probably included communicating with beings from outer space. Indeed, it was in the seven chambers of the Temple of the Sun God that the worthy were initiated into long forgotten supernatural arts.

As we looked around us for any signs of a "visitor," we nearly jumped out of our skin when a bat flew by. We had been told Ashtar might appear, and so we had half come to expect the materialization of a space being and not the appearance of good old Count Dracula.

Suddenly, I felt a presence off to one side. "Do you see anyone standing over there?" I asked Carol, pointing in the direction beyond where any of the tourists were standing. I can't say for certain whether or not I was seeing this in a strict physical sense, or whether my consciousness was now operating on a higher level, but I was able to perceive the vague form of a purple or violet hue a few feet off the ground. Many times Ashtar or other space beings seem to materialize in such a fashion. For example, Carolyn Valentine, an employee with the Naval Research Laboratory, Flight Support Detachment (Patuxent River, Maryland), reported a similar experience to me after having tried an experiment for contacting UFOnauts as described in my "BOOK OF UFO CONTACTS." "Within seconds of concentrating on the Indigo Triangle and the

ALIEN STRONGHOLDS ON EARTH!

name Ashtar, I felt as if I were being pulled upward. I was shown a being, and there seemed to be some vibrating, rotating diamonds, bright green in color, and in the center was an out-of-focus head and shoulders view of a being."

The apparition at Uxmal - if that indeed is what the form represented - lasted only a few seconds and then my mind focused back on our surroundings. There is no way that I can positively state that this was Ashtar putting in an appearance, but later, back in New York, we were given a message received through telepathy that the Commander-In-Chief of the Free Federation of Planets had been with us on what had certainly been an inspiring occasion. I must say, in all sincerity, that a totally tranquil and feeling overcame both of us and it felt like we had briefly been lifted from this dimension and deposited on another planet. Of course, the skeptics will say that we were merely over-excited by the fact that we were so far from home in a land of mystery that we truly believe to be enchanted.

Film maker Kenneth Anger's impression of UFOs and the Sphinx, as portrayed in "Lucifer Rising."

ALIEN STRONGHOLDS ON EARTH!

UFOS AND THE APOCALYPSE

If you should ask Samael Aun Weor about such things as the Space Brothers or traces of ancient astronauts on Mexican soil, he will more than likely nod his head in agreement. For Samael has been very active in both UFOlogy and archeology, operating a group ("Asociacion Gnostica de Estudios Antropologicos y Culturales") which holds weekly meetings in Merida on topics related to this field.

"Scores of UFOs crisscross in space. Some are gigantic, like a large ocean liner. These are called the mother ships, and within them they can carry up to 20 smaller craft. These mother ships can travel not only within our galaxy, but also to distant galaxies. They are equipped to traverse across the infinite reaches of space." Or so says Samael Aun Weor, who asks that the scientific community start to expand their awareness of the universe and not limit themselves to shallow thinking. After all, he explains, "Extraterrestrials are people who have opened their inner mind and become supermen in the true sense of the word."

And if you think Samael is talking out of his hat, basing his opinions strictly on what other parties have told him, you're wrong. Not afraid to stand up and "bear witness before the public," Samael is not ashamed to admit that he has made contact with alien beings in Mexico.

"I was in the Federal District when a UFO descended over a forest. Motivated by curiosity, I walked over to the area where the ship had landed and found the craft resting on steel tripods I went up close to the ship, hoping that the extraterrestrials would take me into their ship. Suddenly, a hatchway opened and an extraordinary man descended down a metal ladder. Behind him, there were two other males and two women of unknown age.

"I said, 'Good morning,' to the man who appeared to be the leader or captain of the crew, and he answered me back in perfect Spanish. These people had copper-colored skin, blue eyes, a high forehead, a straight nose, fine, delicate lips, small ears and were of average height and on the slim side.

"They were moving towards some crates which we were on the ground, and this is when I told them I wanted to go with them to Mars." Samael says a puzzled look came over the leader of the UFO crew when Mars was brought up. "But that's right over there," the spaceship captain indicated, as if it wouldn't be any trouble to make such a voyage. During the course of their

ALIEN STRONGHOLDS ON EARTH!

conversation, one of the space women remarked that she was perplexed by how strange Earth was with all the hate and war that goes on here all the time.

Before the left, the Mexican UFOlogist asked once more if it wouldn't be possible for him to go for a ride to their home planet. "The leader seemed moved when I told him the request wasn't being made for myself, but for humanity, who needs to be informed that such a higher technology exists. Raising his index finger, he said, 'Keep to the path and we shall see.' The path, I believe, is the path to wisdom, the path to perfection."

Moving away to a safe distance, the UFO shot off into space, leaving Samael behind. "The extraterrestrials are from a culture which would never kill anyone, not even a bird, yet we terrestrials fear them and our governments try to shoot their craft from the sky."

As with many contactees in the United States, the UFOnauts who have landed in Mexico warn of the destruction of our planet if we don't keep our warlike behavior in check. They also tell of a major disaster which will come about when the Earth collides with another solid body traveling through space. "When this body reaches us," Samael claims, "it will set off magnetic disturbances which will trigger volcanoes, earthquakes and tidal waves. The entire surface of the Earth will be destroyed." Samael even warns of a polar shift, in keeping with the claims of other UFO contactees.

Samael says that some of us will survive and go on to become a near-perfect race. According to him, a number of humans have already "escaped," having been taken to other planets at their request. Like Adamski, he says there are 12 planets in the solar system and that there is intelligent life on these worlds in space. It would seem difficult to believe that Samael would have access to English published books on the subject, and yet the information he has supposedly received from extraterrestrial sources is amazingly similar to other contacts of this nature.

RETURNING HOME

As we passed through customs we couldn't help but wonder what would be the overall outcome of our travels south of the border. We had heard firsthand some very amazing stories involving our Space Brother. In a sense, we felt as if we had undergone a spiritual uplifting. In subsequent telepathic communications with the Ashtar Command, we had been informed that a "space port" is to be built in the Yucatan, and that when, and if, the "End

ALIEN STRONGHOLDS ON EARTH!

Times" should arrive, this spot will be one of the "lift off" points from which "the chosen" shall be taken up. Ashtar's prediction that we might find a lost artifact did NOT come to pass, though later on we did read an article in a New York paper to the effect that recent archeological findings had been made by a leading Mexican university. Whether or not this is confirmation of what Ashtar had said is not for us to decide.

But perhaps most amazing of all is the recent contact experience of a West Virginia man who claims that the alien he telepathically communicates with told him to "Seek Itzamna," which, according to Peter Tompkins' book, "Secrets of the Mexican Pyramids," refers to the first leader of the Yucatan who was said to be the head of the "Chanes," or "People of the Serpent." This relationship seems to be beyond coincidence and is added fuel to the fire, which suggests that Mexico will play an important role in what is about to transpire on Earth.

ALIEN STRONGHOLDS ON EARTH!

SECTION SIX

HIDDEN HANGARS BENEATH THE SEAS

There are just as many UFOs seen coming from out of the oceans, lakes and rivers of the world as there are craft shooting down from out of the sky. In fact, we can much more easily pinpoint the arrival of a UFO when it is seen jettisoning out of any body of water as opposed to hovering over a peach tree in your grandma's garden.

For those who still believe that Columbus discovered the "New World," there is a UFO sighting associated with his arrival in the region of what became known as the Sargasso Sea. On 16 September Columbus' diary mentions that the ship's compass began reacting to a "magnetic declination." A flock of birds seemed to pick up speed and scatter starboard. No great detail is given to the "unknown light sighting," though it is said to have "crashed" into the ocean waves nearby

There are plenty of reports to consider which show that UFOs are more seaworthy than the best of our ships, past or present. And putting aside King Neptune, some UFOs have been known to drag observers down to Davy Jones' Locker for a hair raising abduction to an underwater UFO base. There is photographic proof of UFOs under the sea, such as the pix taken near the Arctic Circle in December, 1957 by a civilian employee of the U.S. Navy. What in Poseidon's name could that possibly be?

So try to keep as dry as possible as we submerge beneath the waters of some fantastic Atlantis-like blue lagoon (with or without Brooke Shields), hopefully from which we will eventually emerge!

ALIEN STRONGHOLDS ON EARTH!

Photo of mysterious red lights taken from cockpit over the Pacific, August, 2014.

ALIEN STRONGHOLDS ON EARTH!

Chapter Nineteen
BY THE SEA, BY THE "BEAUTIFUL" SEA
By Timothy Green Beckley

Well, let's not take anything for granted as we enter a realm that can be as dark and menacing as any wormhole we are likely to pass through as we voyage in outer space.

For hundreds of years - let's make that thousands - mysterious unidentified lights and objects have been observed hovering, submerging into and emerging from various bodies of water all over the world. These unidentified craft would appear to be using the vast water areas of the Earth as operational bases.

Former NASA Mars mapping expert, Jacques Vallee, an author of compelling books on UFOs has candidly conceded that not only is it likely, but it is most probable that the UFOnauts do have hangars deep under the sea, where they cannot easily be detected.

Some credence to the existence of such entities is seen in the fact that the National Bureau of Standards has stated that it never has been able to identify mysterious radio signals which seem to come from somewhere in the middle of the South Atlantic. These recurring sounds have never been identified or specifically located.

Undersea UFOs have featured in some of the earliest stories of the sea. As long ago as the first century C.E. seagoing men have returned with tales of objects which followed their ships for periods of days - sometimes at sea level and sometimes just below the surface of the water. Many of these objects were reported to be brightly colored. At night they often lit up the sea for miles

ALIEN STRONGHOLDS ON EARTH!

around. Some were circular in shape while others were described as long - "like the body of a whale" - and silver in color.

Charles Fort in his book, "Book of the Damned," describes a case in which Captain EW Banner, skipper of the ship Lady of the Lake, reported seeing a remarkable "object in the sky." It was said to have taken on the appearance of a semi-circle divided into four parts, "the central dividing shaft beginning at the center of the circle and extending far outward, and then curving backward." Fort placed the date at March 22nd, 1870.

FIRST DOCUMENTED SIGHTINGS OF THE WATERY KIND - WITH CREATURES!

William Kiehl and eight witnesses watched anchored UFO with humanoids in Georgia Bay, Canada.

ALIEN STRONGHOLDS ON EARTH!

Whoever ends up inheriting my files - be it a deserving individual or a philanthropic foundation - is going to be in for quite a pleasant surprise if they are able to extract a special report wherever I might have put it aside for "safekeeping," as I do have roughly 50 file drawers filled with letters, documents and affidavit reports from individuals who have come in very close proximity to a UFO over a period of six or seven decades, if not a longer.

One of the most documented accounts of UFOs seen over water - or actually on water! - involves a gentlemen who sent me an eight or nine page handwritten letter about his experience, a most impressive one. I was doubly impressed at the time since his name had become somewhat of an "urban legend" in the annals of UFO research. And his letter was proof that he really existed and that his experience had weighed heavily on his shoulders. As it turns out, Mr. William I. Kiehl lived in San Francisco, but his actual observation took place a long way from home near Georgia Bay, Canada, in August, 1914. To solidify the account, he had eight other witnesses to the odd event, which involved a craft being anchored in the way and the sighting of humanoid occupants. Kiehl penned the following details (the actual letter from him, if I could find it, contained additional data which will have to wait to be explored):

"Wet and chilled, we were gathering wood for a fire when two young girls who were in the party came running excitedly into our make-shift camp in an isolated cove and demanded that we follow them to a nearby beach. A deer was standing there, they said, gazing out onto the water at a strange machine which appeared to be anchored. We followed the girls and there, near the middle of the bay, was a strange machine of a type I had not seen the likes of before nor since.

"I would say that this strange machine was about nine feet high and twelve feet long. On top of the ship were two little men dressed in green and purple tight-fitting clothes. Square yellow masks which seemed to rest on their shoulders covered their faces.

"A light green-colored hose appeared to come out of a small porthole about halfway up the side of the unusual craft. The two little creatures appeared to be trying to get some kinks or knots out of the hose, which was dragging in the water.

"Their task accomplished, three more creatures appeared on the topmost deck of the craft and began adjusting some type of rods which were

ALIEN STRONGHOLDS ON EARTH!

affixed to the upper part of the ship. After what was probably two or three minutes, the five beings went inside the ship by way of the porthole from which the hose was extended.

"The ship then rose from the bay surface, sucking with it a heavy upsurge of water which sprayed the entire sea, leaving a mist above which that did not settle for some time. As the ship continued to move straight up it changed color from red to green, and then it turned and flew off on its side."

Another almost identical story, which received little publicity, appeared in the September- October 1950 issue of "The Steep Rock Echo," house organ of the Steep Rock Iron Company, Ontario, Canada.

A senior executive of the company, accompanied by his wife, was on a boating trip when he pulled into a tiny cove in Sawbill Bay just after dusk on July 2, 1950. "Cliffs rose on all three sides of the cove. Small trees and bushes concealed us and our boat from anyone overhead in a plane, had there been one around that evening," the man reported.

The couple had decided this would be an ideal spot to eat. "Suddenly," relates the executive, "the air seemed to vibrate as if from shock waves from a blasting operation. I had an intuition to climb ten feet up a rock, where a cleft gave onto the bay."

Incident at Steep Rock depicts two witnesses behind boulders in March 1952 edition of Fate.

ALIEN STRONGHOLDS ON EARTH!

There he saw a large shining object in the curve of the shore line, about a quarter of a mile away. "I rushed back to my wife and brought her back to the cleft in the rock," he said. Together they saw the strange shining object which they described as being like "two saucers, one upside down on the top of the other floating on the water."

On the top of the craft were several open hatches and approximately ten "little figures."

The leader of the UFOnauts was standing on a small raised platform. "He wore what seemed to be a red skull cap, or perhaps it was red paint. The caps worn by the others were blue," says the report. "I should say the figures were from three feet six inches to four feet tall - all much the same size. We could not see their faces. In fact, the faces seemed like blank surfaces and the figures appeared to move like automata, rather than living beings."

As the two watched through the fading daylight they saw one of the beings pick up the end of a green hose, lift it from the water, and begin walking to the rear of the ship. As soon as this figure had completed what appeared to be his job, all of them climbed down the open hatches into the interior of the ship. The hatches then closed and the watchers heard a strange hum. Seconds later the UFO took off at high speed.

Days later they returned to the area with an associate. As luck had it, they again saw the object with its hatches open, but the hum from their boat motor apparently attracted the attention of the UFO's crew, who jumped through the ports on the top of the ship which immediately took off.

Photo of a UFO taken from the USS Trepang while on patrol in the Northern Atlantic in March of 1971.

ALIEN STRONGHOLDS ON EARTH!

On August 29, 1964, researchers aboard the Oceanographic Research Ship the USNS Eltanin, were surveying the sea bottom west of Cape Horn. During this survey, they photographed a mysterious object at a depth of 12,808 feet. With an upright antenna-like structure and precise angular geometry it appeared man made. The object became known as the Eltanin Antenna.

The first public mention of the unusual subject of the photograph was a news item which appeared in the "New Zealand Herald" on December 5, 1964, under the heading "Puzzle Picture From Sea Bed."

In 1968, author Brad Steiger wrote an article for "Saga" magazine, in which he claimed that the Eltanin had in fact photographed "an astonishing piece of machinery... very much like the cross between a TV antenna and a telemetry antenna".

ALIEN STRONGHOLDS ON EARTH!

Chapter Twenty
OCEANIC CELESTIAL EVENTS

The U.S. Navy Hydrographic Office issues a weekly publication, "Notice to Mariners," which is a valuable source for those collecting material on the observation of marine phenomena. In recent years this publication has contained several accounts of mysterious celestial events which are still completely unexplained. The following reports have been selected from this publication for a period of a single week in 1959. They are listed under Section VI, "Marine Information," which contains "selected reports from cooperating observers. Mariners are urged to submit reports of their observations of the various marine phenomena. Such reports are evaluated and published as appropriate for the benefit of the maritime community in general." The following are typical:

CELESTIAL PHENOMENON

North Pacific - Second Officer L.R. Bjelde of the American 5.5. "Mariposa," Master S.C. Russell reported:

"On 14 September 1959, at 1318 G.M.T. in lat. 31°26' N., long. 140°04° W., course 061° gyro., speed 19.7 knots, light variable breeze, air temperature 67°F., sea temperature 72°F., CPlctel 30.14 inches, a gigantic explosion was observed in the sky The horizon was brightly illuminated by the blast which left trails that resembled smoke. The phenomenon was on a bearing of 056° true at an altitude of approximately 45°, apparently high above the normal atmosphere."

ALIEN STRONGHOLDS ON EARTH!

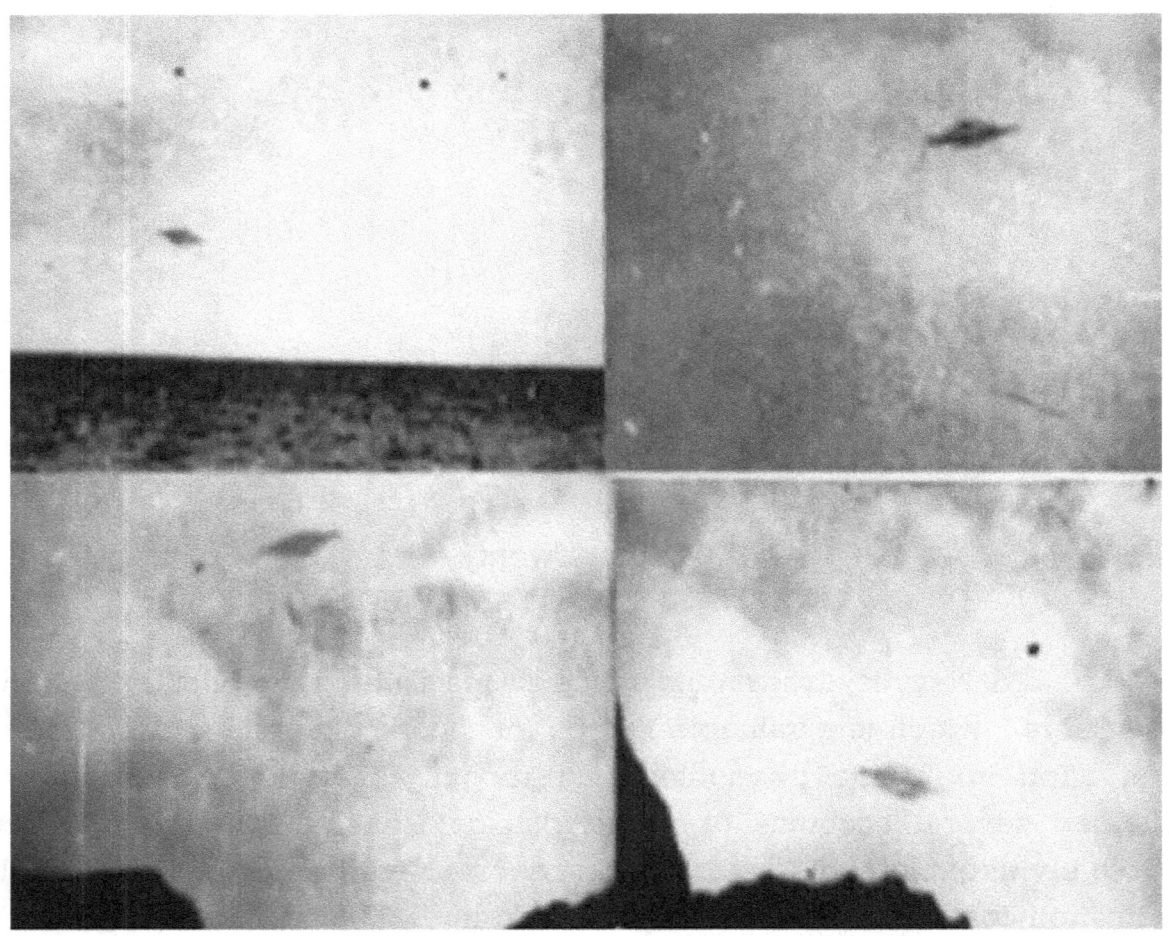

Trindade UFO, Brazil, over the ocean.

CELESTIAL PHENOMENON

South Atlantic - Third Officer W.E. Hughes of the American S.S. Del Mundo, Capt. E.J. Quillin, Master, reported:

"At 0615 G.M.T October 6th, 1959, in lat. 2022'S., long. 38°48'W., on passage from Cabadello, Brazil, to New Orleans, a bright white light with a yellow loom of about 4° was observed just under Castor and Pollux bearing 3SO altitude 38°. A yellow loom trailed the light which traveled southeasterly and set below the horizon bearing 96° at 0622 G.M.T. Mr. Hughes stated the light appeared to be man-made and traveled at a uniform speed and brightness and was observed for approximately seven minutes.

"Weather partly cloudy with good visibility, wind ESE force 3, barometer 29.84 inches, air temperature 78°F., sea temperature 78°F."

ALIEN STRONGHOLDS ON EARTH!

UFO over Trindade Island, January 16, 1958.

MARINE PHENOMENON

Indian Ocean - Capt. Luigi Colombo, Master of the Panamanian S.S. Stanvac Singapore, reported:

"At 1810 G.M.T. April 4th, 1959, in lat. 2°00'N., 59°22'E., course 182, speed 13.5 knots, on passage from Abadan to Maritius Island, the third mate called me to the bridge and I observed a diffuse light on the horizon bearing

ALIEN STRONGHOLDS ON EARTH!

252°. Observing the light through binoculars it appeared as the loom of a city beyond the horizon. It was not due to lightning as the phenomenon lasted for some time and was clearly seen. A similar luminous spot appeared abaft the beam and a third one of lesser intensity was observed abeam. Radar showed four circular targets at 20 miles and three larger ones at 40 miles. The observation lasted from 1810 to 1930 G.M.T. and only one lightning bolt was observed above the three luminous sources.

"Weather clear and good visibility, wind calm, moderate long swell. Barometer 30.00 inches, air temperature 82°F, sea temperature 80°F."

CELESTIAL PHENOMENON

North Atlantic - Second Officer P.V.D. Vrie of the Dutch M.V. Colytto, Capt. R. Ijlstra, Master reported:

"At 0130 Zone Time, February 22nd, 1959, in lat. 18°20'N., long. 58°10'W., I observed an object moving very fast in the sky The height of the object was uncertain but estimated at more than 300 meters (984 feet). It was observed moving from west to east when suddenly its course was altered in the same direction as the ship (235°) which it followed for about three seconds and then turned in the same direction it previously followed, without any change in speed. The color of the object was between orange and red and had a small trail of white-blue gas.

"Weather partly cloudy with good visibility, wind NE force 3-4, slight sea, air temperature 79°F."

Hundreds of similar reports have found their way into mariner journals over the years.

On August 29th, 1964, an amazing photograph taken from the Eltanin, a military sea transportation ship about 1000 miles east of Cape Horn, South Africa, showed what apparently was a complex radio antenna being raised from the ocean at an estimated depth of 2250 fathoms. Dr. Thomas Hopkins, a senior marine biologist who was onboard at the time, remarked that "at that depth there is no light, so photosynthesis could not take place and plants cannot live." Scientific investigation has failed to explain the what-for and why-for of the object photographed by the Eltanin.

In 1964, USO's or Unidentified Submarine Objects, were frequently seen in Australian waters. Henk Hinfelaar, editor of New Zealand's Spaceview,

ALIEN STRONGHOLDS ON EARTH!

personally investigated seven known cases between January and November of that year. One of the reports occurred on January 1, when an unidentified airline pilot (known to Mr. Hinfelaar) was on an assignment from Whenupai (Auckland's Airport) to Kaitaia.

The crew was comprised of the Captain, First Officer and an Operations Officer. As they flew low over the coast line approaching the southern end of Kaipara Harbour something shining drew their attention. The pilot veered the aircraft slightly to port to fly more directly over the object which was just under the surface of the water. He saw that the object, which at first glance might have been mistaken for a whale, was actually a metallic structure.

He observed the following details:

1. It was perfectly streamlined and symmetrical in shape.
2. It had no external control surfaces or protrusions.
3. It appeared metallic and there was a suggestion of a hatch on top, streamlined in shape, not quite halfway along the body as measured from the nose.
4. The shape was not that of a normal submarine.
5. Its length was estimated at 100 feet with a diameter of 15 feet at the widest part.

The March 26th, 1966, edition of the "Miami News" relates how Isaac Lester and John Robert Bair, who were cruising in a motor launch, spotted a strange cigar-shaped object maneuvering in the sky quite low over the water several miles out at sea. To get a closer look, they headed for the object at full speed. When they were within a few hundred yards of it they noticed "eerie pulsations of light around what appeared to be the nose section of the craft." Then, what looked like a greenish volume of light, water or vapor, extended from the underside of the object down to the surface of the water, which they discovered was strewn with dead fish.

The crew of the launch radioed back to the Boca Chica base to report what they had seen, and within several minutes search planes were flying over the area. It was then that the strange craft took off and vanished.

On January 23rd, 1968, the French Submarine Minerve disappeared with 52 men onboard, somewhere in the western Mediterranean. About the same time as the Minerve went down, strange "ping sounds" were heard

ALIEN STRONGHOLDS ON EARTH!

bouncing off a mysterious object beneath the surface. Over 30 ships and dozens of aircraft were called in to take part in the search.

According to the "New York Times," "French officials reported that a destroyer had picked up an echo on its sonar gear which apparently came from a metallic object lying at a depth of 412 to 650 feet." However, several days' extensive search showed no signs of the Minerve.

So what was this metallic object which sonar had tracked?

The submarine USS Scorpion vanished after colliding with an underwater object. Art by Gene Duplantier.

ALIEN STRONGHOLDS ON EARTH!

Chapter Twenty One
CANADA'S UNDERWATER WONDERS
By Timothy Green Beckley

Traveling further north, you'll find any number of UFO bases scattered throughout Canada. Though some of them may be located in the "wilds," from what we hear, there is a stronghold of Dero as well as gray aliens right under Toronto.

LAKE ONTARIO

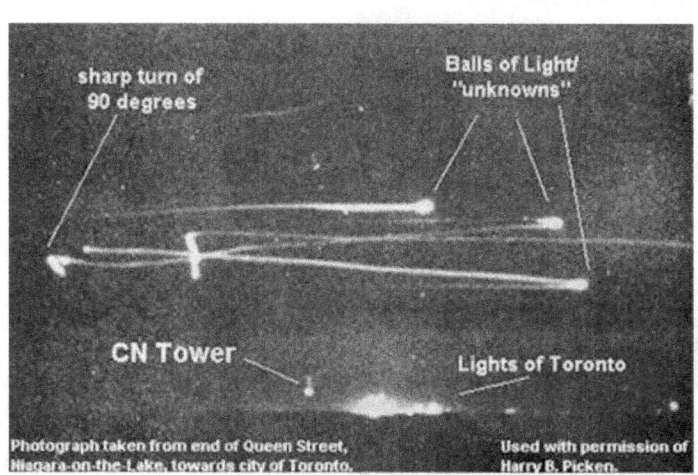

As published in Issue # 1 of the "UFO Review," strange globe-shaped lights have been seen hightailing it above and below Lake Ontario.

When we were publishing the "UFO Review - The Official Flying Saucer Newspaper" back in the Seventies and Eighties we were receiving reports on a regular basis - including some highly sensational photos - of UFOs perching over several of the Canadian Lakes. Lake Ontario in particular seemed to be a hotbed of activity as the craft darted above the lake and submerged into it in front of highly credible witnesses. In fact, I once met up with Tom Grey, who was our publishing associate in Canada. I sat on the stairs of his apartment leading down to the cellar to hear several eyewitnesses who

ALIEN STRONGHOLDS ON EARTH!

had turned up to greet me tell of their experiences. I had even sent a series of these dramatic photos to Harry Lebelson, the late editor of OMNI's UFO Update section for inclusion. He thought they were spectacular, but the publisher nixed them as he was in bed with sci-fi goody-goody two-shoes like Isaac Asimov and Ray Bradbury and didn't want to rock the boat and perhaps have them not contribute to the magazine. Too damn bad I say!

If you're looking for proof, my suggestion would be to take a summer vacation and camp out a couple of hours each night on the banks of Lake Ontario. Some pretty weird things have been seen from both the Canadian and American sides. The UFOs seen here are pretty much always the same. They are orange-colored spheres which have the ability to dart across the heavens at incredible speeds, while at other times they hover silently like diamonds twinkling in the evening sky. First they shoot from out of "nowhere," and then land for a moment or two on the water itself before submerging into the depths of Lake Ontario. If there isn't an underwater UFO base on Lake Ontario, I'll eat my green beret.

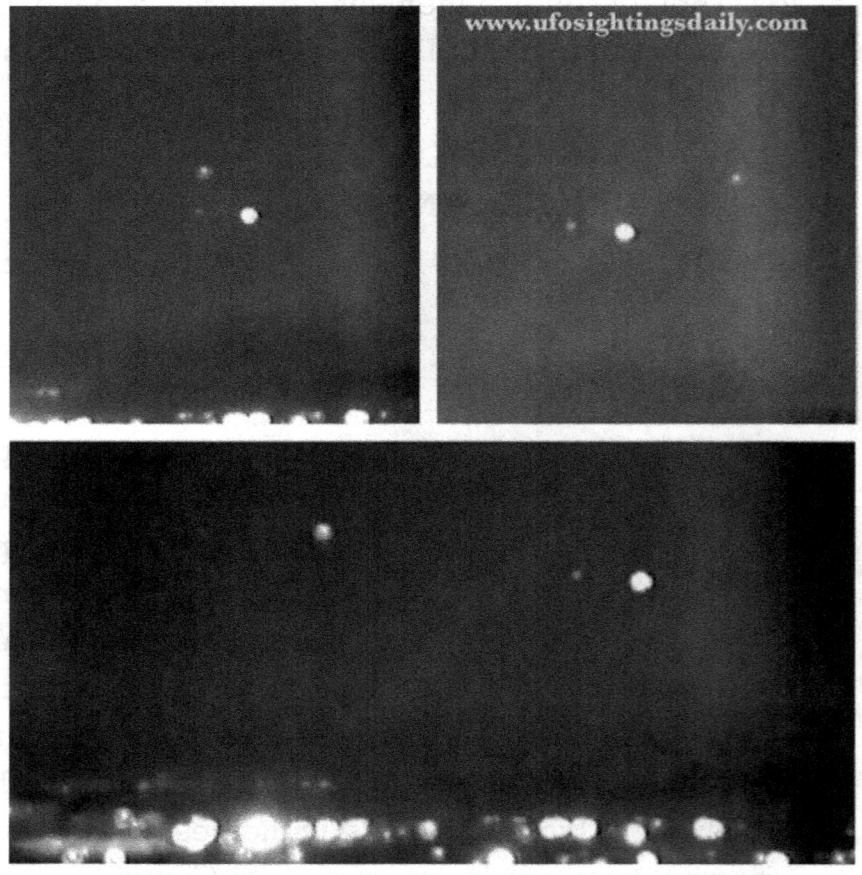

UFOs over Niagara Falls – Canadian Side – Sept 11, 2012.

ALIEN STRONGHOLDS ON EARTH!

Indeed, the strange behavior on the lake has convinced several UFO researchers living in the area that the occupants of these craft have constructed underwater bases from which they are free to roam into nearby space without being easily detected. Further proof that these reports should be taken seriously comes in the form of startling photographic evidence - pictures that show bizarre, highly illuminated lights whose origin remains totally unknown at this date.

According to Malcolm Williams, researcher for the Northeastern UFO Organization, infrared photos taken in the dark of night from the shores of Lake Ontario show all sorts of anomalies which cannot be either conventional aircraft or meteorological phenomena.

Taken on various occasions, the photos show a pattern of lights in the sky which are definitely under intelligent control as they zig-zag about from one position to another in the heavens. One photo shows an object actually resting on top of the water, apparently about ready to make a plunge beneath Lake Ontario.

Many of the photos taken by Malcolm Williams, a former member of the Royal Astronomical Association, were done from a position which would indicate that the main area of interest is over the lake between Oakville and Toronto. This theory is supported by Harry Picken, an aeronautical engineer, pilot and past president of Genair Ltd., a St. Catherine aircraft research firm. Picken, who owns a home right on the banks of the lake, has been keeping tabs on the aerial movements near his property for years. One of the most peculiar things the engineer has noticed is that the lights are usually orange, a color foreign to aircraft lights: "The orange color indicates to me a high sodium content in the light source. Sodium is never used in conventional aircraft lighting," he further points out.

Both Harry Picken and Malcolm Williams believe that the UFO activity over Lake Ontario is somehow related to the fact that a high voltage hydro-generating station is located at nearby Lakeview. The UFOs have been seen repeatedly to lift up from the lake and head in the direction of the plant.

Over the years many odd occurrences have taken place in and around Lake Ontario. In his book, "The Great Lakes Triangle," Jay Gourley tells of several air mishaps in this very locale, adding substance to the theory that something totally "alien" is operating in and around this body of water. "There is little doubt that the pilot of the twin jet CF-101 Canadian Air Force

ALIEN STRONGHOLDS ON EARTH!

interceptor, number 18112, knew he was in trouble on August 23, 1954," Gourley states in his well-researched reference work on the subject.

"He was near Ajax, Ontario, on the north shore of Lake Ontario. He bailed out. He explained later that the aircraft became impossible to control. Publicly, the Canadian Defense Headquarters refused to reveal the cause of the accident. The official cause is a classified secret. I have seen this secret file. It says the scientists who studied the case could not determine what caused the jet to become unmanageable."

It could be that UFOs utilizing highly magnetized equipment beneath the surface could have accidentally or purposely pulled the aircraft out of the sky.

As inspirational artist Carol Ann Rodriguez sees it, there are many secret UFO strongholds on Earth.

ALIEN STRONGHOLDS ON EARTH!

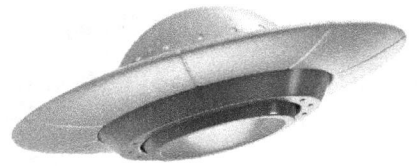

Chapter Twenty Two
DEEP SEA ALIEN DIVING
By Sean Casteel

EDITOR'S NOTE: There is a lot more going on beneath the waves and rough seas than just UFO sightings. We have a multitude of reports coming in from people who have apparently been abducted and taken to some watery stronghold. The odds of this happening to you might be limited, but you can certainly see where it would be a horrific experience if you were on the receiving end of one of these cosmic kidnappings.

According to researcher Preston Dennett, with whom our coauthor Sean Casteel "sat down" recently, the government may know what's going on and might even have a hand in some of these underwater shenanigans. We can't say for what purpose and why they would want to associate themselves with these boogie men of the deep, but apparently they have made a pact or treaty of some sort which we have bought out in previous books by Commander X and other authors.

* * * * * * * * *

Researcher Preston Dennett has written more than 20 books and over 100 articles on UFOs and paranormal phenomena. One of those books, "Undersea UFO Base: An In-Depth Investigation," reveals a great deal of information on a suspected undersea base off the coast of Malibu in Los Angeles County in Southern California. Dennett spoke to us about his

ALIEN STRONGHOLDS ON EARTH!

research and why he continues to believe there is a definite undersea "presence" in the area.

"There are many reasons why I think there might be a base off the coast of Southern California," Dennett said. "The area is very deep, in places up to a mile deep, so there is plenty of room for a base. The number one reason why I think there might be an undersea base is the huge number of USO [Unidentified Submersible Objects] accounts in a sharply defined area over a long period of time. I have documented over 70 UFO cases and 70 USO accounts from the 1920s to the present day. In these cases, objects are seen diving into the water or coming out of the water, sometimes both.

"There are several instances," he continued, "in which boats are targeted by USOs that travel directly beneath them, sometimes causing the electronics on the boats to fail. The objects have been seen to move underwater at high speeds. The witnesses include police officers, the Coast Guard, Navy officers, lifeguards, fishermen, residents, tourists and more. The USO activity is well-known among the locals. The question is, why? Could there be a base?"

SHIPS ARISING FROM THE OCEAN DEPTHS

Dennett says that another argument for an undersea base has to do with "mass sightings" in the region. Some of the UFO/USO cases involve "UFO fleets" with dozens of UFOs, and, in a few cases, hundreds of objects. In these cases, he explained, the UFOs were seen coming from below, not above.

"Where are all these UFOs coming from? If there's not an undersea base," Dennett quipped, "there's a parking lot down there."

And still a third reason Dennett believes in the reality of an undersea base is the large amount of "whistleblower" accounts he has unearthed over the years. People who claim to have worked in intelligence or within the Top Secret area have spoken about a tunnel which leads from Area 51 in Nevada to Edwards Air Force Base in California and on out to sea in the Santa Catalina/San Pedro Channel area.

"Other whistleblowers say that there is an undersea Navy base in this area," he added, "and one claims that it is occupied by both grays and humans."

ALIEN STRONGHOLDS ON EARTH!

THE MYSTERY OF THE "MALIBU ANOMALY"

Perhaps the most compelling reason for this belief is something called "The Malibu Anomaly," an artificial-looking undersea structure located off the coast of Malibu. The anomaly was first given public attention by researcher Robert Stanley in 2010. Dennett first heard about the structure in January 2013, from a private researcher who went by the pseudonym "Maxwell" and informed him of the anomaly's location. The following year, Maxwell used Google applications to obtain photos of the anomaly and published the photos, which quickly went viral on the Internet.

"The so-called Malibu Anomaly," Dennett said, "has three main features that make it look artificial: It has a smooth flat top. It has what appears to be a row of giant columns or pillars. And it also has what appears to be a tunnel leading undersea or underground."

Dennett provided further details.

"The Malibu Anomaly," he went on, "is located about six miles off the coast of Malibu beneath about 2000 feet of water. The object itself is huge, with a roof about 1.35 to 2.45 miles wide. The roof is an estimated 500 feet thick, supported by massive pillars about 600-700 feet tall. The tunnel entrance is about 2,700 feet wide. By coincidence or not, the Malibu Anomaly is located directly in the center of the greatest level of USO activity."

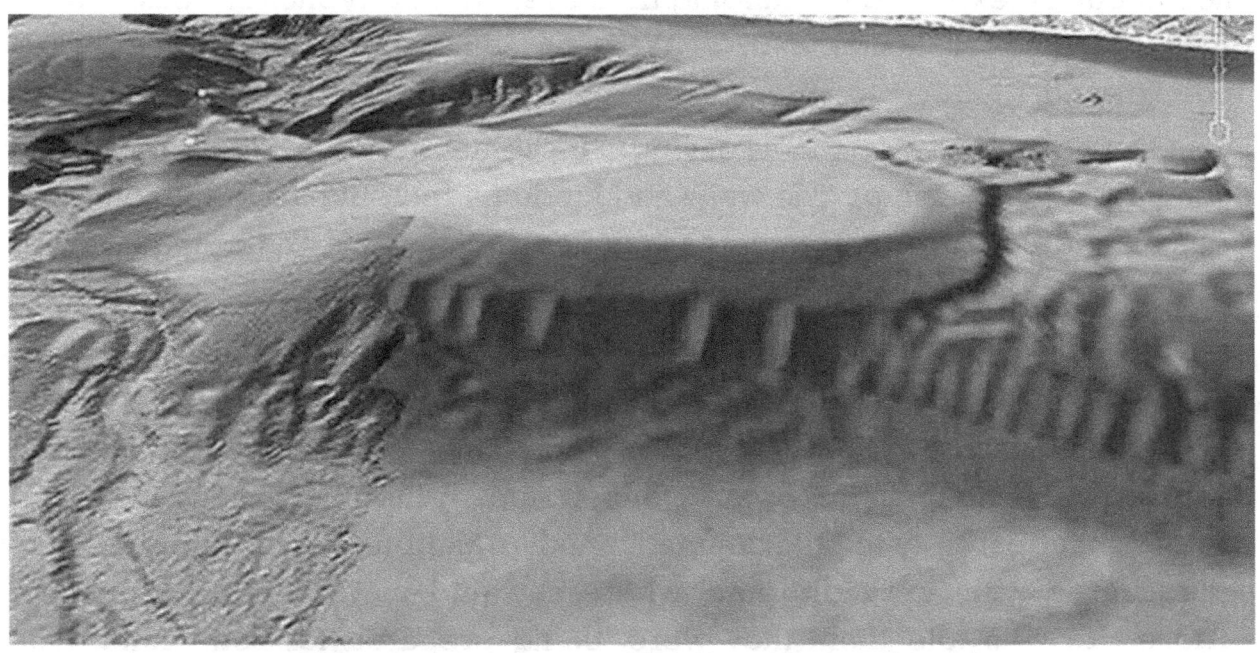

Is there a UFO stronghold off Malibu, California?

ALIEN STRONGHOLDS ON EARTH!

Skeptics admit the object is inarguably there, but contend that the structure is something natural, not an artificial work made by intelligent design. Meanwhile, Dennett received a second-hand report from an elder of the Native American Chumash tribe, who have lived in this area for many thousands of years.

"The elder said they know about the 'structure' and that it was there long before the Chumash," Dennett said. "They have no idea who built it. However big the base is, it has to be big enough to hold at least 200 UFOs at one time."

ABDUCTEES TAKEN UNDERGROUND AND BENEATH THE SEA

Dennett has also collected some unique encounter stories alongside some accounts of the more commonplace kind in the area.

"I documented several cases involving missing time, humanoids and abductions," he said. "Most of these involved standard encounters, but a few were different. In at least two cases, people were taken to what appears to be an underground or undersea base.

"One example comes from a gentleman who is now a medical doctor and private pilot. Back in 1967, twelve-year-old Paul Nelson (pseudonym) and his friend experienced a missing time encounter while staying at Avalon Harbor on Catalina Island, California. Years later, after having more encounters, he explored the missing time event under hypnosis. Nelson didn't recall being taken inside a UFO. What he remembered was being taken underground."

Dennett quotes Nelson as saying, "It seemed to me more underground than it did aboard a ship. The walls had kind of a rock-like facet to them. And I was on a table. There were some machines on the walls. The beings weren't the typical grays. They were more the praying mantis type."

Nelson was examined and then released. His friend, who had also been abducted, appeared to be the primary target of the abduction.

"Nelson is not the only abductee who claims to have been taken to an underground location in this area," Dennett said. "While Nelson and his friend were taken apparently to be examined, another Malibu abductee was taken to a huge area with an 'auditorium' where she and many other people saw various ETs who told them they were 'being prepared for something.' The truth is, we don't know exactly what's going on inside these bases. I do have

ALIEN STRONGHOLDS ON EARTH!

one recent case in which a person 'astral-traveled' inside the base and saw grays and lots of advanced, alien-looking machinery. Likely the ETs are conducting a wide variety of research projects."

NEW CASES COME FLOODING IN

After Dennett had a few media appearances under his belt in which he talked about the undersea base and the USOs that come and go in its vicinity, he received a flood of letters, emails, etc., from new witnesses. One incident reported to Dennett took place on August 4, 2006.

"Retired attorney David Russo was on the beach at Long Beach," Dennett recounted, "when he saw a small triangular-shaped object swoop down out of the sky, then stop and hover about fifteen feet above the ocean's surface. It remained for a few moments, rotating and glowing bright blue. Then it turned red and took off at high speed.

"Another case occurred in 1995," he continued, "to Paul Castardo, a Navy ex-submariner. He and a friend were taking a sailboat north up the coast. They had just traversed the Santa Catalina Channel and were north of the area when they encountered a bright yellow object floating on the water in an area where it was known to be too rocky for boats. At this point, the electronics on their boat failed. The USO darted in front of them and passed alongside their ship, where it stopped for several moments. The witnesses described the USO as having what looked like 'stadium lights.' Neither one of them could identify it."

A 1983 incident involved Dr. Gary Wagoner, who was aboard a nuclear-powered guided missile cruiser called the U.S.S. Long Beach at the time.

"They were on the outward side of Catalina Island," Dennett said, "when they saw an object apparently on the surface of the water or hovering above it. It looked like a half moon with a notch

cut out from the bottom. It would dim and flare in brightly, and blink in strange patterns. Wagoner observed it with about twenty other shipmates. The object did not appear on radar."

WHAT DOES THE GOVERNMENT KNOW ABOUT ALL THIS?

Dennett is confident that the government is more than aware of this kind of activity in the area.

ALIEN STRONGHOLDS ON EARTH!

"It's impossible to conceive that they do not know about it," Dennett declared. "Many of the encounters involve government and military officials. In several of the cases, the objects were chased by military jets. They've known about the activity here for a long time. In 1947, the Navy sent a survey ship called 'Maury' to investigate 'a large mass underwater' that kept moving and changing locations, causing havoc with ships. The Navy tracked the object south down the coast of California to Southern California, where it turned, went out to see and was lost."

Another case involving government knowledge happened in February 1956, when numerous people, including lifeguards, police officers, a night watchman and numerous residents saw an object swoop down from the sky and submerge itself in the water off Redondo Beach, California. The object was described as twenty feet wide. It remained in the area long enough for lifeguards to row a boat out its location, at which point it disappeared.

"The Navy sent divers the next day," Dennett said, "but found nothing. Following the incident, the Coast Guard released a statement saying the witnesses had seen a 'light buoy.'"

Which sounds, of course, like the familiar debunking one frequently hears in the wake of UFO sightings and incidents.

"Researchers Idabel Epperson and Leonard Stringfield both investigated the case," Dennett said, "and disagree with the explanation given by the Coast Guard."

MORE CASES OF APPARENT GOVERNMENT AWARENESS

According to Dennett, there are still more similar incidents.

Researcher Mel Podell investigated a 1967 case at San Juan Capistrano where a family of four and several others watched a large triangular-shaped object dive into the water. The witnesses contacted the Air Force, who expressed enough interest in their experience to send over two agents to investigate and obtain their firsthand testimony.

Bill Hamilton reports on a 1994 case in which witnesses were watching "glowing discs" coming in and out of the water off the coast of Rancho Palos Verdes. They were chased away from the area by black helicopters and what appeared to be government agents who threatened them and told them to leave the area immediately.

ALIEN STRONGHOLDS ON EARTH!

"Or take what happened on September 3, 2012," Dennett said. "Mike (a pseudonym) observed a strange 'sparkling light' dive into the water between Palos Verdes and Catalina Island. Immediately, the government appeared to investigate. Says Mike, 'Now a 300-foot-long ship from the Scripps Institute of Oceanography positions itself five hours later, 4:00 A.M., where the light object entered, and has been there ever since. It is still positioned there today, two days later.'

"As can be seen, the government is clearly aware of the activity," Dennett went on. "In 2017 MUFON researcher Chase Kloetze contacted the Underwater Construction Unit located at Port Hueneme Naval Base, who admitted that they were aware of the 'underwater base rumors,' and that they were not true."

ALIEN AND HUMAN COWORKERS

Another aspect of potential government cover-up is the interrelatedness of the various rumored underground/undersea bases.

"In my research," Dennett said, "several sources reported that the areas of Santa Catalina Channel, Edwards Air Force Base and Area 51 were connected by tunnels. These tunnels likely continue to other bases, which are also connected. I find it interesting that at both Area 51 and Edwards AFB there are reports of aliens working with humans. This same claim has also been made about the Santa Catalina USO base. It does appear that the bases are being used as a location where aliens and humans can meet in private, undisturbed by the public. ETs have never announced themselves publicly. They continue to perform their activities in secrecy, and undersea/underground bases would be a logical choice.

"Any other choice," he added, "would lead to open contact, which the ETs are apparently not quite ready to do. But I wouldn't be surprised if it happened one day soon."

We don't know exactly what's going on in these hidden bases, Dennett admitted, but there are numerous reports that indicate the presence of ETs, advanced machinery, large chambers, ships and various experiments.

"We know the ETs have various agendas," he said, "that they are actively pursuing. They have an interest in genetics. They often provide messages warning of environmental destruction or nuclear proliferation. They speak about alternative energy sources and seem also to be interested in

ALIEN STRONGHOLDS ON EARTH!

teaching people healing and psychic awareness. I'm guessing these are the types of activity they are pursuing in these underground/undersea bases."

Dennett again cited the case of Paul Nelson, who said he was physically examined, as well as the woman who said she and others were "being prepared for something."

"It's clear that the ETs are monitoring us closely," Dennett said. "The Santa Catalina base is located mere miles away from one of the largest population centers on this planet. It's a perfect place to have access to a large population base and still remain utterly undetectable."

THE WORLDWIDE PHENOMENON OF UNDERSEA OBJECTS

Preston's audio book on underwater anomalies.

But Dennett also affirms that the USO phenomenon exists outside his home turf of Southern California and that he has collected similar cases from around the world.

"One case came from the Haiti area," he said, "while another was off the East Coast of the United States. Another was in the Bahamas. A few were in lakes, one in Florida and the other in Arkansas. USOs can appear even in small bodies of water. Most of our planet is covered in water. Only recently have we begun to recognize the high levels of USO activity across the planet. It wouldn't surprise me if there a lot of bases across the planet."

Meanwhile, the government's silence continues.

"As far as I know," Dennett said, "there has been no official governmental admission that undersea bases exist, human or otherwise. The government has failed to acknowledge any of the UFO/USO activity or provide any positive statements regarding the reality of extraterrestrials. To admit the presence of undersea bases will bring up the UFO question, which is a subject the government is still actively covering up.

ALIEN STRONGHOLDS ON EARTH!

"ETs have multiple agendas," he continued. "Many of them directly involve humans. And it does not appear that the UFOs will go away anytime soon. They are here to stay. We must learn to deal with them and hopefully benefit from them. It looks like we're moving toward disclosure and open official contact. If that happens, the question of the presence of these controversial underground and undersea bases just might be answered. Until then, I think it's important that we fight for the truth from our government on the subject of UFOs."

SUGGESTED READING BY PRESTON DENNETT

UFOS OVER ARIZONA

UFOS OVER COLORADO

UFOS OVER CALIFORNIA

UFO authority Preston Dennett.

ALIEN STRONGHOLDS ON EARTH!

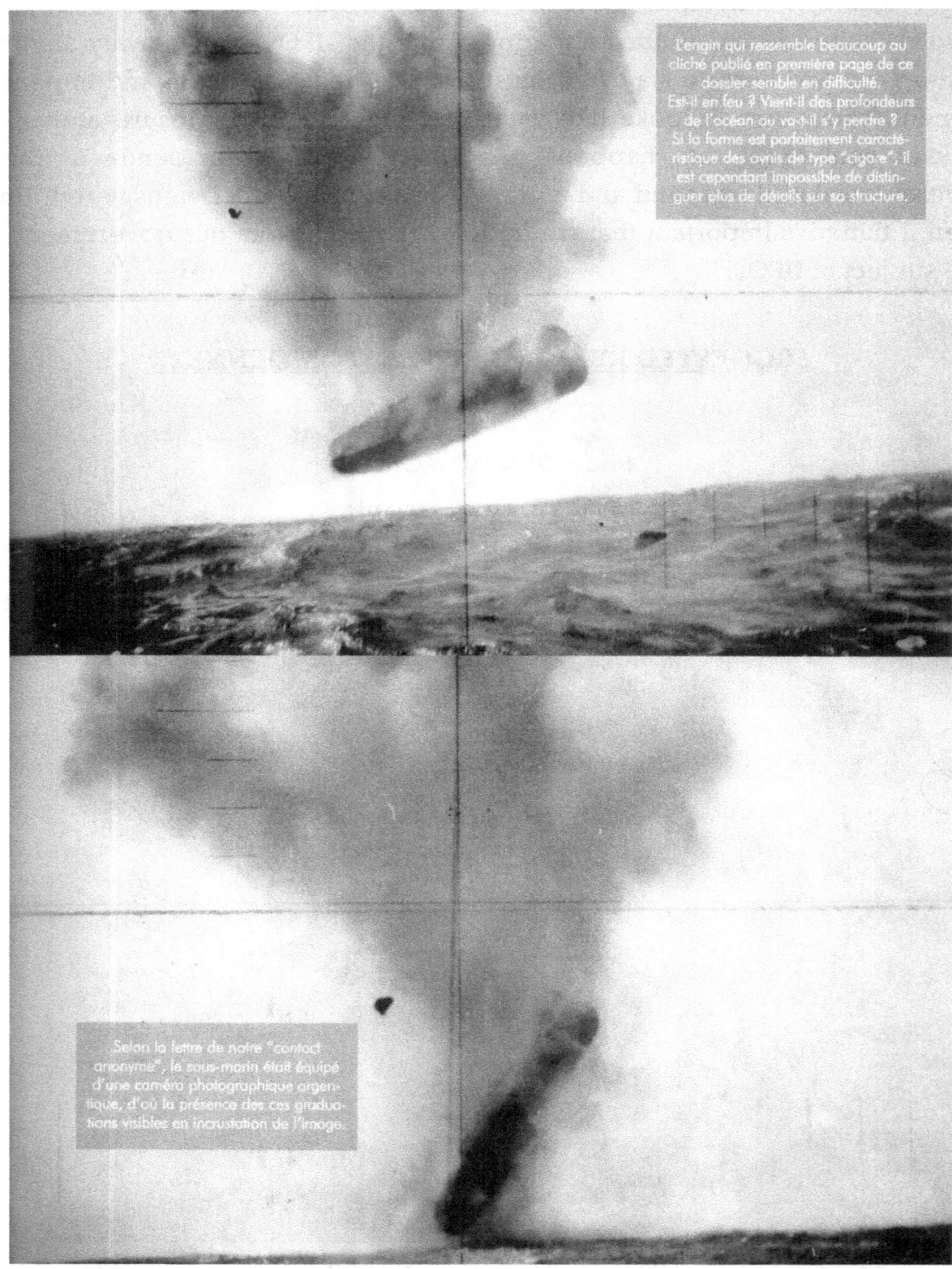

These are two of a series of UFO pictures published in the French magazine *"Top Secret."* The images were allegedly taken by the submarine USS Trepang in March 1971 in the Northern Atlantic between Iceland and Jan Mayan Island.

ALIEN STRONGHOLDS ON EARTH!

Chapter Twenty Three
ARE UNDERSEA BASES USED FOR ALIEN ABDUCTIONS?
By Sean Casteel

Are aliens taking abductees to their underwater lairs to administer frightening physical examinations out of the way of prying eyes?

Is a "secret invasion" about to take place that is being kept veiled for the time being because the ETs - or whoever they are - have hidden themselves in our vast bodies of water?

There is now ample evidence that existing alongside the UFO phenomenon is an equally complex but less well known phenomenon with the acronym USO, which stands for Unidentified Submerged Object, or alternately, Unidentified Submarine Object. While they are seen much less frequently than the aboveground UFOs, they are nevertheless observed often enough to warrant extensive study as a related phenomenon.

In an interview I conducted with world-renowned UFO researcher Stanton Friedman, he told me, "There have been a number of reports over the years of objects that do several things. Navy submarines have apparently

ALIEN STRONGHOLDS ON EARTH!

seen things moving along much faster than they can underwater, without going in or coming out. Others have seen UFOs come down in the water and move around and then take off from the water. And there have been reports of things that just come bursting forth out of the water."

WHAT A USO IS CAPABLE OF

Another story was told to me by Don Ledger, the coauthor of a book on the famous Shag Harbor incident. Ledger received training in the fields of marine navigational aids and radar. In the course of that training, he spoke to a man at a sonar shop at a naval base in Halifax, Canada.

"He was working as a repairman for the navy on sonar," Ledger recalled. "I asked him, 'Did you ever see anything unusual down there, like whales or something besides submarines?' And he said, 'Oh, yeah, every once in a while we'll run across something that seems to be moving way too fast for a submarine.' I said, 'What do you mean by fast?' And he said, 'Well, one time we recorded one going about 150 miles an hour underwater. That's impossible.' So I said, was there something wrong with the equipment? And he said, no, the equipment all checked out."

The sonar repairman also said it hadn't been the first time such an object had been sighted and it would not be the last time, either. The repairman also said the USO had reached an incredible depth of two miles, which is also well in excess of the abilities of manmade submarines. It is amazing that they can handle the pressure without killing the occupants, especially when that fact is coupled with the extremes of speed these objects can reportedly attain. Perhaps, Ledger speculates, the objects are surrounded by an energy field that operates equally well both in the air and underwater.

"They're probably in an envelope all their own," Ledger said. "It doesn't really matter how deep these things go. It probably doesn't affect them whatsoever."

THE USO SHAG HARBOR INCIDENT

I also spoke to Chris Styles, Don Ledger's research partner and his coauthor for the book "Dark Object: The World's Only Government-Documented UFO Crash," published in 2001. The book deals with a sighting

ALIEN STRONGHOLDS ON EARTH!

that took place in Shag Harbor, on the southern coast of Nova Scotia in Canada.

"On October 4, 1967," Styles told me, "around 11:20 PM, several people called the nearby RCMP detachment and reported seeing simply lights. Some reported that an airplane had crashed into the 'Sound,' as they called it, Shag Harbor."

When the police arrived, they found a pale yellow light floating on the water. The light began moving under its own power and left a heavy, dense trail of yellow foam on the water. When they saw the light sink beneath the surface, they commandeered a local boat and went out in the harbor to look for it, but found no physical evidence.

The search resumed at first light the next day, and ships were sent by the Canadian navy as well as seven divers. After five days, the search was called off, with nil results. No aircraft were ever reported missing, and it was generally believed that the object was the crash of a UFO. The government documents that declare the object to be a downed extraterrestrial craft are freely available in Canada, according to Styles.

Before it disappeared, the object was reported by several witnesses to be at least 60 feet across and to display flashing colored lights that repeated in the same sequence over and over. But Styles emphasized that it was not the public who called the object a UFO. The neighboring residents had only initially reported strange lights. It was the Canadian authorities themselves who referred to the incident as a "UFO search," contrary to normal expectations surrounding such things.

When asked why the extraterrestrial occupants would operate underwater, Styles said, "I think water provides a perfect medium for hiding; it's great for stealth. You're out of sight and out of mind. I mean, off the coast of Nova Scotia, so many feet down, there's not a whole lot of traffic there, right? I know some people have wondered, is there a base down there? These things are always fun to speculate about, but I'm more into getting the data. We'll find something and then we'll worry about the interpretation."

For Stanton Friedman, it's a matter of the USOs exploiting what's down there of value.

"Besides just hiding from the guys above," Friedman said, "there are a lot of resources at the bottom of the ocean. There are nodules of all kinds of metals, almost pure metals. There are loads of diamonds, for instance, off the

ALIEN STRONGHOLDS ON EARTH!

coast of Africa that are underwater. There are nodules of manganese and cobalt and other things at the bottom of the ocean, besides all kinds of strange sea creatures from which they may extract some very interesting biological or chemical things."

A JOURNEY BENEATH THE SEA TO THE MUSEUM OF TIME

Having established a little background on USOs, let us now examine a case of abduction from undersea.

Betty Andreasson Luca is a housewife, mother and grandmother, and is also one of the most important alien abductees ever to be investigated and documented. Researcher and author Raymond Fowler has written a series of books about Betty, which tell the continuing story of Betty's mind-bending encounters with diminutive gray aliens she believes to be angelic servants of Jesus Christ.

In April 1980, Betty underwent yet another session of regressive hypnosis to retrieve the buried memories of some of what happened to her at the hands of the aliens. As the session began, she reported being abducted into an alien spacecraft, which may seem fairly routine at this point. But this time, she recalled the ship started hurtling toward a body of water. Under hypnosis, with the tape recorder rolling, she becomes terrified that the ship was about to "crash" into some water. Betty was so frightened that the hypnotist interrupted the session to allow her to calm down.

When the examination of this memory resumed a few days later, Betty recalls the craft entering the water and being wholly submerged beneath it. The ship proceeds to enter a cave or tunnel with walls of solid ice and icicles throughout. The underwater place is brightly lit. Betty sees people, "people like me," she says.

What Betty next reports is astounding. She is seeing what Fowler later called "The Museum of Time" - living people encased in the ice in what we call "tableaux" in earthly terms. Each museum person on display has his or her own scenery appropriate to their time, wearing the correct clothes, etc. The figures look neither dead nor stuffed, and include babies and children as well as many different races. Betty repeatedly calls the clothing "funny and old-fashioned." There are too many cubicles for Betty to count.

When Fowler listened to a cassette of this particular regression session several days later, he found his mind "rebelling," unable to believe what

ALIEN STRONGHOLDS ON EARTH!

Betty had said. Yet how, he wondered, could Betty spontaneously and emotionally relive such detailed and intricate experiences unless they were true?

Fowler would later write, "A cold chill coursed through my body when Betty was describing people and animals enclosed in glassy cubicles in an icy cavern. Perhaps Betty was privy to the aliens' Museum of Time!"

Does all this offer a clue as to what the USO occupants are really up to down there? In any case, they appear to be the same entities as the more familiar airborne UFOs, with the same proclivity for abducting their Chosen Ones and subjecting them to frightening confrontations with as yet unknown and perhaps ultimately incomprehensible alien truths. Do the aliens maintain a kind of museum of human history? Are they proudly and affectionately displaying specimens of their creation, humankind? Or is there a darker mockery at work here, a kind of contemptuous collecting of samples of a shamefully lower form of life?

THE MOST SPECTACULAR USO ABDUCTION CASE OF ALL TIME!

Like Betty Andreasson Luca, Filiberto Cardenas was abducted by a USO. Cardenas was also given many strange prophecies by his captors, prophecies which came electrifyingly true shortly thereafter.

It all began on the evening of January 3, 1979, when Cardenas was in his gift shop in Hialeah, Florida, and received a phone call from his friend, Fernando Marti. Marti asked Cardenas to accompany him to buy a pig from the local merchants to roast the next Sunday. Marti and his wife and daughter arrived at Cardenas' place of business and they set out on their errand. After stopping at two different farms, they were still unable to find an acceptable 'puerco" for their feast. As they continued their drive, they turned off onto a rural road that was in poor condition. At that point, the car began to lose power.

ALIEN STRONGHOLDS ON EARTH!

The two men examined the engine but were unable to see what the problem was. Then the engine began to reflect red and violet lights in sequence. At the same moment, they heard a strange noise, like a swarm of bees. Next the car began to shake, and Marti's wife began to scream in panic, believing it was an earthquake. When Cardenas tried to approach her to calm her down, he became paralyzed, frozen under the hood of the car. Then the same force that had paralyzed him began to lift him and suspend him in the air. Cardenas began to shout, "Don't take me! Don't take me!" The noise and lights ceased and everything seemed to return to normal. Then Marti looked up and saw a UFO ascending into the sky. He shouted, "They have taken Filiberto!"

After several attempts, he was able to start the car. He felt compelled to tell the police, but feared he would not be believed, or worse, that he would be accused of having himself harmed Cardenas. He decided to inform the police anyway and also called Cardenas' wife, saying, "A light took Filiberto away."

Meanwhile, Cardenas awoke onboard the UFO, in a seat that seemed to hold him in place by some kind of suction and restrained all his movements. He saw three strange figures, one of whom placed a strange helmet on his head and spoke to him in a language he thought sounded like German. He was shown projected images, as on a television, of scenes from the past, present and future of humankind. He was then taken to a smaller ship that discharged from the mother-ship. He saw a beach approaching, and then the UFO plunged into the sea. Everything was obscured by the incredible velocity at which the ship moved.

The ship veered to the right and began to lose speed. Cardenas could now see a tunnel with walls that seemed illuminated as if they were phosphorescent. The ship entered the tunnel and then emerged in a place that was completely dry. The area was huge. He noticed two symbols, one of them being a serpent as large as "an electric light pole," Cardenas later said. The other image was similar but smaller. His captors took him from the ship and told him to sit down on a large rock.

At this point, one must note the similarity to what happened to Betty Andreasson Luca. As with Luca, the UFO that transported Cardenas quickly plunged into the sea and emerged in a dry alien environment. While in Luca's

ALIEN STRONGHOLDS ON EARTH!

case the surroundings were icy, it is still remarkably similar to the large cave to which Cardenas was taken.

IN THE UNDERWATER CAVES

In the cavern area, Cardenas was welcomed by a human-looking figure who said he was from the Earth and had long worked with the UFO entities. He seemed to be saying that Cardenas was most fortunate to be receiving instructions from "beings like us." After some further conversation, and a quick trip to what was apparently an undersea alien city, Cardenas was returned to a pasture near where he had been originally abducted. The aforementioned predictions Cardenas received from the aliens included everything from the future succession of the popes to the 1980 election of President Ronald Reagan, the 1985 earthquake in Mexico City and the demonstration by Chinese students in Tiananmen Square in 1989. Cardenas, armed with the prophecies from the aliens, was also able to accurately predict the assassination in 1981 of Egyptian president Anwar Sadat and the Gulf War against Saddam Hussein in 1990.

As is demonstrated by the experiences of Betty Andreasson Luca and Filiberto Cardenas, the aliens are at home in our skies and in our bodies of water. They have a firm grasp on mankind's past and can see into our future. And they do it all from hidden bases throughout our world.

SUGGESTED READING

Sean Casteel

UFO ABDUCTION FROM UNDERSEA NIGHTMARE ALLEY: FEARSOME ACCOUNTS OF ALIEN ABDUCTION: YOU COULD BECOME THEIR NEXT VICTIM!

ALIEN STRONGHOLDS ON EARTH!

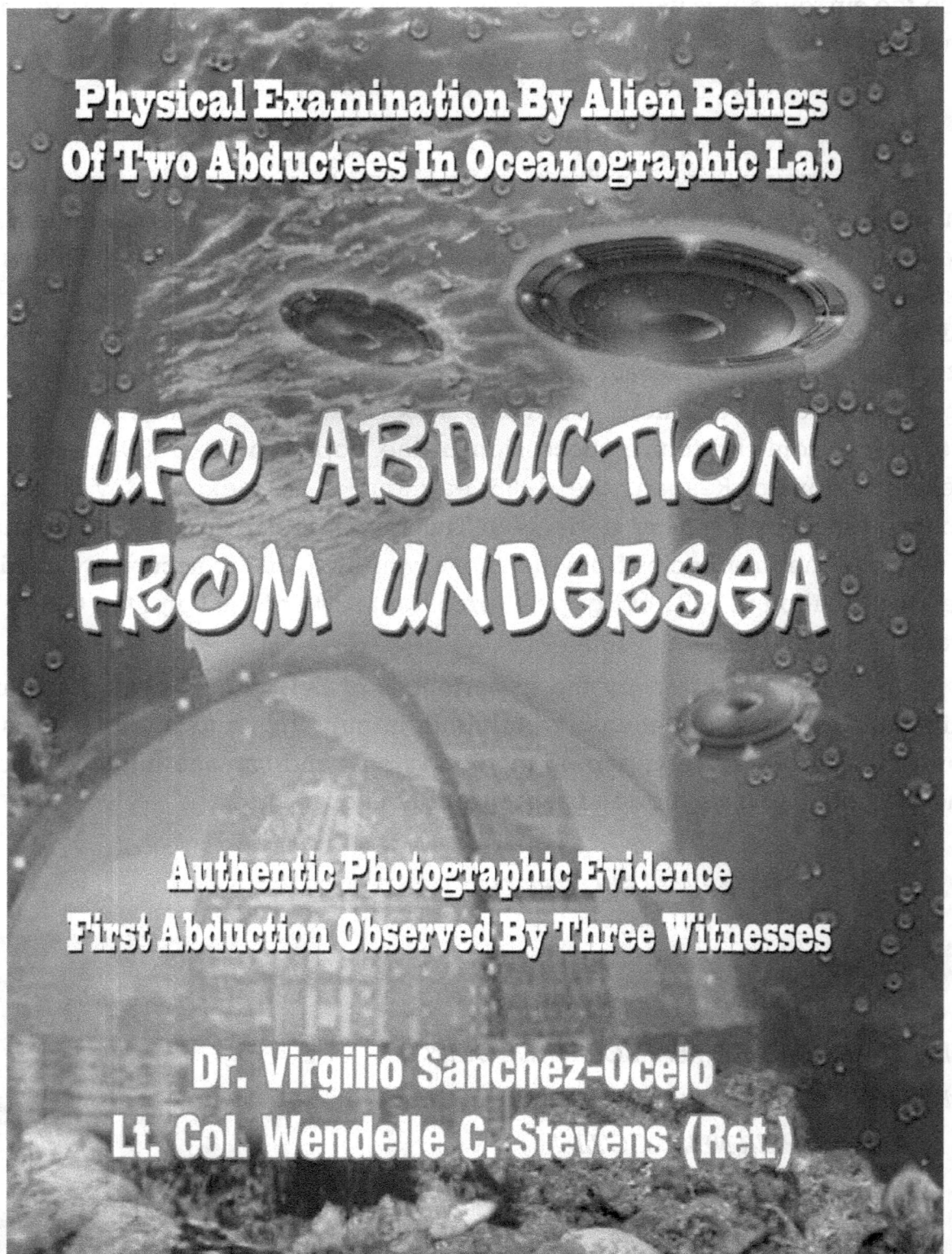

"UFO Abduction From Undersea"
Inner Light/Global Communications.

ALIEN STRONGHOLDS ON EARTH!

SECTION SEVEN

UNDERGROUND ALIEN BASES

Are strange, inhumane experiments taking place in underground alien bases?

Strange things happen underground that are totally baffling, and, furthermore, most of the time we never hear anything about the puzzling phenomena associated with natural hollows, caverns, extended tunnel systems and military bases carved into canyon walls.

Many a miner or spelunker has told twisted tales of being confronted by an unknown race of beings, some frightfully ugly and antagonistic, while others seem totally benign.

Some of these underground fortresses appear to be occupied or guarded by aliens, or unknown races of subterranean dwellers, and a few by MK Ultra-style guards, a militaristic branch of the New World Order with ties to the "secret government." Much has been written on the subject. We suggest "Underground Alien Bases" and "Screwed by the Aliens" as your Underground 101 primer. There are so many acknowledged underground bases that we could never possibly cover them all, but here is an overview along with some tantalizing tales of alien and military mind control.

ALIEN STRONGHOLDS ON EARTH!

Underground bases may even be on the moon, as depicted in the 1952 edition of Gray Barker's Saucerian Bulletin, his first UFO-zine ever.

ALIEN STRONGHOLDS ON EARTH!

Chapter Twenty Four
THE ALIENS GO UNDERGROUND
By Nigel Watson

EDITOR'S NOTE: We have come to rely on Britisher Nigel Watson as a source of profound paranormal research material, some of which we would not have access to on this side of the pond. Nigel has researched and investigated historical and contemporary reports of UFO sightings since the 1970s. He is the author of "Portraits of Alien Encounters" (VALIS, 1990), "Phantom Aerial Flaps and Waves" (VALIS, 1990), "Supernatural Spielberg" (with Darren Slade, VALIS, 1992), editor/writer of "The Scareship Mystery: A Survey of Phantom Airship Scares," 1909 - 1918 (DOMRA, 2000), "The UFO Investigations Manual" (Haynes, 2013), and "UFOs of the First World War" (The History Press, 2015). For the UneXplained Rapid Reads e-book series he wrote: "UFOs: The Nazi Connection," "Spontaneous Human Combustion," "UFO Government Secrets," "The Great UFO Cover-Up" and "Ghostships of the Skies" (all 2015). He has also written for numerous other books, publications and websites, including Magonia, Paranormal Magazine, Fortean Times, Wired, Flipside, How It Works, All About Space, Fate, Strange Magazine, Beyond, History Today, Aquila, Alien Worlds, UniLad, The Unexplained, Flying Saucer Review, UFO Magazine India and UFO Magazine (USA). In the 1980s, he gained a BA degree in Psychology (Open University) and a BA (with Honors) degree in Film and Literature (University of Warwick). He has recently contributed to several books published by Tim Beckley including, "UFO Hostilities" and "Screwed by the Aliens." He has also

ALIEN STRONGHOLDS ON EARTH!

appeared on the podcast "Exploring the Bizarre" with Tim Beckley and Tim Swartz.

* * * * * * * * * *

"UFOs - Nazi Secret Weapons?" - Published by Inner Light/Global Communications.

The concept of superior races that originated in mythic civilizations like Atlantis and Thule helped give credos to white supremacist Nazi ideology. Many of their assumptions derived from occult teachings and mystical beliefs in 'gods' and advanced 'adepts' living inside mountains or caves. Ironically, Hitler had to seek refuge in underground bunkers, where he ultimately took his life, and since then there has been a growing belief that aliens secretly live in underground bases throughout the world.

Supporters of the idea that the flying saucers are of Nazi origin claim that they established an underground base at Antarctica after World War II. Mattern-Friedrich, in his book "UFOs, Nazi Secret Weapon" (Samisdat, 1975), even stated that Hitler faked his own death and escaped to continue the war in secret. With or without Hitler, they continued to develop, with the help of the aliens, flying saucers and associated advanced technology.

From here it has been suggested that this alliance has worked with the CIA and the US 'military-industrial complex' to create vast underground bases at Dulce (New Mexico); Area 51 (Nevada); Camp Hero (Long Island); and Denver International Airport. Similar bases are reputed to exist in Australia and Europe.

According to such theories, literally thousands of abductees have been taken to these bases to be "programmed" and returned to their homes to act as agents of the aliens, or they have been used in hybrid breeding projects, or used as slaves inside these underground bases.

ALIEN STRONGHOLDS ON EARTH!

They claim this all began in 1945, when the German rocket scientist Werner von Braun surrendered to Major Clay Shaw, who was working as an agent for Project Paperclip. This project was designed to secure advanced Nazi knowledge, technology and personnel and bring it back to the US before the Soviets got hold of it. Bavarian Intelligence and their sympathizers, like Shaw, infiltrated this CIA project, thereby allowing Werner von Braun and other top Nazi scientists to successfully bring into reality the Apollo moon landing project under the auspices of NASA.

The presence of an alien base in Antarctica was "confirmed" by the writings of Albert K. Bender. In 1952, he set up the International Flying Saucer Bureau (IFSB) in Bridgeport, Connecticut, and it quickly gained branches throughout the USA and the world. Bender came unstuck in September 1953 when he wrote to a friend to say he had found the "true" answer to the riddle of the flying saucer phenomenon. Not long afterwards, he was shocked when three MIB came to his home brandishing the letter. They confirmed that his ideas about the flying saucers were correct and that if the public knew the truth there would be mass hysteria and a breakdown of civilization as we know it.

As far back as 1952, researcher Albert K. Bender claimed that the Men In Black were being used to guard certain UFO facilities. Researcher Gray Barker wrote about these misadventures in his "They Knew Too Much About Flying Saucers."

He was told to close down his organization - or else. The experience was so frightening that he promptly did what he was told. In 1962, when he felt he was safe enough from the menace of the MIB, he wrote "Flying Saucers and the Three Men." This revealed that the three MIB were tall, dark-skinned and slant eyed, and turned into serpent-like creatures during his encounter. Later on, they also took him on an astral journey to an underground base in Antarctica. Regarding this trip he wrote: "How much time this floating consumed I do not know, but it seemed like days."

ALIEN STRONGHOLDS ON EARTH!

Bender's room full of horrors might have attracted the attention of the dreaded MIB.

His MIB are more like ghosts and his experiences following their appearance are nightmares on the edge of reason. Some think he told these wild tales to finally put-off, or at least, appease the demands of the UFO enthusiasts who kept asking him about the MIB. Others think it proves the MIB are not human secret agents but supernatural, or, as Keel called them, ultra-terrestrial beings who have plagued humanity since time began.

The MIB are just the modern-day manifestation of the Devil or, more prosaically, they are fantasies triggered by watching too many gangster B-movies.

The concept that there are UFO bases got an enormous boost on 29 December 1987 when John Lear posted a 4000-word document on the Internet. What is now known as the "Lear Document" claimed that, in 1979, sixty-six US Special Forces soldiers were killed in a gunfight with alien forces while trying to rescue human workers in an underground alien base near Dulce, New Mexico.

This was partly inspired by the conspiratorial ramblings of Paul Bennewitz. This chain of events began in 1980, when Bennewitz attended hypnotic regression sessions with abductee Ms. Myra Hansen, conducted by Dr. Leo Sprinkle. During these sessions, Hansen and her son claimed they saw aliens mutilating animals.

Furthermore, she recalled being flown by a spacecraft to New Mexico, where she was taken inside an underground base. Here she saw human body parts floating in huge tanks. It was Bennewitz's contention that Hansen had been fitted with an alien implant, a device they might use to control her thoughts and actions. Using his skills as an electronics expert, he attempted to intercept and block the signals he believed were being transmitted to the woman's implant. At one stage, he used metal foil to block the signals, and then he decided to intercept electronic low frequency (ELF) transmissions. He was successful in finding ELF signals, but they seem to have been transmitted

ALIEN STRONGHOLDS ON EARTH!

by the nearby Kirtland Air Force Base in the process of conducting secret experiments as part of the SDI "Star Wars" project.

When the USAF warned him not to continue his work, he was even more convinced that he had intercepted alien signals. Indeed, he contacted anyone who would listen about the UFO threat and he created a computer program to decode the signals. In response, the department of Air Force Office of Special Intelligence (AFOSI) bombarded him with as much disinformation as possible to make him look like a fully-certified UFO nut.

Under these pressures, Bennewitz suffered a mental breakdown. Even worse was the revelation that UFO researcher William Moore confessed that he had unwittingly aided the AFOSI by passing on disinformation to Bennewitz.

The disinformation material about alien bases, cattle mutilations, implants and abductions done with the aid and knowledge of the US government also became the subject of Linda Moulton Howe's book "Alien Harvest," which included a full transcript of Dr. Sprinkle's original hypnotic regression sessions with Hansen.

Howe alleged that documents shown to her later became the evidence used to prove the existence of a secret government project called Majestic 12 (MJ-12). Lear used the same material to claim that trapped workers at the Dulce underground base "had become aware of what was really going on" - that aliens were implanting devices in the brains of abductees, impregnating female abductees, conducting genetic experiments, and worse, they were terminating "some people so that they could function as living sources for biological material and substances," and assassinating "individuals who represent a threat to the continuation of their activity."

A witness even came forward to say that he was one of the survivors of the "fire fight" at Dulce. Philip Schneider said he was involved in extending the underground military base at Dulce when the alien nature of the base was accidentally revealed. He managed to shoot two aliens before he was shot in the chest by an alien weapon. This emanated from a box attached to the chest of an alien and it gave him a dose of cancer-inducing cobalt radiation. Schneider was the only "talking survivor"; two others were under close guard. It was his contention that the Eisenhower administration signed a treaty with aliens in 1954, which gave them permission to abduct and implant US citizens. In return, the US government has been given new technologies that

ALIEN STRONGHOLDS ON EARTH!

enable them to enslave and dupe the population. Thousands of "black helicopters" and stealth aircraft are used to monitor our activities.

In addition, AIDS was invented in 1972 through the genetic engineering of human, animal and alien excretions. The late UFO conspiracy theorist, Milton William Cooper, used the Lear Document to assert that aliens and a secret government are planning to establish colonies on other planets, and that they have introduced "deadly microbes to control or slow the growth of the Earth's population. AIDS is only ONE result of these plans."

More recently numerous Ufologists have found artificial structures on the Moon and Mars by viewing NASA pictures. These are usually explained as being of erosional features or caused by the way the pictures were processed.

Whatever the "mundane" explanation, I think we are more fascinated by the idea that there are people secretly living beneath the surface of Mars and that they are part of some secret space program. Such a project would need vast resources and would be very hard to keep covered up, yet many think this is what is happening and that these activities are being carried out in conjunction with one or more alien species.

Certainly there is plenty to dig up regarding this aspect of Ufology.

SUGGESTED READING

ALIEN BLOOD LUST

SCREWED BY THE ALIENS

UFOS OF THE FIRST WORLD WAR

Britisher Nigel Watson.

ALIEN STRONGHOLDS ON EARTH!

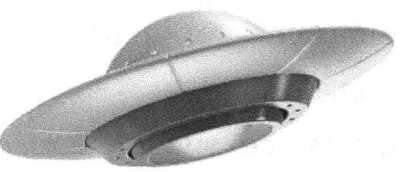

Chapter Twenty Five
THE DULCE BASE

EDITOR'S NOTE: In the corner of a small town in America's Southwest, something very strange is going on. Indeed, is an alien "Fifth Column" already active on Earth preparing total conquest via implantation and mind control?

According to the author Branton - who used only his first name for privacy reasons (and because he was deathly afraid!) - "The repercussions of what is taking place here will soon be felt throughout the whole country, when the beast has reached out with its deadly tentacles to invade our seemingly impregnable fortress, causing it to crumble and fall."

****

Did U.S. military forces perish recently in hand-to-hand combat with a group of hostile Grays who subsequently seized control of one of our Top-Secret underground bases? And has the New World order established an unholy alliance with this group of ETs? In Dulce, New Mexico, seemingly everything has gone haywire, becoming the epicenter of: cattle mutilation phenomena; energy grids; secret societies; underground anomalies; conspiracies between townsfolk and "outsiders"; unexplained legends and mythology concerning various "lost civilizations"; geomagnetic enigmas; abductions and missing time; hostile alien beings; peculiar sounds and "movements" coming from beneath the Earth. [As discussed on the History Channel, Coast to Coast, and TheParaCast.]

Though the account is long and complex, researcher Lon Stickler sums the case up very nicely in his "Monsters and Phantoms" blog:

ALIEN STRONGHOLDS ON EARTH!

Do you believe an alien base exists below Dulce, New Mexico?

Archuleta Mesa rises a few thousand feet over the small rural community of Dulce - hub of the Jicarilla-Apache Indian Reservation. A broad aesthetic plateau, it dominates the northern skyline.

Archuleta rock, as locals call it, appears normal. But it's not what's on the surface that creates an infamous chapter in the volumes of UFO stories.

It's what is said to lie beneath.

Ufologists claim Dulce is the site of a massive underground facility operated by the U.S. government and one or more alien races: a seven-story complex that connects to Nevada's Area 51 and Los Alamos National Laboratory in New Mexico. The deeper you go, the darker it gets.

Some call Dulce a Cold War-era government fallout shelter, far removed from alien races. Undeniably, residents of Dulce, a two-hour-plus drive southeast of Durango, seem to acknowledge that something is out of the ordinary.

Strange activity has been reported around Archuleta Mesa for decades.

ALIEN STRONGHOLDS ON EARTH!

A STRONG BELIEF IN UFOS

Theodoria Burns, a first responder with the Jicarilla-Apache Medical Service, said many Dulce residents believe in UFOs.

"Sometimes, weird things happen, like lights in the sky, different colors that vanish right away," she said. "You think it's an airplane, but it's not."

She said she has never seen a base, "but they say it does exist."

The UFO researchers claim reports of strange lights, unidentified flying objects and cattle mutilations are higher surrounding the mesa.

In many accounts, a man named Thomas Edwin Castello, a character many say is fictional, claimed to be a senior security guard at the mesa's secret underground base. According to lore, he came forward in 1979 with radical allegations.

Castello described a research facility, emphasizing the ominous sixth level, dubbed Nightmare Hall, where appalling operations and experiments were conducted by both humans and aliens.

Structural engineer Phil Schneider claims he had an all-out battle with grays at the Dulce underground facilities.

He claimed alien abductions led to this unremarkable mesa, and what occurs, including cross-breeding and fertilization, is unimaginable.

Drawings surfaced of human-like fetuses in beakers, mutant captives in cages and vats of liquid containing human and inhuman body parts.

Among popular UFO community accounts, Castello claims to have quit his position as a security guard, going into hiding after a purported battle with the aliens inside the mountain, in which 70 humans supposedly were killed.

The resulting "Dulce Papers" proclaim infinite, shocking detail about aliens and secret technologies.

ALIEN STRONGHOLDS ON EARTH!

I HEAR THINGS

Calvin Martinez of Farmington has family in Dulce.

"I hear things. There are a lot of stories," he said. "But one time I was at a cookout, and there was this light that came up, and it slowly merged across (the southern sky). People were taking pictures. It went around in circles and then back the way it came."

Martinez mentioned a widely repeated UFO story of a woman who was found - unclothed - running from the mesa near the Navajo River.

"They picked her up, and she said she wasn't from here, that they were doing all kinds of tests on her in that mountain," he said.

Are grays going about molesting Earth women in the lower levels of the Dulce Base? Perhaps impregnating them?

While many maintain Castello is a fictional character, Paul Bennewitz is not. The Albuquerque electronics specialist ran Thunder Scientific Laboratories in the 1970s when he stumbled on what he claimed were UFO transmissions he traced to Archuleta Mesa, where he learned about the Dulce base. Later, he became convinced of a government conspiracy to discredit him.

In "The Dulce Report," a published report by political scientist Michael E. Salla, formerly of American University and George Washington University, Salla wrote that when the U.S. Air Force Office of Special Investigations became aware that Bennewitz was gaining attention, they developed an effort to discredit him by providing him erroneous information. Ufologist William

ALIEN STRONGHOLDS ON EARTH!

Moore later went public, saying that he was involved in a plot by the Office of Special Investigations to misinform Bennewitz, keeping him from collecting more accurate information.

Strange tales of aliens in league with the government and strange experiments are common among the UFO community.

New Mexico State Patrol Trooper Gabe Valdez, investigating various local reports, joined Dulce cattle rancher Edmund Gomez, whose cattle were being mutilated, and four other men to explore Archuleta Mesa in 1988. The group saw a UFO, said ufologist Jason Bishop, as well as lights coming from and fading into the mountain.

Several newspapers reported an "experimental boomerang aircraft" in the area, according to Bishop's account. But Gomez and Valdez were suspicious.

Valdez wrote "Dulce Base," a book about his investigations, and even appeared on the History Channel's "UFO Hunters" in 2009. He revealed images: disturbing mutilations of cattle and what he claimed was a human hybrid found inside a cow.

A COW'S STRANGE DEATH

A resident, who gave only a first name of Dee and who works at Players Sports Bar & Grill in Dulce, shared her own story from her family's ranch.

"Our ranch has a canyon, real long, and the cows were way up at the end," she said. "I guess something chased one down because you could see where it ran into the trees. It died, and where it laid there were three holes in the ground. There were no tracks, and that cow had no blood."

Dee said she returned the next night, and the cow's internal organs were gone.

"It had udders, but it was all burned out," she said.

Cattle mutilations have been reported around Dulce for decades, Valdez said. But it's the government, not alien activity, he said.

Dee said: "It was happening all over. I don't know what it was, but the cows wouldn't go up there for a long time."

Dulce resident Shane Engle doesn't believe in UFOs. Still, he can't explain the time his mother's car was taken over by an "unknown force" before she regained control. He also can't account for the lights he's seen. He does, however, believe in the mutilations.

"My uncle owned a ranch," he said, pointing south. "One morning, he came out, and all the cows were hollow. No cuts, no wounds. They were hollow."

Several Dulce residents declined to be interviewed but said that "something is going on up there."

Norio Hayakawa, director of Civilian Intelligence Central, which bills itself as an oversight committee on government accountability, revealed the name of the base at a conference in 2010: Rio Arriba Scientific & Technological Underground Auxiliary.

One man said that, while exploring the mesa, he was stopped by "uniformed men who came out of nowhere."

"That's all I'm going to say," he said, and walked away.

Maybe you don't believe, like Engle, as he described eerie lights over an endless desert sky.

"I don't believe in that stuff," he said, "but I've seen it." - The Durango Herald

SUGGESTED READING

Dulce Base The Truth and Evidence From the Case Files of Gabe Valdez

The Dulce Wars: Underground Alien Bases and the Battle for Planet Earth

Underground Alien Bio Lab At Dulce: The Bennewitz UFO Papers

www.phantomsandmonsters.com/search?q=ufo+base

ALIEN STRONGHOLDS ON EARTH!

Chapter Twenty Six
MILITARY MIND CONTROL AND THE UFO EXPERIENCE
By Tim R. Swartz

EDITOR'S NOTE: Tim Swartz is a good buddy and a damn good researcher. Tim R. Swartz is an Indiana native and Emmy-Award winning television producer/videographer, and is the author of a number of popular books including "The Lost Journals of Nikola Tesla," "America's Strange and Supernatural History," "Secret Black Projects, Evil Agenda of the Secret Government," "Time Travel: A How-To-Guide," "Richard Shaver-Reality of the Inner Earth," "Admiral Byrd's Secret Journey Beyond the Poles," and is a contributing writer for the books, "Sir Arthur Conan Doyle: The First Ghostbuster," "Brad Steiger's Real Monsters, Gruesome Critters, and Beasts from the Darkside", and "Real Ghosts, Restless Spirits and Haunted Places."

As a photojournalist, Tim Swartz has traveled extensively and investigated paranormal phenomena and other unusual mysteries from such diverse locations as the Great Pyramid in Egypt to the Great Wall in China. He has worked with television networks such as PBS, ABC, NBC, CBS, CNN, ESPN, Thames-TV and the BBC. He has also appeared on the History Channel's program "Ancient Aliens" and the History Channel Latin America series "Contacto Extraterrestre."

* * * * * * * * *

ALIEN STRONGHOLDS ON EARTH!

Since the 1960's (and possibly even earlier), some witnesses to UFO events have reported that they were abducted by the alleged alien pilots. In the 1970's these other-worldly kidnappings entered the once-supposed sanctity of the home as people reported being taken from their beds against their will in the middle of the night.

These abduction reports followed a very predictable pattern: a person, or even several people, is taken from their car or home by small, humanoid creatures that are gray in color, have large jet-black eyes and almost no nose, mouth or ears. The abductees are usually given physical exams that are often painful and humiliating. Sometimes there is some form of communication where the abductee is shown images, often apocalyptic in nature. But just as often there is no communication, giving the abductee the impression of being experimented on like a lab animal by unfeeling technicians.

Even more disturbing is the fact that most abductees say that these abductions are not a one-time-only occurrence, as they are taken for experiments numerous times throughout their lives. Frighteningly, children of abductees are also more prone to report abduction experiences of their own more often than children whose parents have not had abductions.

Is there an evil alien race hidden among us and calling the shots?

ALIEN STRONGHOLDS ON EARTH!

Some researchers have uncovered evidence that some abductees are also being targeted by a group, or groups, that are not from outer space, but from planet Earth. Investigator Helmut Lammer has noted that UFO abductions are generally a very strange and complex phenomenon, and that it has gotten even stranger as some UFO abductees have reported that they have also been kidnapped by human military intelligence personnel (MILAB) and taken to hospitals and/or military facilities, some of which are described as being underground.

Very few of the popular books on the subject of UFO abductions have mentioned these experiences. Especially odd is the fact that abductees recall seeing military intelligence personnel together with alien beings, working side by side in these secret facilities. The presence of human military and civilian personnel occupying the same physical reality as alien beings exceeds the mind-sets of the skeptics and the open-minded researchers by several orders of magnitude. The skeptics would rather believe that stories of aliens and military personnel in governmental underground facilities are fabrications designed to elicit attention from conspiracy believers or hallucinations in general.

Some witnesses to UFO events have reported that they were abducted by the alleged alien pilots. These "alien" kidnappers entered homes and took their victims from their beds in the middle of the night.

ALIEN STRONGHOLDS ON EARTH!

Researchers in the field of mind control suggest that these cases are evidence that the whole UFO abduction phenomenon is staged by the intelligence community as a cover for their illegal experiments. The open-minded researchers who are trying to gain respect for abduction research ignore these stories, since they represent only a minor fraction of the cases in their files. Abduction cases involving reports of being taken by the military as well as alien beings are very important for two reasons:

1. If the UFO community has evidence that a covert military intelligence task force is involved in the abduction phenomenon, we would know that this phenomenon represents a matter of national security.

2. The alleged military involvement in the abduction phenomenon could be evidence that the military uses abductees for mind control experiments as test-targets for microwave weapons. Moreover, the military could be monitoring and even kidnapping abductees for information gathering purposes during, before and after a UFO abduction.

A HISTORY OF MIND CONTROL

The subject of human mind control has long been consigned to the realm of lurid spy novels and grade B action movies. Most people consider the possibility of mind control by outside influences to be nothing more than the ravings of lunatics and psychotics. However, over the years, governments and intelligence agencies have spent millions of dollars in research to determine whether the mind can be regulated, influenced and controlled.

The phrase "mind control" has been defined to mean many different things, and all these definitions have their advocates. Some believe that mind control involves the harassment of individuals for the purpose of disorienting them, or decreasing their ability to discuss issues of importance. This includes the use of less-than-lethal technologies such as microwaves, electromagnetic irradiation, sonic-waves and other techniques.

Other research concerns individual mind control by means of what is called "structured abuse," what L. Ron Hubbard once identified as "drug/pain/hypnosis" conditioning. Discussions on this topic can be found in books and articles related to satanic ritual abuse, alien abductions, and the "false memory syndrome" debate.

Many investigators claim that experiments done in the 1940's, 50's and 60's have led to Top Secret electronic machines that are capable of influencing the minds of chosen individuals anywhere in the world. Others say that microwaves delivering direct-voice communication to the brain are being used to harass American citizens. There is also good evidence suggesting that unwilling victims of sophisticated forms of hypnosis are being secretly programmed to act as assassins when needed.

Because of the outrageous nature of such evidence, the media and the public have been unwilling to consider that their most precious freedom - independent thought - could be seriously compromised.

Mind control can trace its origins to mankind's distant past with the use of magical rites and Shamanism. Techniques of mind control developed in our western culture are believed to have been field-tested by various mystery religions, secret societies and political organizations.

The modern era of hypnosis began with the Viennese physician Franz Anton Mesmer who theorized that the "tidal" influences of the planets also operate on the human body through a universal force, which he termed "animal magnetism."

One of the earliest attempts at mind control involved "Mesmerism," or as it is known today, Hypnotism. Primitive societies have used hypnotic phenomena throughout the ages for physical and spiritual benefits. Tribal drums and ritualistic dances have been a part of many societies worldwide. Believed to have the power to heal, kings of middle age Europe would touch commoners with remarkable results. Priests and ministers would use a laying on of hands to affect changes in the health and fortune of their church members.

There have even been paintings and sculptures in ancient Greece and Egypt that depict a "curing sleep" induced in subjects by their leaders to affect healing or change of mental attitude. This interesting condition gained the attention of doctors and scientists in the 18th century all because of a man whose name would later become the name of the mental phenomena. That name is Mesmerism.

Considered to be the father of hypnotism, Franz Anton Mesmer was born in Vienna, Austria in 1734. Mesmer in his youth considered first becoming a priest and then a lawyer. He finally decided to be a doctor in Vienna at the age of thirty-two. In 1773 Mesmer, started working with a Jesuit priest by the name of Maximilian Hell, who was also the Royal Astronomer of Vienna, Austria.

The two men treated their patients with magnets and magnetized baths. Hell thought the magnets cured with physical properties, interrupting the sick person's magnetic field. Mesmer thought there was a fluid mineral that pulsated throughout the person's body as well as throughout the universe. He called it "animal magnetism."

Even though Mesmerism was eventually considered a fraud by leading experts of the day, as time went by, further research on Mesmerism led many scientists to conclude that Mesmer had indeed accidentally discovered a hidden feature of the human mind, a state of mind called "High Suggestibility." Because of this, Franz Anton Mesmer is credited with the discovery of what is now known as hypnosis.

The history of hypnotism is replete with tales of good people led astray under the spell of an evil hypnotist. The name Svengali has come to mean someone who has an unnatural influence on another, usually with hypnotism. One of the favorite dogmas of modern hypnotism is that "hypnotism can't make a person do anything against his or her moral code."

Some past incidents suggest that certain hypnotists apparently could make some people do whatever they wanted. One such event occurred in 1865 in the French village of Sollies-Farliede. A beggar named Thimotheus Castelan was invited to stay for a night with a man and his adult daughter, Josephine. During the night, Thimotheus hypnotized the woman, then raped and abducted her.

For two weeks the pair kept to the back roads, appearing only for single evenings spent in the homes of other villagers. Thimotheus was seen to make strange signs over Josephine and to mumble instructions. Josephine carried out his every wish.

ALIEN STRONGHOLDS ON EARTH!

Finally the authorities caught up with Thimotheus and his unwilling companion. Thimotheus was sentenced to twelve years of hard labor, while Josephine suffered through various nervous afflictions for several months afterwards. The two physicians testified in the case were unanimous in their opinion that the "magnetic effect" destroyed Josephine's moral freedom and her ordinary restraint was lost.

In 1937 a young German woman was hypnotized by a man who falsely claimed he was a doctor. For seven years the woman suffered from various false ailments allegedly induced by the hypnotist. Upon his suggestion she actually murdered her husband, believing he was a stranger out to attack her. When the case came to trial, her hypnotically induced suggestions were so complex that it took a court psychiatric consultant nine months to make sense of the situation. The woman was found not guilty. However, the hypnotist managed to escape and was never caught. This case and others like it suggested that mind control was possible.

In 1977, a Senate subcommittee on Health and Scientific Research, chaired by Senator Ted Kennedy, focused on the CIA's testing of LSD on unwitting citizens. Only a mere handful of people within the CIA knew about the scope and details of the program. The Kennedy subcommittee learned about the CIA Operation MK-ULTRA through the testimony of Dr. Sidney Gottlieb.

The purpose of the program, according to his testimony, was to "investigate whether and how it was possible to modify an individual's behavior by covert means." Claiming the protection of the National Security Act, Dr. Gottlieb was unwilling to tell the Senate subcommittee what had been learned by these experiments.

He did state, however, that the program was initially started by a concern that the Soviets and other enemies of the United States would get ahead of the U.S. in this field. Through the Freedom of Information Act, researchers were able to obtain documents detailing the MK-ULTRA program and other CIA behavior modification projects.

In 1953, CIA director Allen Dulles, speaking before a national meeting of Princeton alumni, distinguished two fronts in the then-current "battle for men's minds:" a "first front" of mass indoctrination through censorship and propaganda, and a "second front" of individual "brainwashing" and "brain changing."

ALIEN STRONGHOLDS ON EARTH!

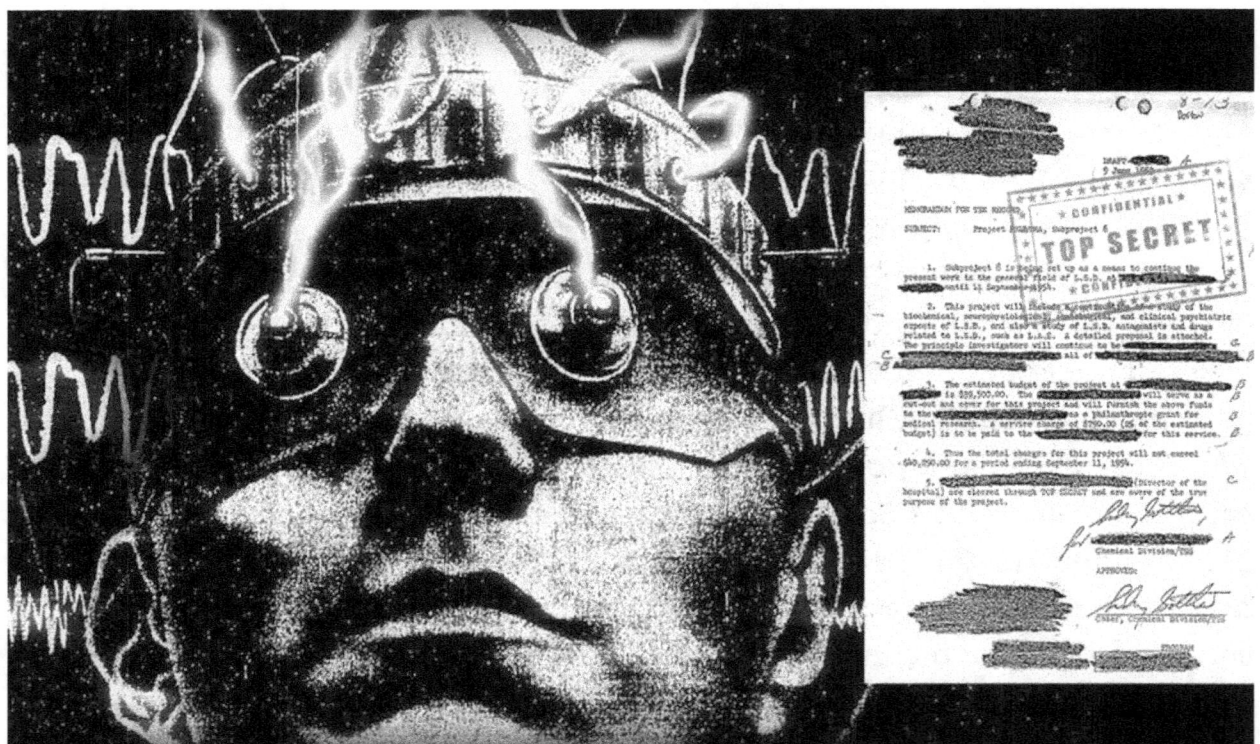

Is there still an MK-Ultra program within the secret government?

The same year, at CIA deputy director Richard Helm's suggestion, Dulles approved the MK-ULTRA project, and exempted it from normal CIA financial controls. From this point on, U.S. research and development of various forms of mind control are believed to have accelerated at an alarming rate. Using the excuse of battling the "Communist Menace," the U.S. government, military and various intelligence groups, received secret black budget funding in an effort to learn how to control and manipulate the human mind.

Even though the CIA claims that they stopped all mind control research in the 1970s, it is foolish to think that decades of successful research would be thrown away so cavalierly. What is more likely is that the research and implementation of human mind control has been covered up and compartmentalized to such an extent that only those who are "in the loop" have any knowledge of what is really going on. There are, however, some tantalizing clues on the frightening direction that these underground groups have taken in their quest for the ultimate control of the human mind.

ALIEN STRONGHOLDS ON EARTH!

THE REALITY OF ELECTRONIC IMPLANTS

The largest newspaper in Scandinavia, "Helsingin Sanomat," wrote in the September 9, 1999 issue that "Scientific American" magazine estimates that in the 21st century, perhaps all people will be implanted with a "DNA microchip." How many people realize what it actually means? Total loss of privacy and total outside control of the person's physical body functions, mental, emotional and thought processes, including the implanted person's subconscious and dreams, for the rest of his life.

The July 25, 2017 edition of the "New York Times" reported that employees at Three Square Market, a technology company in Wisconsin, can choose to have a chip the size of a grain of rice injected between their thumb and index finger. Once that is done, any task involving RFID technology - swiping into the office building, paying for food in the cafeteria - can be accomplished with a wave of the hand.

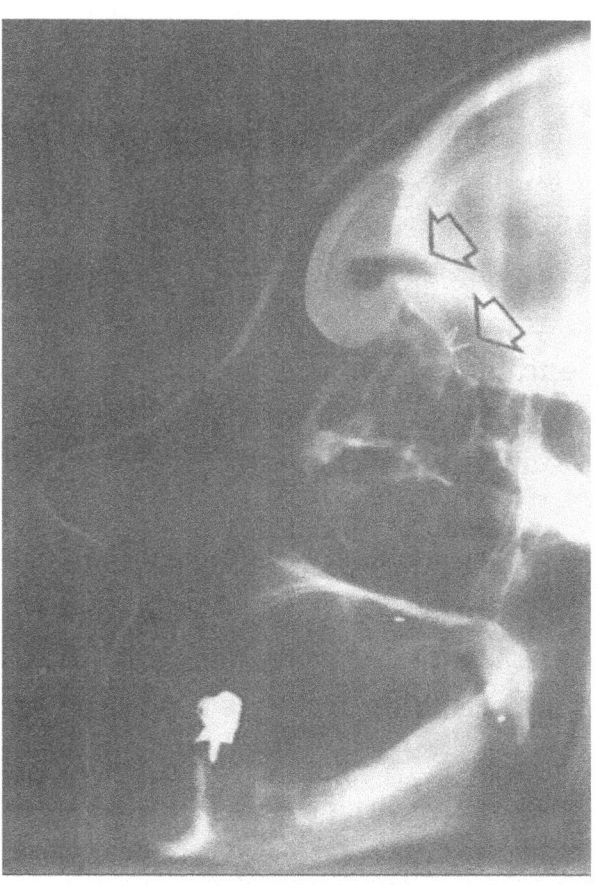

X-ray of electronic implants in the brain of Swedish mind-control victim Robert Naeslund.

The program is not mandatory, but so far, more than 50 out of 80 employees at Three Square's headquarters in River Falls, Wis., had volunteered. Even though employees seemed to be eager to try out this new technology, it does raise a variety of questions, both privacy and health-related.

Alessandro Acquisti, a professor of information technology and public policy at Carnegie Mellon University's Heinz College says that technology designed for one purpose may later be used for another. A microchip implanted today to allow for easy building access and payments could, in theory, be used later in more invasive ways: to track the length of employees' bathroom or lunch breaks without their consent or even their knowledge.

ALIEN STRONGHOLDS ON EARTH!

"Once they are implanted, it's very hard to predict or stop a future widening of their usage," Dr. Acquisti said.

It sounds like science fiction, but it is secret military and intelligence agencies' mind control technology, which has been experimented with for almost half a century, totally without the knowledge of the general public and even the general academic population.

Supercomputers in Maryland, Israel and elsewhere with a speed of over 20 billion bits/sec can monitor millions of people simultaneously. In fact, the whole world population can be totally controlled by these secret brain-computer interactions, however unbelievable it sounds for the uninformed.

Human thought has a speed of 5,000 bits/sec and everyone understands that our brain cannot compete with supercomputers acting via satellites, implants, local facilities, scalar or other forms of biotelemetry.

Each brain has a unique set of bioelectric resonance/entrainment characteristics. Remote neural monitoring systems with supercomputers can send messages through an implanted person's nervous system and affect their performance in any way desired. They can of course be tracked and identified anywhere.

Neuro-electromagnetic involuntary human experimentation has been going on with the so-called "vulnerable population" for about 50 years, in the name of "science" or "national security" in the worst Nazi-type testing, contrary to all human rights. Physical and psychological torture of mind control victims today is like the worst horror movies. Only, unlike the horror movies, it is true.

It happens today in the United States, Russia, China, Japan, and Europe. With few exceptions, the mass media suppresses all information about the entire topic.

Mind control technology in the U.S. is classified under "non-lethal" weaponry. The name is totally misleading because the technology used is lethal, but death comes slowly in the form of "normal" illnesses, like cancer, leukemia, heart attacks, Alzheimer's disease with loss of short term memory first. No wonder these illnesses have increased all over the world.

When the use of electromagnetic fields, extra-low (ELF) and ultra-low (ULF) frequencies and microwaves aimed deliberately at certain individuals, groups, and even the general population to cause diseases, disorientation, chaos and physical and emotional pain breaks into the awareness of the general population, a public outcry is inevitable.

Reports from persons targeted by neuro-electromagnetic experimentation show that not everyone is implanted. The fact that those few victims who have had implants removed cannot get custody of the implants means someone has a keen interest in controlling the use of covert implants and preventing the publication of this practice.

Who is behind a sinister plan to microchip and control and torture the general population? The United States Patent Office has granted patents for purposes of mental monitoring and mind alteration.

An apparatus and method for remotely monitoring and altering brainwaves, methods for inducing mental, emotional and physical states of consciousness in human beings and a method of and apparatus for desired states of consciousness are among some of them.

People who have been implanted, involuntarily or through deception, have become biological robots and guinea pigs for this activity under the guise of national security. The real consequences of microchip implantation (or with today's advanced hidden technology, using only microwave radiation for mind control,) are totally hidden from the public. How many know the real dangers of microwaves through cell phones?

SOCIAL MEDIA IS SPYING ON US

How many believe the disinformation that microwave radiation is not causing health problems? The economic issues in the cell phone industry are enormous. Therefore health issues are deliberately brushed aside.

However, the same thing is inevitable in the future as with the tobacco industry. When economic compensation for health damages becomes big enough, as in the tobacco industry, health hazards will be admitted and users are then responsible for their tobacco-related illnesses.

Using cell phones for mind control has amazing potential. At this point, practically everyone has a cell phone and at least one social media account. Much has been written on how Russia may have influenced the 2016 Presidential election by the clever use of social manipulation through outlets such as Facebook and Twitter. This is all the result of decades of research on human psychology and social media companies are beyond a doubt

ALIEN STRONGHOLDS ON EARTH!

exploiting psychological vulnerabilities to manipulate and control people's time and attention.

It is now well-known that social media companies sell our demographic information to advertisers who use it to target us. However, they don't stop there. Facebook also tracks users' Internet usage: Every website that has a Facebook pixel will report your visit to Facebook.

Facebook buys information from companies that sell credit reports, which contain information like income and lawsuit involvement. The company even purchases information from supermarket loyalty programs, so they may know what your grocery bill looks like. Unless you've changed your privacy settings, Facebook tracks your location. Recently, Facebook users discovered that Facebook even keeps log histories of phone calls and texts.

With this information, Facebook categorizes you according to a database of about 52,000 attributes. It is possible to view your categories in the ad settings on Facebook. The information they've collected is used to target us with ads. Troublingly, social media companies will sell the information they have gathered about us to virtually anyone, including the same Russian operatives that seek to influence the country's politics.

Military and police agencies can follow every user, influence their thoughts through microwaves, cause healthy people to hear voices in their heads and if needed burn their brains in a second by increasing the current 20,000 times.

That probably happened to Chechnyan leader General Dudayev who died talking on a cell phone. Heating effect of tissues with the speed of light is a known effect of high power microwave and electromagnetic pulse weapons.

According to Navy studies they also cause fatigue states, depression, insomnia, aggressiveness, long and especially short term memory loss, short catatonic states, cataracts, leukemia, cancer, heart attacks, brain tumors and so forth. Alteration of behavior and attitudes has been demonstrated as well.

Dr. Ross Adey has found out that by using 0.75 mille-watts per square centimeter intensity of pulse modulated microwave at a frequency of 450 MHz it is possible to control ALL aspects of human behavior.

Microwave radiation excites the hydrogen bond in the cells and can interfere with meiosis, which leads to tumors. All our emotions, moods, and thoughts have a specific brain frequency which has been catalogued. If these

ALIEN STRONGHOLDS ON EARTH!

records fall into the wrong hands, our behavior and attitudes can be manipulated by persons whose ethics and morals are not in our best interest.

CONTROLLING THE WORLD'S POPULATION

Both military and intelligence agencies have been infiltrated with secret operatives whose goals seem to be to manipulate the population. The Director of the Swiss Secret Service had to resign in September 1999 because of his agency's involvement in illegal arms deals and a plan to create an organization within the legal Secret Service. This globally infiltrated organization has "octopus type" activities in all major intelligence services in the world, working together with the Mafia and terrorists. It has recruited people from all important government institutions, state and local administrations.

It owns Star Wars technology which is used against military and civilian populations, claiming it is "non-lethal" weaponry. "Down and out" people, jobless, freed prisoners, mental outpatients, students and orphans are trained by this organization to harass, follow, and torture innocent people, who for whatever reason have been put on the organization's hit list. They are already in every neighborhood.

Deception is the name of the game, so recruits are told untrue sinister stories of their victims to keep them motivated. The media, large corporations, religious and political leaders are also infiltrated.

Who are the targets? Experimentation with soldiers and prisoners may continue, as well as handicapped children, UFO witnesses, mental patients, homosexuals and single women. However, anyone can become a target, even those who invented the system.

Researchers who find out about this secret radiation of the population become targets themselves. The U.S. Senate discussed the issue on January 22, 1997. The U.S. Air Force's "Commando Solo" aircraft have been used to send subliminal radio frequency messages to manipulate even the minds of foreign nations in their elections. Haiti, Bosnia and Iraq are a couple of recent examples.

In July 1994 the U.S. Department of Defense proposed the use of "non-lethal" weapons against anyone engaged in activities the DoD opposes. Thus opposing political views, economic competitors, counterculture individuals and so forth can be beamed to sickness or death.

ALIEN STRONGHOLDS ON EARTH!

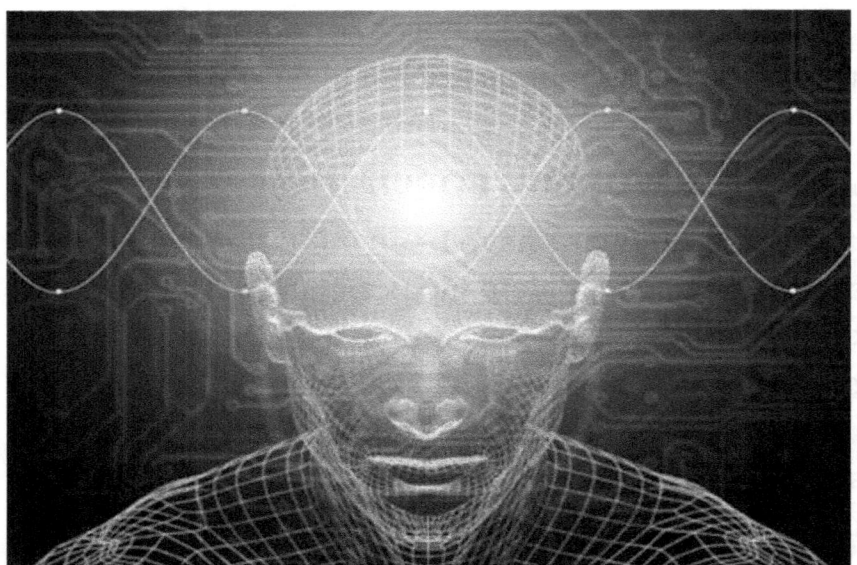

In July 1994 the U.S. Department of Defense proposed the use of "non-lethal" weapons against anyone engaged in activities the DoD opposes.

The Psychiatric Diagnostic Statistical Manual (DSM) for mental disorders has been a brilliant cover up operation in 18 languages to hide the atrocities of military and intelligence agencies' actions towards their targets. The manual lists all mind control actions as signs of paranoid schizophrenia.

If a target is under surveillance with modern technology via TV, radio, telephone, loudspeakers, lasers, microwaves, poisoned with mind altering drugs via air-ducts, giving off familiar smells which cause headache, nausea and so forth, if he claims his clothes are poisoned, his food or tap water as well - all medical schools teach their students that the person is paranoid, especially if he believes the government, intelligence agencies, or UFOs are behind it all.

Never is the medical profession told that these are routine actions all over the world by intelligence agencies against their targets. Thus, victims of mind control are falsely considered mentally ill and get no help since they are not believed and their suffering is doubled by ignorant health professionals.

The unethical abuses of power by individuals in charge of biomedical telemetry are incomprehensible to normal people. The goal of mind control is to program an individual to carry out any mission of espionage or assassination even against their will and self-preservation instinct and to control the absolute behavior and thought patterns of the individual. The purpose of mind control is to disrupt memory, discredit people through aberrant behavior, to make them insane or to commit suicide or murder.

How is it possible that this technology is not stopped by political top authorities? They themselves will also be targets someday, a fact they have not always realized. How much are they involved?

ALIEN STRONGHOLDS ON EARTH!

After the 9/11 terrorist attacks, the U.S. congress gave carte blanche approval to President Bush's notorious Patriot Act, this despite the fact that few lawmakers were even allowed to read the act and the attack on civil liberties its approval would allow. Many congressmen stated after the fact that they could not explain why they voted for the Patriot Acts approval.

In fact, in 2006, congress once again voted to extend the Patriot Act, even though most of the country's voters were dead-set against the draconian measures allowed within it. It was as is the country's lawmakers had no will of their own.

ALIEN ABDUCTIONS AS A COVER

In recent years, various information on remote mind control technology has filtered into the conspiracy research community through publications such as Conspiracy Journal, as well as a Finnish gentleman by the name of Martti Koski and his booklet "My Life Depends On You." Over the last decade, Koski has been sharing his horrifying tale, documenting the discovery of rampant brain tampering committed upon himself and countless others.

The perpetrators of these evil doings allegedly include the Royal Canadian Mounted Police (RCMP), the CIA and Finnish Intelligence, among various other intelligence agencies. At one point during a mind control programming episode, the "doctors" operating on Koski identified themselves as "aliens from Sirius." Apparently, these "doctors" were attempting to plant a screen memory to conceal their true intentions.

What this suggests is a theory that alien abductions were a cover for MK-ULTRA mind control experiments perpetrated by secret intelligence agencies.

According to author Walter Bowart, in the revised edition of "Operation Mind Control," one alleged mind control victim said that in the late 70s the victim had been the recipient of a mock alien abduction, the intention of which was to create a screen memory that would conceal the actual mind control programs enacted on the victim. The subject in this instance claimed to have seen a young child dressed in a small alien costume, similar in appearance to the aliens in Steven Spielberg's movie ET.

None of this, of course, dismisses outright the theory that UFOs are alien spacecraft. Nevertheless, its implications are staggering when one considers the impact and subsequent commercialization of the alien abduction

ALIEN STRONGHOLDS ON EARTH!

phenomenon, and how it has reshaped the belief systems and psyches of millions upon millions of the planet's inhabitants, in essence creating a new paradigm on the reality of visitors from other planets that prior to thirty years ago was virtually non-existent.

As chronicled in Walter Bowart's "Operation Mind Control," in the late 70s Congressman Charlie Rose (D-N.C) met with a Canadian inventor who had developed a helmet that simulated alternate states of consciousness and realities. One such virtual reality scenario played out by those who tried on this helmet was a mock alien abduction.

Much to Rose's amazement, the simulated alien abduction scenario seemed incredibly realistic.

This device sounds quite similar to the late Dr. Michael Persinger's much-touted "Magic Helmet," which received a fair amount of press. Equipped with magnets that beam a low-level magnetic field at the temporal lobe, the "Helmet" affects areas of the brain associated with time distortions and other altered states of consciousness.

Although Bowart did not specifically name the inventor of the helmet in "Operation Mind Control," chances are it was Persinger to whom he was referring. Persinger's name has also been bandied about by mind control researcher, Martin Cannon - in his treatise "The Controllers" - as a behind the scenes player in intelligence operations related to MK-ULTRA.

This takes us back to Helmut Lammer and his Project MILAB. His studies indicate that MILAB abductees are harassed by dark, unmarked helicopters that fly around their houses. Lammer has discovered that the helicopter activity associated with UFO abductions has increased from the 80s to the present day. Dan Wright has ten cases in the MUFON Transcription Project files where helicopters were seen flying in the area of the abductee's home within hours of an alleged UFO abduction. Lammer has also found that many abduction researchers in North America have, on average, about three helicopter cases connected with UFO abductions in their files.

Most abductees report interaction with military intelligence personnel after the helicopters begin to appear. Debbie Jordan reports, for instance, in her book "Abducted!" that she was stunned by an alleged friend and taken to a kind of hospital where she was examined by a medical doctor. This doctor removed an implant from her ear.

ALIEN STRONGHOLDS ON EARTH!

MILABs could be evidence that a secret military intelligence task force has been operating in North America since the early 80s and is involved in the monitoring and kidnapping of alleged UFO abductees.

The abduction experiences of Leah Haley and Ms. K. Wilson are full of MILAB encounters. Some of Ms. Wilson's experiences are comparable with mind control experiments. For example, she writes of a flashback from her childhood where she remembers being forced into what appears to be a Skinner Box-like container which may have been used for behavior modification purposes.

Because of these types of experiences, Ms. Wilson published an article on her web site titled Project Open Mind: Are Some Alien Abductions Government Mind Control Experiments? Beth Collins and Anna Jamerson included hypnosis transcripts of an abduction by human military personnel in their book "Connections," and the late Dr. Karla Turner investigated MILABs in her books: "Into the Fringe" and "Taken: Inside the Alien-Human Abduction Agenda."

Lammer reports that MILABs involve the following elements: Dark, unmarked helicopter activity, the appearance of strange vans or buses outside the houses of abductees, exposure to disorienting electromagnetic fields, drugging, and transport by a helicopter, bus or truck to an unknown building or an underground military facility. Usually after the military kidnappings, there are physical after-effects such as grogginess and sometimes nausea.

There is also a difference when the abductors appear. In most UFO abduction cases, the beings appear through a closed window, wall, or the abductee feels a strange presence in the room. Most abductees report that they are paralyzed from the mental power of the alien beings.

During MILABs the abductee reports that the kidnappers give him or her a shot with a syringe. It is also interesting that MILAB abductees report

ALIEN STRONGHOLDS ON EARTH!

that they are examined by human doctors in rectangular rooms and not in round sterile rooms, as they are described during most UFO abductions. The described rooms, halls and furniture are similar to terrestrial hospital rooms, laboratories or research facilities and have nothing to do with "UFO" furniture.

During a MILAB, the examination is similar to UFO abductions. However, the MILAB victim is not paralyzed, but rather tied to an examination table or a gynecological chair. Sometimes, the abductee gets a strong drink before the examination. This is perhaps a contrast-enhancing fluid.

MILAB doctors are usually dressed in white lab coats and show an interest in implants as well as gynecological examinations. In some MILAB cases military doctors searched for implants and sometimes even implanted the abductee with a military device. Therefore, surgeons extracting alleged alien implants should be prepared in the event they find military devices since human implant technology is very advanced.

It should be considered that some of the information received from MILAB abductees may be cover stories, induced by the hypno-programming processes of military psychiatrists. There is also the possibility that the military uses rubber alien masks and special effects during a MILAB.

Facts such as these lead some mind control researchers to believe that all alien abductees are used in secret mind control and/or genetic experiments staged by a powerful black arm of the United States government. However, investigators should not jump to any conclusions until all of the facts are in. Serious researchers should investigate all possibilities. Some UFO abductees may indeed be mind control victims or they may have been used in black-ops genetic experiments from the 80s or earlier.

Lammer speculates that the alien/human abduction scenario is more complex than previously thought. It seems that there is evidence that more than one human agenda may be involved in the unexplained alien abduction phenomenon. Each of these agendas probably has their own interest in alleged alien abductees.

It also seems that the first group is interested in mind and behavior control experiments. There is evidence of sensory deprivation experiments, liquid breathing experiments, experiments on electromagnetic stimulation of the temporal lobes, brain research and implant research.

ALIEN STRONGHOLDS ON EARTH!

The second group seems to be interested in biological and/or genetic research. Some MILAB victims recall that they saw humans in tubes filled with liquid and genetically altered animals in cages during their kidnappings inside military underground facilities. It should be noted that alien abductees "without" military contacts remember similar scenarios inside UFOs.

The third group seems to be a military task force, which has operated since the 80s and is interested in the UFO/alien abduction phenomenon for information gathering purposes. This would be a logical consequence if one with the right "Need to Know" considers that some alien abductions may be real.

It could be that the leaders of this military task force think that some alien abductions are real and that they have national security implications. It could be that the second and third group works together, since they could share their interest in genetic studies and findings from alleged alien abductees.

"Information Operations: A New War-Fighting Capability," was a paper published in 1996 for the "Air Force 2025" study. The authors write about a brain implanted cyber situation. In this paper the authors propagate implanted microscopic brain chips which perform two functions: The bio-chip connects the implanted individual to a constellation of integrated or smart satellites (IIC) in low earth orbit, creating an interface between the implanted person and the information resources. The implant relays the processed information from the IIC to the user.

Second, the bio-chip creates a computer generated mental visualization based upon the user's request. The visualization encompasses the individual and allows the user to place him into a selected "battle space." Further a wide range of lethal or non-lethal weapons will be linked to the IIC, allowing special authorized implanted users (super-cyber-soldiers) to directly employ these weapons. This means, a soldier sees the normal world plus an overlay of information identifying and describing specific objects in his field of view. He can now evaluate the threat these targets represent and order a variety of weapon systems to engage and destroy these targets from a great distance.

One can see from such military studies that secret research in human-brain-machine and virtual reality implant research is going on. Most of the references in this paper refer to military research institutes and are classified for the public. Since the authors write that implanting things in peoples raises

ALIEN STRONGHOLDS ON EARTH!

ethical and public relation issues today, one should ask where the guinea pigs of these futuristic research projects are.

MILABs could be evidence that a secret military intelligence task force has been operating in North America since the early 80s and is involved in the monitoring and kidnapping of alleged UFO abductees. They monitor the houses of their victims, then kidnap and possibly implant them with military devices shortly after a UFO abduction experience. It appears that they are searching for possible alien implants as well. Their gynecological interest in female abductees could be explained if they are searching for alleged alien-hybrid embryos. One thing is certain: this task force and the people who are behind these kidnappings are using advanced mind control technology which is currently being tested illegally on individuals who have nothing to do with UFO abductions.

SUGGESTED READING

GEF THE TALKING MONGOOSE

THE LOST JOURNALS OF NIKOLA TESLA

MIND STALKERS

TIME TRAVEL - FACT NOT FICTION!

MEN OF MYSTERY

Tim R. Swartz guards the Great Pyramid.

Write us for our FREE catalog of books and other unusual items.

INNER LIGHT/GLOBAL COMMUNICATIONS

P.O. Box 753
New Brunswick, NJ 08903

mrufo8@hotmail.com

www.conspiracyjournal.com

OCCULT SECRETS OF HITLER AND THE THIRD REICH

Hitler was the top Priest of the Nazi religion, a Godless pagan, Satanic cult. He sacrificed six million souls for the Fatherland. We expose the terror of his plot to take over the world through occult means, even employing UFOs or Foo Fighters. *Check desired titles.*

☐ **NEW! — OCCULT SECRETS OF THE THIRD REICH - $21.95**
Shocking revelations detail the Fuhrere's fascination with the occult and the formation of the SS storm troopers to propagate the virtues of the Aryan race and its supposed superiority. Why did they believe that such artifacts as the Spear of Destiny were essential in their world conquest? —"^

☐ **OMEGA FILES: SECRET NAZI BASES REVEALED — $21.95**
This 258 page dossier contains the most intricate and intimate details of a global conspiracy which seems to be rooted in an alien - military - industrial collaboration which is intent on bringing all freedom-loving peoples of this world under its control, through the implementation of a global government which has commonly been referred to as the 'New World Order."

☐ **NAZI UFO TIME TRAVELERS — $18.95**
Beware of the Nazi "Wonder Weapons" in our sky. Nazi scientists develop the Glocke ("The Bell") a time travel device constructed with the help of Nordic-looking star beings. Have the Nazis "returned" to the present to reinstate their claim to world domination? Said Wernher von Braun, "We find ourselves faced by powers which are far stronger than we had hitherto assumed, and whose base of operations is at present unknown to us."

☐ **UFO'S NAZI SECRET WEAPONS? — $18.85** Authored by Christof Friedrich and banned in 12 countries. Here are diagrams of the various flying discs under construction and in operation at the end of WWII. This edition is not endorsed by: The Publisher Or Any Known UFOlogist, Conspiracy Buff, or the "Space Brothers."

☐ **ALL FOUR TITLES ABOVE — $59.00 + $10 S/H**
TIMOTHY BECKLEY, BOX 753, NEW BRUNSWICK, NJ 08903
PayPal to mrufo8@hotmail.com

FREE LEMURIAN SEED TELECRYSTAL

NOW IN ONE VOLUME!
Rare And Out Of Print For More Than 30 Years!

Venusian Health Magic And Secret Sciences

Two Transformational Programs In One Unique Study Guide 14 Individual Lessons

Presented once again to combat the negativity of these explosive times! Cosmic Masters And Interplanetary Travelers Provide Mystical Revelations Of Great Importance To Our Spiritual Growth And Development. Good Health Tips - Pyramid Principles - Importance Of A New Age Diet -- Achieving Harmonic Perfection - Modulating Yourself Upward - Virtues Of The Golden Sphere. - Venusian Vigor And Vitality.

Michael X talks extensively of working with a Telolith or Teleacrystal which will assist in breaking through to higher dimensions and at the same time enable you to retain a firm balance in this earthly realm.

Your **VENUSIAN SECRET SCIENCE AND HEALTH MAGIC Course/Study Guide and FREE Telecystal**

REDUCED PRICE NOW JUST $27.00 + $5 S/H
Timothy Beckley · Box 753 · New Brunswick, NJ 08903

Researchers Promote Use Of The Crystal Power Rod As A Modern Day

WiSHiNG ROD

THE CRYSTAL POWER ROD AS A "WISH MACHINE"

Also Known Widely As The COSMIC GENERATOR this device is believed to have originated in Atlantis and supposedly operates with energy generated by the operator's mind, amplified by emotions, feelings, desires. Once amplified, these "wishes" can be projected over vast distances to influence others.

WISH MACHINES – MIND MACHINES

They come in various forms and are known as Radionics, Ociloclasts, or Hieronymous Machines, Detector Rods, Symbolic Machines or, put most simply, Black Boxes regardless of their appearance.

SUPER SECRET DOSSIER INCLUDED WITH YOUR POWER ROD

Your Crystal Power Rod (may vary slightly from illustration) and Mind Machine Study Guide is sold as a unit for $85.00 + $5.00 S/H and is obtainable only from:
Timothy Beckley · Box 753 New Brunswick, NJ 08903

THE TRUTH AT LAST! HARD-TO-FIND BOOKS
RADIONICS BOXES — MOLDAVITE — TREE OF LIFE

☐ **#1—NIKOLA TESLA 3-BOOK SUPER SPECIAL!**

"The Miracle of Tesla's Purple Energy." The benefits of the purple plates are said to be almost supernatural, yet are firmly rooted in scientific principles. *"Men of Mystery."* The untold story of Tesla and his student, Otis T. Carr, who claimed to be building an anti-gravity device to take us to space as early as 1959. *"Tesla's Death Ray and the Columbia Space Shuttle Disaster."* Earth shaking facts NASA wants kept under wraps. Who was responsible?
ALL THREE BOOKS—JUST $25.00

☐ **#2—2 BOOKS: MISSING DIARY OF ADMIRAL RICHARD BYRD & NAZI UFO TIME TRAVELERS**

Are there secret polar entrances leading to a paradice inside the Earth, inhabited by giants, as discovered by Admiral Byrd and revealed in his secret diary? Proof that the Germans developed a bell-shaped device capable of space and time travel based upon contacts with ETs, made as early as 1919. Hundreds of large-format, provacative pages.
2 VOLUMES—$25.00

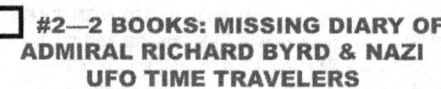

☐ **#3 MATRIX CONTROL SYSTEM OF PHILIP K. DICK AND THE PARANORMAL SYNCHRONICITIES OF TIM BECKLEY**

Are we living in a computer simulation—mere robotic creations of ancient technology played upon an eternal chessboard? Can we reside in parallel univeses simultaneously, leading multiple lives? The role of bizarre "coincidences" that control our destiny fully revealed!
450 LARGE FORMAT PAGES—$23.00

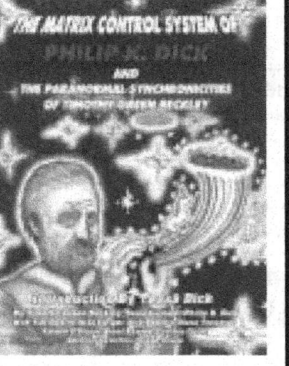

☐ **ALL 6 BOOKS AND FREE UNCLASSIFIED DVD—$59.00**

☐ **RARE TRANSFORMATIONAL GEM FROM SPACE**

Moldavite opens multidimensional portals with its beautiful green extraterrestrial energy. This rare stone arrived in a meteor some million years ago and is found only in one place on Earth. Powerful aid for increasing sensitivity to guidance, intuition and telepathy, and ability to receive and understand messages from higher realms. COMPLETE MOLDAVITE KIT includes the stone in an elegant setting, a 178-page workbook, and "Divine Fire" audio CD. Individually crafted; stones and setting vary.
MEDIUM STONE—$79 • LARGE STONE—$92

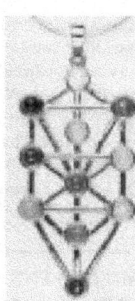

☐ **BLACK BOXES TWO ECONOMY VERSIONS OF OUR "WISH MACHINES"**

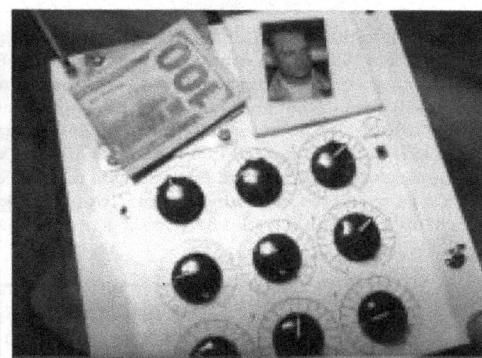

Other Rife, Harmonious or Radionics Machines sell for $2,000 or more! Our are two of the most economical, yet most powerful available. Includes comprehensive, *"Mind Machines"* book, and a dossier of scientific research describing their capabilities. No medical claims made. For experimental purposes. Actual box are custom-made and will vary.
MOST ECONOMICAL—$292
UPGRADED—$449 *(Plug-in model, antenna, light and toggle switch)*

☐ **TREE OF LIFE PENDANT ENERGY ACCUMULATOR**

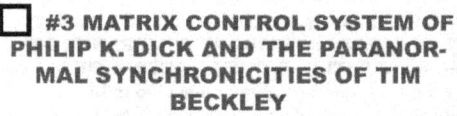

The Tree Of Life was understood by Old Testament prophets as an energy accumulator. This beautiful, individually crafted pendant is cast in silver with ten faceted stones. It acts to ammplify your deepest desires, broadcasting them to the highest powers to bring awareness, wisdom and knowledge. Casts a deep reflection of the eternal mysteries. In the Kabbalah, the Tree Of Life represents a "telephone" to the heavens. Includes pendant, study guide and 70-minute audio CD. Designs, stones and settings may vary.
TREE OF LIFE PENDANT—$125

Check desired items. Include your name, postal address and ZIP. Check, Money Order or PayPal to Tim Beckley, 11 East 30th Street, #4R, New York, NY 10016. Secure Phone: 646-331-6777. Speak slowly and clearly name, address, items desired.

Timothy G. Beckley • Box 753 • New Brunswick, NJ 08903 • PayPal to mrufo8@hotmail.com
FREE CONSPIRACY JOURNAL • NO REFUNDS • email mrufo8@hotmail.com if paying via PayPal

LARGEST INDEPENDENT PUBLISHER OF ALTERNATIVE BOOKS SINCE 1965

EXPLORE THESE "WAY-OUT" WORLDS

NEW RELEASE!

❏ **PROJECT MAGNET — THE LIGHTS IN THE SKY ARE NOT STARS!**
ONE MAN ALONE IS SAID TO HOLD THE KEY TO THE SECRETS OF THE FLYING SAUCERS ARD HOW THEY ARE ABLE TO PERFORM INCREDIBLE MANEUVERS IN OUR ATMOSPHERE — AND HE CLAIMS THEY HAVE ESTABLISHED FACE-TO-FACE CONTACT WITH HUMANS. HERE IS THE COMPLETE TOP-SECRET HISTORY OF UFOS AND HUMANOID SIGHTINGS IN CANADA,

Wilbert B. Smith was a Canadian engineer responsible for the technical aspects of broadcasting between the U.S and his country during the1950s. Because of the number of UFO sightings over Canadian air space, Smith convinced his government to establish a UFO monitoring system, which eventually did detect anomalous phenomena in the sky which Smith felt certain was of an off-world origin. Dying of cancer, Smith made arrangements with his wife to hide his "sensitive" files so they would not fall into the hands of those who would use his findings for their own un-scrupulous ends. "They will be coming to ransack all my work," Smith proclaimed. And he was right! As predicted, Canadians, Americans and Soviets approached his widow, requesting she turn over her husband's work as it would help to further expedite their unprincipled labors. Tales of crashed saucers. Human looking ETs here now. Govt sponsored cover ups. ❏ $19.95

❏ **THE CASE FOR UFO CRASHES – FROM URBAN LEGEND TO REALITY** — WHAT IS HIDDEN IN THE MYSTERIOUS "BLUE ROOM" AT WRIGHT-PATTERSON AIR FORCE BASE? DOES "HANGAR 18" CONTAIN WRECKAGE OF A CRASHED UFO AND PRESERVED BODIES OF ALIENS FROM OUTER SPACE? — For over 50 years the late Senator Barry Goldwater, was denied access. : "I was told in such an emphatic way that it was none of my business — what was in this "room" —that I've never tried to make it my business since." EVERY PRESIDENT SINCE TRUMAN HAS BEEN PART OF THE "GRAND DECEPTION" – NOW IS THE TIME TO EXPOSE THE "COSMIC WATERGATE!" Here are dozens of unpublished Crashed Saucer stories uncovered by the author Tim Beckley during the course of his research, including . .* The night a UFO came crashing down over an Ohio shopping mall. . . * A bizarre tale of an "alien artifact" uncovered by a jogger and displayed in the lobby of a Florida movie theater before it was mysteriously removed and vanished completely. . . * An unbelievable eye witness account of a UFO that fell inside New York City's bustling Central Park after being shot at by the military. .
❏ **Order CASE FOR UFO CRASHES, $22.00. Includes bonus DVD.**

❏ **THE ASTOUNDING UFO SECRETS OF JIM MOSELEY INCLUDES FULL TEXT OF UFO CRASH SECRETS AT WRIGHT PATTERSON AIR FORCE BASE — THIS IS NOT JUST ANOTHER BOOK ABOUT UFO SIGHTINGS OR THE CRASH AT ROSWELL! —** IT'S AN EXTRAORDINARY REMEMBRANCE OF THE COURT JESTER — THE GRAND TROUBADOUR — THE NUMERO UNO TRICKSTER — OF ALL OF UFOLOGY. In addition to the musings and gossip of those that he remained closest to in life, Jim (with the help of endeared drinking buddy and ghost writer Gray Barker) fans out across the country to personally investigate some of the most perplexing UFO cases of all time –Cases personally pondered over by Moseley in this book include: ** "I Met Two Men From 'Venus' — And They Had No Fingerprints!" ** What Happened To The "Authentic" UFO Film That Vanished Without A Trace? ** Kidnapped By Aliens? – A Most Strange And Unusual Case. ** The Angels Of Oahspe. ** Adamski, Williamson And The Case For The UFO Contactees. ** Behind The Barbed Wire Fence At Wright-Patterson Air Force Base. ** The OSI And The Lubbock Lights. ** ETs And Alien Wreckage - The Strange Story Of An Air Force Whistleblower. ** The Earth Theory And UFOs From The Antarctica.
❏ **Order SECRETS OF JIM MOSELEY -$20.00**

❏ **UMMO AND THE EXTRATERRESTRIAL PAPERS — THE ALIENS ARE AMONG US! THEY WISH TO COMMUNICATE! AND HAVE EVEN CONSTRUCTED CITIES IN REMOTE PLACES WHILE THEY ARE HERE!** The story of UMMO starts with a series of letters and phone calls to various Spanish UFO researchers in 1965 that purportedly came from an extraterrestrial race. While the most commonly reported method of ET contact is clearly by telepathy, the aliens in this case tried a more direct, decidedly earthly method of communication. The letters contained highly detailed discourses on such weighty topics as physics and medicine that could only have been written by experts on the cutting edge in those rarified fields that are light years beyond what a lay hoaxer could have come up with. One of the letters also predicted that a UFO sighting would occur on a certain day at a certain location in Spain, and the ship did indeed appear on schedule and at the appointed place. Photos of their ships and unique symbol have been taken as added verification. A similar account has popped up in Canada and is included. This book is over 250 large size pages and contains never before revealed info on this fascinating episode. ❏ **Order UMMO AND THE ET PAPERS - $25.00**

❏ **SUPER SPECIAL –ORDER ALL ITEMS THIS PAGE - $69.00 + $8 S/H AND WE WILL INCLUDE A BONUS DVD ON AN INTRIGUING ASPECT OF THE UFO MYSTERY**
Timothy Beckley, Box 753, New Brunswick, NJ 08903

ALL KITS AND PROFUCTS SOLD FOR EXPERIMENTAL USE ONLY

NIKOLA TESLA MAN OF MYSTERY
NEW – NIKOLA TESLA JOURNEY TO MARS UPDATE

With Shocking Photos That Show Evidence Of Life On Mars!

Thanks to technology developed by the "wizard Nikola Tesla," Mars is no longer the Mystery Planet! What is the truth about a supposed Secret Space Program outside the jurisdiction of NASA?

For centuries astronomers have peered through their telescopes for signs of life on the Red Planet. Some thought they saw canals or strange lights that roamed the surface. Jules Verne — and other early pioneers of science fiction — wrote what were then considered to be far-fetched stories about the exploration of the moon and the planet Mars. They based their classic literary works not just on their own fertile imaginations, but on "wild rumors" circulating that such voyages had already been made, accomplished by a group of scientists — all members of the same secret lodge or society that had tapped into an unknown power source, using it to facilitate the birth of flight, years before the Wright Brothers were able to leave the ground.

Contacted by this secret fraternal order, Nikola Tesla is said to have furthered their cause, coming up with his own method of interplanetary travel, soon to be stolen and used by Hitler and perhaps the New World Order.

Here is proof that scientists and engineers regularly travel back and forth between colonies that have been set up on the Martian surface and deep underground. *Update* is all part of a super-secret space program that the public has been told nothing about. ☐ Large format. $15.95

OTHER TITLES OF INTEREST

☐ TESLA AND THE INCREDIBLE TECHNOLOGIES OF THE NEW WORLD ORDER — Does Area 51 hold the key to many modern day mysteries? — $15.00

☐ MEN OF MYSTERY - NIKOLA TESLA AND OTIS T. CARR — A ship to get us off the planet was constructed in the 1950s. Suppressed Plans — $20.00

☐ NIKOLA TESLA FREE ENERGY AND THE WHITE DOVE — Was Tesla a space man or a time traveler? Here are the suppressed stories and rumors. — $18.00

☐ THE EXPERIMENTS, INVENTIONS, WRITINGS AND PATENTS OF TESLA - 396 large format pages for serious students who want to view hundreds of his papers and documents. - $27.00

☐ THE LOST JOURNALS OF NIKOLA TESLA - Tim Swartz uncovers Time Travel, Alternative Energy and the secret of Nazi flying discs. - Large Format, $21.95

☐ NEW — THE MIRACLE OF TESLA'S PURPLE ENERGY PLATES — The plates are said to be almost supernatural. — $10.00 (add $25 for one 4x5 plate).

ALL BOOKS AS LISTED $120.00 + $10 SHIPPING

Timothy Beckley, Box 753, New Brunswick, NJ 08903 (Available via PayPal - mrufo8@hotmail.com)

www.ingramcontent.com/pod-product-compliance
Lightning Source LLC
Chambersburg PA
CBHW080242170426

43192CB00014BA/2539